D1384175

THE
Protestant
Mystics

THE
Protestant
Mystics

✠ ✠ ✠

selected and edited by
ANNE FREMANTLE

with an introduction by
W. H. AUDEN

LITTLE, BROWN AND COMPANY · BOSTON · TORONTO

LIBRARY OF CONGRESS CATALOG CARD NO. 64–10472

FIRST EDITION

ACKNOWLEDGMENTS

The authors wish to acknowledge with appreciation permission to
quote from the following works in copyright:

LUTHER'S WORKS: CAREER OF THE REFORMER IV,
edited by Lewis W. Spitz and Helmut T. Lehmann, Vol. 34,
translated by Philip Wayne, by permission of Fortress Press.

THE CONFESSIONS OF JAKOB BOEHME, translated by Frederick D. Maurice, compiled and edited by W. Scott Palmer, introduction by Evelyn Underhill, by permission of Methuen &
Company Limited.

A METHOD OF PRAYER by Johannes Kelpius. Copyright by
Harper & Brothers 1951. Reprinted by permission of Harper &
Row, Publishers, Incorporated.

AN ANTHOLOGY OF GERMAN POETRY FROM HÖLDER-
LIN TO RILKE, edited by Angel Flores, by permission of the
author.

RELIGION ON THE AMERICAN FRONTIER: THE BAP-
TISTS, 1783-1830, "Autobiography of Jacob Bower," pages 190-
195, by William Warren Sweet, by permission of Mrs. William
Warren Sweet.

*Published simultaneously in Canada
by Little, Brown & Company (Canada) Limited*

PRINTED IN THE UNITED STATES OF AMERICA

KIERKEGAARD, selected and introduced by W. H. Auden, by permission of Curtis Brown Limited.

FAR AWAY AND LONG AGO by W. H. Hudson. Copyright, 1918, by E. P. Dutton & Co., Inc. Renewal, 1946, Royal Society for the Protection of Birds. Reprinted by permission of E. P. Dutton & Co., Inc., Royal Society for the Protection of Birds, and The Society of Authors.

VAN GOGH: A SELF PORTRAIT, selected by W. H. Auden, by permission of the New York Graphic Society and Vincent W. Van Gogh, Director, Van Gogh Foundation.

THE QUAKER READER, selected and introduced by Jessamyn West, "A Small Town Boy" by Rufus M. Jones, by permission of the Girard Trust Corn Exchange Bank.

THE CELTIC TWILIGHT by William Butler Yeats, reprinted by permission of Mrs. William Butler Yeats, Macmillan & Co. Ltd., and The Macmillan Company of Canada Ltd.

FORBES ROBINSON, DISCIPLE OF LOVE, edited and with an introduction by M. R. J. Manktelow, by permission of the Lord Bishop of Woolwich.

SONG AND ITS FOUNTAINS by Æ, by permission of Macmillan & Company Limited.

SO LONG TO LEARN by John Masefield. Copyright 1951 by John Masefield. Reprinted with the permission of The Macmillan Company, The Society of Authors, and Dr. John Masefield, O.M.

THE PAVILION by Stark Young. Copyright 1951 Stark Young. Reprinted with the permission of Charles Scribner's Sons.

A WRITER'S DIARY by Virginia Woolf, copyright, 1953, 1954, by Leonard Woolf. Reprinted by permission of Harcourt, Brace & World, Inc., and Leonard Woolf.

LETTERS BY A MODERN MYSTIC by Frank C. Laubach, Copyright © 1937, 1958 by Frank C. Laubach, by permission of Fleming H. Revell Company.

AN AUTOBIOGRAPHY by Edwin Muir, "The Adoration of the Beasts," by permission of The Hogarth Press Limited.

COLLECTED POEMS 1921-1951 by Edwin Muir, "The Transfiguration," Copyright © 1957 by Edwin Muir, by permission of Grove Press, Inc., and Faber and Faber Limited.

FOUR QUARTETS, "East Coker," Copyright, 1943, by T. S. Eliot. Reprinted by permission of Harcourt, Brace & World, Inc., and Faber and Faber Limited.

A TESTAMENT OF DEVOTION by Thomas R. Kelly. Copyright by Harper & Brothers 1941. Reprinted by permission of Harper & Row, Publishers, Incorporated.

POEMS 1923-1954 by E. E. Cummings. "i thank You God," Copyright, 1950, by E. E. Cummings, and "O sweet spontaneous,"

Preface

THE flat statement by a distinguished philosopher (a Protestant), Dr. W. T. Stace, that "there are *no* Protestant mystics" brought about this book. W. H. Auden and I set out to prove there were. But we found, as we did our homework, that many Protestants agreed with Dr. Stace. Calvinists, *en masse*, thought that even if there were mystics, there shouldn't be any; other Protestants claimed (though they themselves belonged to other persuasions) that only the Society of Friends could claim genuine Protestant mystics. There certainly is, we found, a difference between Catholic and Protestant mystics that is historically true for all except the members of the Church of England and of the Protestant Episcopal Church in the United States. In the Christian tradition, everyone is called to be a mystic — that is, to enjoy that direct relationship with God for which every human soul is created. *Cor ad cor loquitur*: heart must speak to heart in the final most intimate encounter that is nearer to the self than breathing, for the perception, however feeble, by the soul of its Creator must eventually be direct. But — and this is perhaps where the difference between mystics who happen to be Catholic and those who happen to be Protestant seems to lie — Catholic mystics travel a well-worn, well-known, well-marked and easily identified road. There are the same stages, more or less the same, in Cassian as in Newman — fifteen hundred years apart though they be; in Augustine of Hippo, a fourth-century African, or Father Augustine

Baker, a sixteenth-century Englishman; in St. Irenaeus,
martyred by the Romans, and Edith Stein, martyred by the
Germans. Whether described by Teresa of the Castle or
Teresa of the antimacassars, the slow, painful, clearly
marked journey is the same: the dark nights of the senses,
of the soul — the purifications, the progress from petition-
ary prayer to meditation, from meditation to contemplation, from contemplation to infused prayer, and thence
— for the proficient — to unitive prayer, to the mystic marriage, and, finally, to a state of union. But in this anthology
none of these maps or manuals or "ways" will be found to
be described. For the mystic who happens to be a Protestant, although he is not more isolated than the Catholic —
the flight is always, as Plotinus called it, from the alone to
the Alone — the fellow climbers are not roped. For the
Catholic there are "recognitions" everywhere. But for Jakob
Boehme the sixteenth-century shoemaker, or John Wesley
the founder of Methodism, or George Fox the Quaker, or
Emanuel Swedenborg, there was no benefit of clergy, no
scaffolding to hang onto, few guidebooks, and little in history to help.

Fifty thousand words already chosen had to be cut for
exigencies of space; some great Protestant writers, such as
Henry More the Cambridge Platonist, Archbishop Laud
and King Charles I, Lancelot Andrewes, Sir Thomas Browne
and Evelyn Underhill are not here because they wrote meditations rather than revelations. We realize we have short-
changed the Scandinavians and the German Pietists, for
lack of translations into English, and we should have been
far more catholic had we had but space enough. We have,
however, tried to represent the main centuries and currents
of Protestant experience, as expressed by Protestants who
were mystics.

ANNE FREMANTLE

Contents

THE
Protestant
Mystics

Introduction

IN his great book *The Mystical Element of Religion*, von
Hügel defines a living religion as a tension-in-unity between three elements, the Institutional, the Intellectual
and the Mystical. This holds in every sphere of human life.
As individual members of an animal species, composed of
living matter and mortal, we are all identically subject to
the same physical and chemical laws. In this aspect of our
being, the pronoun *We* is singular not plural, for the pronoun *I* has no meaning. It is meaningless to say *I* have a
four-chambered heart. When the human species is compared with other species, the most conspicuous difference
is that, aside from basic biological processes like breathing,
digestion and physical growth, we seem to be born with no
behavior-directing instincts; even the most elementary behavior required for physical survival and reproducing our
kind has to be learned by each of us, either through imitation of or instruction by others. As Hazlitt said: "Without
the aid of prejudice and custom, I should not be able to
find my way across the room." This difference is particularly
striking when one compares man with those creatures
whose sociality rivals his, the social insects, for it is precisely among them that instinctive behavior is almost all-
powerful and learning capacity almost nil. A bee or an ant
society endures in time from one generation to another
automatically; a human society can only endure by conscious effort, the passing on of a tradition from the older

generation to the younger. Human society, that is to say, is always institutionalized, governed not by instinct or force, but by authority. As members of the human race, born without knowledge or sense of direction, the primary attitude of each individual towards authority must be one of faith: we cannot begin by doubting. A father points to an animal and says to his small son: "Look. A fox." It is conceivable that the father has never read any books on natural history and seldom been in the country so that he has mistaken a badger for a fox, but unless his son has faith in his father and believes that he knows the right names for all animals, if he begins by doubting, then he will never learn to speak.

All religions begin not with the present but the past for, when we ask a question about the meaning of the existence of ourselves and the universe, we and the universe are already in existence; all religions must therefore begin with cosmogonies, theogonies, creation myths. In addition, what we call, with detestable snobbery, the Higher Religions base their claims upon some event in historical time which has already taken place; each asserts that some divine revelation has been made, in and through such a person in such a place at such a time, and that this historical revelation is, for all future time, divine and redemptive. An institution which makes it its professional business to keep alive the memory of the event — otherwise later generations will be unaware that it occurred — and to assert its redemptive importance — otherwise later generations will take it as one historical event on a par with an infinite number of other historical events and devote no special attention to it — is essential.

The function of the Church as an institution is not to convert — conversion is the work not of men but of the Holy Spirit — but to make conversion possible by continuing to preach its good news in words and liturgical acts. She must go on repeating herself, no matter whether her repetition be passionate or, when faith is low, lifeless and mechanical, to preserve that possibility. Frost's lines are as true for peoples and generations as they are for the individual.

> Our very life depends on everything's
> Recurring till we answer from within.
> The thousandth time may prove the charm.

In relation to any institution, ecclesiastical or secular, on all matters of fact and theory concerning which we know ourselves to be ignorant, and in all matters of conduct where uniformity is obviously necessary or convenient, we are or ought to be catholics (with a small c). To doubt for the sake of doubting, to differ for the sake of being different is pride. Private judgment is a meaningless term, for no one is omniscient and omnipotent and every man derives most of his thoughts, opinions and principles from others. Obedience to some authority is inescapable; if we reject the authority of tradition, then we must accept the authority of local fashion.

We are created animals gifted with intelligence, that is to say, we cannot be content merely to experience but must seek to make sense of it, to know what is its cause and significance, to find the truth behind brute fact. Though some individuals have greater intelligence and curiosity than others, the nature of intelligence is identical in every individual. It is impossible for something to be true for one mind and false for another. That is to say, if two of us disagree, either one of us is right or both of us are wrong.

In our relation to one another as intelligent beings, seeking a truth to which we shall both be compelled to assent, We is not the collective singular We of tradition, but a plural signifying a You-and-I united by a common love for the truth. In relation to each other we are protestants; in

relation to the truth we are catholics. I must be prepared
to doubt the truth of every statement you make, but I must
have unquestioning faith in your intellectual integrity.

The basic stimulus to the intelligence is doubt, a feeling
that the meaning of an experience is not self-evident. We
never make a statement about what seems to us self-evidently the case. That is why the positive content of a proposition, what it asserts to be true, is never so clear as what it
excludes as being false. Dogmatic theology, for example,
came into being more to exclude heresy than to define orthodoxy, and one reason why theology must continue to be
and grow is that the heresies of one age are never the same
as the heresies of another. The Christian faith is always a
scandal to the imagination and reason of the flesh, but the
particular aspect which seems most scandalous depends
upon the prevailing mentality of a period or a culture. Thus,
to both the gnostics of the fourth century and the liberal
humanists of the eighteenth, the Cross was an offense, but
for quite different reasons. The gnostic said: "Christ was
the Son of God, therefore He cannot have been physically
crucified. The Crucifixion was an illusion." The liberal humanist said: "Christ was physically crucified, therefore He
cannot have been the Son of God. His claim was a delusion." In our own day, the stumbling block is again different. I think most Christians will find themselves in understanding sympathy with Simone Weil's difficulty: "If the
Gospels omitted all mention of Christ's resurrection, faith
would be easier for me. The Cross by itself suffices me."

Besides defending the Church against heresy, theology
has another perennial task to perform, instructing the devout, both the institutional authorities and the mass of the
laity, in the difference between the things of God and the
things of Caesar. In addition to the absolute presupposi-
tions which we consciously hold by faith as necessary to
salvation, we all of us hold a large number of notions about

what constitutes the beautiful in art, what is the just form of social structure, what the natural universe is like, etc., which we hold not by faith but by habit — they are what we are used to and we cannot imagine them otherwise. Along comes a new style of art, a social change, a scientific discovery, and our immediate reaction is to think that such changes are contrary to our faith. It is one of the tasks of the theologian to show that this is not the case, and that our fright is unnecessary. If this is not done, we shall presently find that we have changed either our faith or our God.

Whatever the field under discussion, those who engage in debate must not only believe in each other's good faith, but also in their capacity to arrive at the truth. Intellectual debate is only possible between those who are equal in learning and intelligence. Preferably they should have no audience, but if they do have one, it should be an audience of their peers. Otherwise, the desire for applause, the wish, not to arrive at the truth but to vanquish one's opponent, becomes irresistible. Never were the fatal effects of publicity in debate so obvious as in the sixteenth century. As Professor C. S. Lewis has written:

The process whereby "faith and works" became a stock gag in the commercial theatre is characteristic of that whole tragic farce which we call the history of the Reformation. The theological questions really at issue have no significance except on a certain level, a high level, of the spiritual life; they could have been fruitfully debated only between mature and saintly disputants in close privacy and at boundless leisure. Under these conditions formulae might possibly have been found which did justice to the Protestant assertions without compromising other elements of the Christian faith. In fact, however, these questions were raised at a moment when they immediately became embittered and entangled with a whole complex of matters theologically irrelevant, and therefore attracted the fatal attention both of government and the mob. It was as if men were set to conduct a metaphysical argument at a fair, in competition or (worse still) forced collaboration with the cheapjacks and roundabouts, under the eyes of an armed and vigilant police force who frequently changed sides. Each party increasingly misunderstood the other and triumphed in refuting positions which their opponents did not hold: Protestants misrepresenting Romans as Pelagians or Romans misrepresenting Protestants as Antinomians.

In addition to being members of a species gifted with intelligence, each of us is created in the Image of God, that is to say, each is a unique person who can say *I*, with a unique perspective on the universe, the exact like of whom has never existed before nor will again. As persons, each of us has his biography, a story with a beginning, middle and end. As St. Augustine, following St. James, says: "Man was created in order that a beginning might be made." The dogma of the descent of all mankind from a single ancestor, Adam, is not, and should never have been imagined to be, a statement about man's biological evolution. It asserts that, in so far as he or she is a unique person, every man and woman, irrespective of race, nation, culture and sex, *is* Adam, an incarnation of all mankind; that, as persons, we are called into being, not by any biological process but by other persons, God, our parents, our friends and enemies. And it is as persons, not as members of a species, that we become guilty of sin. When we speak of being "born in sin," of inheriting the original sin of Adam, this cannot mean, it seems to me — I speak as a fool — that sin is physically present in our flesh and our genes. Our flesh, surely, is not in itself sinful, but our every bodily movement, touch, gesture, tone of voice is that of a sinner. From the moment consciousness first wakes in a baby (and this may possibly be before birth) it finds itself in the company of sinners, and its consciousness is affected by a contagion against which there is no prophylaxis.

The personal I is by necessity protestant (again with a small p), for no one else can have my experience for me or be responsible for my history. This I, though, exists only in the present instant: my past memories are never of myself alone. Towards my immediate experience, what is required of me is neither faith nor doubt but a self-forgetful concentration of my attention upon the experience which is only mine in the sense that it has been given to me and not to someone else. The *I* is only truly itself when its attention to experience is so intense that it is unaware of its own existence. I must not ask whether the experience is like or unlike the experience of others, a hallucination or objectively real, expected or unexpected, pleasant or painful. All these questions are to be asked later, for the answers are bound to be erroneous if, through distraction of attention, I fail to experience fully. When I do ask them, I shall usually find, of course, that however novel the experience may have been to me, most people have had similar experiences, and that the explanation and significance have long been known. But, occasionally, there may have been some element in it which is really novel. In that case, though I must beware of exaggerating its importance simply because it happened to me, I must neither deny it nor hug it as private secret, but make it public though all the authorities on earth, administrative or intellectual, should laugh at me or threaten me with penalties. In any case, it is only through the sharing of personal experience, important or trivial, that our relation with others ceases to be that of one member of a social species to another and becomes that of one person to another. So, too, in my relation to God; it is personal experience which enables me to add to the catholic *We believe still* the protestant *I believe again*.

When von Hügel calls all that is not institutional or intellectual mystical, he obviously includes under this division many experiences which are not, in a technical sense, mystical. He includes any firsthand religious experience. But mystical experiences, whether concerned with God or with his creatures, have, of all experiences, the most right to be called firsthand, as owing least to either tradition or impersonal ratiocination.

II

There seem to be four distinct kinds of mystical experience:

> The Vision of Dame Kind
> The Vision of Eros
> The Vision of Agape
> The Vision of God

Before considering the differences between them one should consider what they have in common which makes comparison possible.

(1) The experience is always "given," that is to say, it cannot be induced by an effort of will. In the case of the Vision of Dame Kind, it can in some cases, it seems, be induced by chemical means, alcohol or the hallucigenic drugs. (I have myself taken mescaline once and L.S.D. once. Aside from a slight schizophrenic dissociation of the I from the Not-I, including my body, nothing happened at all.) In the case of the Vision of God, it does not seem to be granted to anyone who has not undergone a long process of self-discipline and prayer, but self-discipline and prayer cannot of themselves compel it.

(2) The experience seems to the subject not only more important than anything he experiences when in a "normal" state, but also a revelation of reality. When he returns to a normal state, he does not say: "That was a pleasant dream but, of course, an illusion. Now I am awake and see things as they really are"; he says: "For a moment a veil was lifted and I saw what really is. Now the veil has fallen again and reality is again hidden from me." His conclusion is similar to that of Don Quixote who in his bouts of madness sees windmills as giants, but when in his lucid intervals

he sees them as windmills, says: "Those cursed magicians delude me, first drawing me into dangerous adventures by the appearance of things as they really are, and then presently changing the face of things as they please."

(3) The experience is totally different from that of "seeing things" whether in dreams or waking visions. In the case of the first three kinds which are concerned with visible creatures, these are seen with extraordinary vividness and charged with extraordinary significance, but they are not physically distorted; square objects do not become round or blue ones red, nor does the subject see objects which are not there when the vision fades. Again, one thinks of Don Quixote. He may see a windmill as a giant, but he doesn't see a giant unless there is a windmill there. In the case of the Vision of God, in which, whatever explanation one cares to make, what the subject encounters is not a visible creature, the mystics are unanimous in saying that they do not see anything in a physical sense. Thus St. Theresa says that in her true visions and locutions "she never saw anything with her bodily eyes, nor heard anything with her bodily ears." Sometimes they do "see and hear" things, but they always recognize these as accidental and irrelevant to the real experience, and to be regarded with suspicion. When his followers came to St. Philip Neri to tell him about their delightful visions of the Blessed Virgin, he ordered them the next time they had such a vision to spit in her face, and it is said that, when they did so, a devil's face was at once revealed.

(4) Though the experience is always given and surprising, its nature is never entirely independent of the subject. In the case of the Vision of Dame Kind, for example, it is commoner in childhood and adolescence than in maturity, and the actual content of the vision, the kind of creatures transformed and the hierarchy of importance among them seem to vary from person to person. To one color is the

most significant, to another form, and so on. In the case of the Vision of God, the religious beliefs of the subject seem to play a part. Thus, when one compares the accounts given by Christian, Mohammedan and Indian mystics, it is impossible to say with certainty whether they are accounts of different experiences or accounts of the same experience described in different theological languages, and, if the first, whether the differences are due to the mystic's beliefs. If a Hindu mystic, for example, were to become converted to Christianity, would his mystical experience show a change?

As an example of the difficulty of separating observation from interpretation of experience, let me take a trivial personal one. Many people have given accounts of what they experienced while having a tooth extracted under nitrous oxide, and these show close similarities. Thus William James says:

The keynote of it is invariably a reconciliation. It is as if the opposites of the world, whose contradictions and conflict make all our difficulties and troubles, were melted into unity.

My experience, like his, was of two opposites, love in the sense of agape, and hate, but in my case they did not melt into a unity. I felt an absolute conviction about two things: (a) that, ultimately the power of love was greater than the force of hate; (b) that, on the other hand, however great any human being might estimate the force of hate to be, he would always underestimate it. The actual quantity of hate in the universe was greater than any human imagination could conceive. Nevertheless, the power of love was still greater. Would I, I ask myself, have had precisely *this* experience if I had not been brought up in a Christian home and therefore been a person to whom the Christian notion of agape was a familiar one, and I find myself unable to say yes or no with any certainty.

(5) From a Christian point of view, all four kinds of

experience are, in themselves, blessings and a good; there is nothing in any of them that is contrary to Christian doctrine. On the other hand, all of them are dangerous. So long as the subject recognizes them as totally unmerited blessings and feels obligated by gratitude to produce, in so far as it lies in his power, works which are good according to their kind, they can lead him towards the Light. But if he allows himself either to regard the experience as a sign of superior merit, natural or supernatural, or to idolize it as something he cannot live without, then it can only lead him into darkness and destruction.

III

The Vision of Dame Kind

The objects of this vision may be inorganic — mountains, rivers, seas — or organic — trees, flowers, beasts — but they are all non-human, though human artifacts like buildings may be included. Occasionally human figures are involved, but if so, they are invariably, I believe, strangers to the subject, people working in the fields, passers-by, beggars, or the like, with whom he has no personal relation and of whom, therefore, no personal knowledge. The basic experience is an overwhelming conviction that the objects confronting him have a numinous significance and importance, that the existence of everything he is aware of is holy. And the basic emotion is one of innocent joy, though this joy can include, of course, a reverent dread. In a "normal" state, we value objects either for the immediate aesthetic pleasure they give to our senses — this flower has a pleasant color, this mountain a pleasing shape, but that flower, that mountain are ugly — or for the future satisfaction of our desires which they promise — this fruit will taste delicious, that one horrid. In the Vision of Dame Kind, such distinctions, between the beautiful and the ugly, the serviceable and the unserviceable, vanish. So long as the vision lasts the self is "noughted," for its attention is completely absorbed in what it contemplates; it makes no judgments and desires nothing, except to continue in communion with what Gerard Manley Hopkins called the inscape of things.

> Each mortal thing does one thing and the same:
> Deals out that being indoors each one dwells;
> Selves — goes itself; *myself* it speaks and spells
> Crying *What I do is me: for that I came.*

In some cases, the subject speaks of this sense of communion as if he were himself *in* every object, and they in him. Thus Wordsworth in *The Ruined Cottage:*

> . . . sensation, soul and form
> All melted in him. They swallowed up
> His animal being; in them did he live
> And by them did he live.

In his book *Mysticism, Sacred and Profane,* Professor Zaehner calls this the pan-en-henic vision, which he considers the definitive sign of the natural mystic; for him, an account which does not speak of this fusion of identities cannot be an account of a genuinely mystical experience. I think Professor Zaehner is mistaken. In their accounts of the Vision of God Christian mystics sometimes seem almost to say that they *became* God, which they cannot, of course, have believed; they are trying to describe, presumably, a state in consciousness so filled with the presence of God that there is no vacant corner of it detachedly observing the experience. The natural mystic who speaks in pan-en-henic terms does not really mean that he becomes a tree or that a tree becomes him. No one, for example, was more convinced than Richard Jeffries, who does speak in these terms, that "there is nothing human in nature." He would certainly say that in the vision he feels capable of imaginatively entering into the life of a tree, but that no more means he becomes a tree than imaginatively entering into the life of another human being means that one ceases to be oneself and becomes him.

The joy felt by the natural mystic may be called innocent. While the vision lasts, the self and its desires are so completely forgotten that he is, in fact, incapable of sin. On the other hand, unlike the religious mystic, he is unaware of sin as a past fact and a future possibility, because his mystical encounter is with creatures who are not persons, and to which, therefore, the terms moral good and moral evil do not apply. For the same reason, Eros plays no conscious role. No accounts of the Vision of Dame Kind ever use, as accounts of the Vision of God often do, the experience of sexual union as an analogy.

The interpretations of the Vision of Dame Kind and even the language in which it is described vary, of course, according to the religious beliefs of the subject, but the experience itself seems to be independent of them, though not entirely independent, I think, of either the personality or the culture of the subject. In our own culture, in various degrees of intensity, many persons experience it in childhood and adolescence, but its occurrence among adults is rare. In so-called primitive cultures it may persist longer. Colonel Van Der Post's account of the African Bushmen suggests to me that among them it may persist uninterrupted throughout life. Even in our Western culture, its frequency is not evenly distributed. It is to be observed that nearly all the accounts have been written by members of the Northern peoples — the Mediterranean countries have contributed very little — which means that in fact, though the fact may be irrelevant, most of them have been written by persons with a Protestant upbringing. My own, very tentative, explanation for this is that in the Mediterranean countries the individual experience of Nature as sacred is absorbed and transformed into a social experience, expressed by the institutional cults, so common around the Mediterranean, of the local Madonna and the local saint. Whether it is possible completely to Christianize in spirit what is plainly polytheistic in form, I shall not presume to say. If I have my doubts, it is because of the enormous aesthetic pleasure such cults give me and my nostalgic regret when I am in countries which lack them.

Though the Vision of Dame Kind is not specifically Christian, there is nothing in it incompatible with the Christian belief in a God who created the material universe and all its creatures out of love and found them good: the glory in which the creatures appear to the natural mystic must be a feeble approximation to their glory as God sees them. There is nothing to prevent him from welcoming it as a gift, however indirect, from God. To a Gnostic for whom matter is the creation of an evil spirit, it must, of course, be a diabolic visitation and to the monist who regards the phenomenal world as an illusion, it must be doubly an illusion, harmless, maybe, but to be seen through as soon as possible. To a philosophical materialist for whom the notion of glory has no meaning, it must be an individual delusion, probably neurotic in origin, and to be discouraged as abnormal and likely to lead the patient into the more serious and socially harmful delusion of some sort of theism. When such a staunch atheist as Richard Jeffries can speak of praying "that I might touch the unutterable existence even higher than deity," the danger of allowing people to take solitary country walks becomes obvious.

Believing Christians who have had the vision have always been explicit as to what it was *not*. Thus Wordsworth:

> He did not feel the God; he felt his works;
> Thought was not. In enjoyment it expired.
> Such hour by prayer or praise was unprofaned,
> He neither prayed, nor offered thanks or praise,

His mind was a thanksgiving to the power
That made him. It was blessedness and love.

And thus George Macdonald:

I lived in everything; everything entered and lived in me. To be aware of a thing was to know its life at once and mine, to know whence it came and where we were at home — was to know that we are all what we are, because Another is what He is.

And they give thanks to God for it, not only for the joy that accompanies it, but also because it safeguards them, as even the Vision of God cannot, against a Gnostic undervaluation of the creaturely. Even in the Vision of God, the Christian must remember that, as Suso says:

The being of the creatures in God is not that of a creature, but the creatureliness of every creature is nobler for it, and more useful, than the being it has in God. For what advantage has a stone or a man or any creature in its status as a creature, from the fact that it has been eternally in God?

To those who have never been Christians or, for one reason or another, have lost their faith, the very innocence of the experience can be an occasion of error. Since it involves neither the intellect nor the will, it is always possible for the intellect to misunderstand and the will to abuse it. The intellect can take the encounter with a numinous creature for an encounter with deity itself. Hence animism, polytheism, idols, magic and the so-called natural religions in which the non-human creation, including, of course, those physical and biological elements and forces which man shares with all other creatures, is the ultimate source of power and meaning and, therefore, responsible for man. Pantheism, as we find it in Goethe and Hardy, is really a sophisticated and sensitive form of humanism. Since man is, at present and so far as we know, the only creature in nature with consciousness, moral conscience, reason, will and purpose, a

God (or Goddess) solely immanent in Nature must, unless He can create a new species, be at man's mercy; only man can tell Him what his will is or carry it out; one can pray to an idol, but it is difficult to see how one could *pray* to His Immanence, though one might revere Him.

The other temptation, more dangerous in a culture like ours than it was to the pagan world because in ours the experience is probably rarer and more temporary, is to idolize the experience itself as the summum bonum and spend one's life either gloomily regretting its loss and so falling into a state of accidie, or trying by artificial means, like alcohol and drugs, to recapture and prolong it. The hallucigenic drugs are not, so far as we know, habit-forming, but no one has yet made a habit of taking them day after day for years. When this has been done, as it surely will be, I suspect that the law of diminishing returns will be found to apply to them as it applies to the more traditional artificial aids. If this should not turn out to be the case, if it should become possible for anyone to enjoy the Vision of Dame Kind whenever he wishes, the consequences might be even more serious. It is a characteristic of the world which this vision reveals that its only human inhabitant is the subject himself, and a continual indulgence in it could only lead to an increasing indifference towards the existence and needs of other human beings.

The vision of the splendor of creation, like all kinds, lays a duty upon one who has been fortunate enough to receive it, a duty in his turn to create works which are as worthy of what he has seen as his feeble capacities will permit. And many have listened and obeyed. It has been, I am quite certain, the initial cause of all genuine works of art and, I believe, of all genuine scientific inquiry and discovery, for it is the wonder which is, as Plato said, the beginning of every kind of philosophy.

IV

The Vision of Eros

Half the literature, highbrow and popular, produced in the West during the past four hundred years has been based on the false assumption that what is an exceptional experience is or ought to be a universal one. Under its influence so many millions of persons have persuaded themselves they were "in love" when their experience could be fully and accurately described by the more brutal four-letter words, that one is sometimes tempted to doubt if the experience is ever genuine, even when, or especially when, it seems to have happened to oneself. However, it is impossible to read some of the documents, *La Vita Nuova*, for example, many of Shakespeare's sonnets or the *Symposium* and dismiss them as fakes. All accounts of the experience agree on essentials. Like the Vision of Dame Kind, the Vision of Eros is a revelation of creaturely glory, but whereas in the former it is the glory of a multiplicity of non-human creatures which is revealed, in the latter it is the glory of a single human being. Again, while in the vision of Nature, conscious sexuality is never present, in the erotic vision it always is — it cannot be experienced by eunuchs (though it may occur before puberty) and no one ever fell in love with someone they found sexually unattractive — but physical desire is always, and without any effort of will, subordinate to the feeling of awe and reverence in the presence of a sacred being: however great his desire, the lover feels unworthy of the beloved's notice. It is impossible to take such accounts as a fancy poetization of any of the three kinds of unmystical erotic experiences with which we are all familiar. It is not simple lust, the detached recognition of another as a desirable sexual object, for in relation to

anything one regards as an object one feels superior, and
the lover feels inferior to the beloved. Nor is it sexual in-
fatuation, the experience of *Vénus toute entière à sa proie
attachée*, in which desire has invaded and possessed the
whole self until what it craves is not sexual satisfaction only
but a total absorption of the other self, body and soul, into
itself; in this condition the dominant feeling is not of unworthiness but of anguish, rage and despair at not being
able to get what one craves. Nor, again, is it that healthy
mixture of mutual physical desire and *philia*, a mutual personal liking based on common interests and values, which
is the securest foundation for a happy marriage for, in this
state, the dominant feeling is of mutual respect between
equals.

Moreover, all the accounts agree that the Vision of Eros
cannot long survive if the parties enter into an actual sexual
relation. It was not merely the social conditions of an age
in which marriages were arranged by the parents which
made the Provençal poets declare that married couples
could not be in love. This does not mean that one must
under no circumstances marry the person whose glory has
been revealed to one, but the risk in doing so is proportion-
ate to the intensity of the vision. It is difficult to live day
after day, year after year, with an ordinary human being,
neither much better nor much worse than oneself, after one
has seen her or him transfigured, without feeling that the
fading of the vision is the other's fault. The Vision of Eros
seems to be much more influenced by social conditions than
any of the others. Some degree of leisure and freedom from
financial anxiety seems to be essential; a man who must
labor ten hours a day in order not to starve has other matters to attend to: he is too occupied by practical necessities
to think of more than his sexual need for a woman and his
economic need for a good housekeeper and mother. And
it would seem that the beloved must belong to a class of

persons whom the lover has been brought up to regard as his social equals or superiors. One cannot, it seems, fall in love with someone whom one has been trained to think of as being less of a person, more of a thing than oneself. Thus Plato, though he came in later life to disapprove of homosexuality, can only conceive of the beloved as a male in his adolescence or early manhood because, in the Athens of his time, women were regarded as essentially inferior creatures.

The effect of the vision on the lover's conduct is not confined to his behavior towards his beloved. Even in his relations to others, conduct which before he fell in love seemed natural and proper, judged by his new standard of what he feels it should be to be worthy of her, now seems base and ignoble. Further, in most cases, the experience does not lead, as one might expect, to a sort of erotic quietism, a rapt contemplation of the beloved to the exclusion of others and the world. On the contrary, it usually releases a flood of psychic energy for actions which are not directly concerned with the beloved at all. When in love, the soldier fights more bravely, the thinker thinks more clearly, the carpenter fashions with greater skill.

The Church, whose institutional and intellectual concern in sexual matters is, and must be, primarily with marriage and the family, has always, very understandably, regarded the Vision of Eros with the utmost suspicion. Either she has dismissed it as moonshine, or condemned it offhand, without trying first to understand it, as idolatry of the creature and a blasphemous parody of the Christian love of God. Knowing that marriage and the vision are not compatible, she has feared that it will be, as it very often is, used as an excuse for adultery. Condemnation without understanding, however, is seldom effective. If the lover idolizes the beloved, it is not what we ordinarily mean by idolization, in which the worshipper makes his idol responsible for his existence. This kind of idolization can certainly occur in the relation between the sexes. Cases of men and women who shoot themselves and each other because the object of their affection does not return it, or loves somebody else, may be read of almost every day in the newspapers, but one knows at once that they cannot have been truly in love. The true lover would naturally rather his beloved returned his love than refused it, he would rather she were alive and visible than dead and invisible, but if she cannot return his love, he does not try to compel her by force or emotional blackmail, and if she dies, he does not commit suicide but continues to love her.

The two most serious attempts to analyze the Vision of Eros and give it a theological significance are Plato's and Dante's. Both agree on three points: (a) the experience is a genuine revelation, not a delusion; (b) the erotic mode of the vision prefigures a kind of love in which the sexual element is transformed and transcended; (c) he who has once seen the glory of the Uncreated revealed indirectly in the glory of a creature can henceforth never be fully satisfied with anything less than a direct encounter with the former. About everything else they disagree radically. One of the most important differences between them is obscured by the inadequacy of our vocabulary. When I say, "X has a beautiful profile," and when I say, "Elizabeth has a beautiful face," or "the expression on Mary's face was beautiful," I have to use the same adjective, though I mean two totally different things. Beauty in the first statement is a given public quality of an object; I am talking about a quality the object *has*, not about what it *is*. If (but only if) a number of objects belong to the same class, I can compare them and arrange them in order according to the degree of beauty they possess, from the most beautiful to the least. That is why, even among human beings, it is possible to hold beauty contests to elect Miss America, and possible for an experienced sculptor to state in mathematical terms the proportions of the ideal male or female figure. Beauty in this sense is a gift of Nature or of Chance, and can be withdrawn. To become Miss America, a girl must have inherited a certain combination of genes and have managed to escape any disfiguring diseases or crippling accident, and, diet as she may, she cannot hope to remain Miss America forever. The emotion aroused by this kind of beauty is impersonal admiration; in the case of a human being, it may also be impersonal sexual desire. I may want to sleep with Miss America, but I have no wish to hear her talk about herself and her family.

When I say, "Elizabeth has a beautiful face," I mean something quite different. I am still referring to something physical — I could not make the statement if I were blind — but this physical quality is not a gift from Nature, but a personal creation for which I hold Elizabeth to be responsible. The physical beauty seems to me a revelation of something immaterial, the person whom I cannot see. Beauty in this sense is unique in every case: I cannot compare Elizabeth and Mary and say which has the more beautiful face. The emotion aroused by it is personal love, and, again, this is unique in every case. To the degree that I love both Elizabeth and Mary, I cannot say which I love more. Finally, to say that someone is beautiful in this sense is never simply a favorable aesthetic judgment; it is always a favorable moral judgment as well. I can say "X has a beautiful profile but is a monster," I cannot say, "Elizabeth has a beautiful face but is a monster."

As creatures, human beings have a double nature. As members of a mammalian species which reproduces itself sexually, each of us is born either male or female and endowed with an impersonal need to mate with a member of the opposite sex; any member will do so long as he or she is not immature or senile. As unique persons we are capable of, but not compelled to, enter voluntarily into unique relations of love with other persons. The Vision of Eros is, therefore, double too. The beloved always possesses some degree of that beauty which is Nature's gift. A girl who weighs two hundred pounds and a woman of eighty may both have beautiful faces in the personal sense, but men do not fall in love with them. The lover is, of course, aware of this, but what seems to him infinitely more important is his awareness of the beloved as a person. Or so, at least, Dante says. What is so puzzling about Plato's description is that he seems unaware of what we mean by a person. By beauty, he always seems to mean impersonal beauty and by love impersonal admiration.

[The lover] should begin by loving earthly things for the sake of the absolute loveliness, ascending to that as it were by degrees or steps, from the first to the second, and thence to all fair forms; and from fair forms to fair conduct, and from fair conduct to fair principles, until from fair principles he finally arrive at the ultimate principle of all, and learn what absolute Beauty is.

The more I study this passage, the more bewildered I become, and I find myself talking to Plato's ghost and saying:

"(1) As regards earthly things, I agree that I can compare two horses, or two men, or two proofs of the same mathematical theorem, and say which is the more beautiful, but will you please tell me how I am to compare a horse, a man and a mathematical proof and say which is the most beautiful?

"(2) If, as you say, there are degrees of beauty and that the more beautiful should be loved more, then, at the human level, it must be the moral duty of all of us to fall in love with the most beautiful human being known to us. Surely, it is very fortunate for all concerned that we fail to do our duty.

"(3) It is quite true, as you say, that a fair principle does not get bald and fat or run away with somebody else. On the other hand, a fair principle cannot give me a smile of welcome when I come into the room. Love of a human being may be, as you say, a lower form of love than love for a principle, but you must admit it is a damn sight more interesting."

How different, and much more comprehensible, is Dante's account. He sees Beatrice, and a voice says, "Now you have seen your beatitude." Dante certainly thinks that Beatrice is beautiful in the public sense that any stranger would call her beautiful, but it would never enter his head to ask if she were more or less beautiful than other Florentine girls of her age. She is Beatrice and that is that. And what is the essential thing about her is that she is, he is absolute certain, a "graced" person, so that after her death, he is convinced, as a believing Christian, that her soul is among the redeemed in Paradise, not among the lost in Hell. He does not tell us exactly what the sins and errors were which had brought him near to perdition nor, when they meet again, does Beatrice, but both speak of them as acts of infidelity to her, that is to say, if he had remained faithful to his vision of one human creature, Beatrice, he would not have committed offenses against their common Creator. Though unfaithful to her image, he has, however, never completely forgotten it (the Platonic ladder makes the forgetting of an image on a lower rung a moral duty), and it is this memory, the fact that he has never completely ceased to love her, which makes it possible for Beatrice to intervene from Heaven to save his soul. When, at last, they meet again in the earthly paradise, he re-experiences, though infinitely more intensely, the vision he had when they first met on earth, and she remains with him until the very last moment when he turns towards "the eternal fountain" and, even then, he knows that her eyes are turned in the same direction. The Vision of Eros is not, according to Dante, the first rung of a long ladder: there is only one step to take, from the personal creature who can love and be loved to the personal Creator who is Love. And in this final vision, Eros is transfigured but not annihilated. On earth we rank "love" higher than either sexual desire or sexless friendship because it involves the whole of our being, not, like them, only a part of it. Whatever else is asserted by the doctrine of the resurrection of the body, it asserts the sacred importance of the body. As Silesius says, we have one advantage over the angels: only we can each become the bride of God. And Juliana of Norwich: "In the self-same point that our Soul is made sensual, in the self-same point is the City of God ordained to him from without beginning."

v

The Vision of Agape

The classic Christian example of this is, of course, the vision of Pentecost, but there are modes of it which are not overtly Christian. Since I cannot find a specific description among these selections, I shall quote from an unpublished account for the authenticity of which I can vouch.

One fine summer night in June 1933 I was sitting on a lawn after dinner with three colleagues, two women and one man. We liked each other well enough but we were certainly not intimate friends, nor had any one of us a sexual interest in another. Incidentally, we had not drunk any alcohol. We were talking casually about everyday matters when, quite suddenly and unexpectedly, something happened. I felt myself invaded by a power which, though I consented to it, was irresistible and certainly not mine. For the first time in my life I knew exactly — because, thanks to the power, I was doing it — what it means to love one's neighbor as oneself. I was also certain, though the conversation continued to be perfectly ordinary, that my three colleagues were having the same experience. (In the case of one of them, I was able later to confirm this.) My personal feelings towards them were unchanged — they were still colleagues, not intimate friends — but I felt their existence as themselves to be of infinite value and rejoiced in it.

I recalled with shame the many occasions on which I had been spiteful, snobbish, selfish, but the immediate joy was greater than the shame, for I knew that, so long as I was possessed by this spirit, it would be literally impossible for me deliberately to injure another human being. I also knew that the power would, of course, be withdrawn sooner or later and that, when it did, my greeds and self-regard would return. The experience lasted at its full intensity for about two hours when we said good-night to each other and went to bed. When I awoke the next morning, it was still present, though weaker, and it did not vanish completely for two days or so. The memory of the experience has not prevented me from making use of others, grossly and often, but it has made it much more difficult for me to deceive myself about what I am up to when I do. And among the various factors which several years later brought me back to the Christian faith in which I had been brought up, the memory of this experience and asking myself what it could mean was one of the most crucial, though, at the time it occurred, I thought I had done with Christianity for good.

Compared with the other kinds of vision, the Vision of Agape has several peculiarities. In the Vision of Dame Kind, there is one human person, the subject, and a multiplicity of creatures whose way of existence is different from his. The relation between him and them is therefore one-sided; though they are transfigured for him, he does not imagine that he is transfigured for them. In the Vision of Eros two human persons are involved, but the relation between them is unequal; the lover feels unworthy of the beloved. If it should so happen that both experience the vision simultaneously in regard to each other, both will still feel unworthy. In the Vision of God, two persons are again involved, the soul and God, and the relation of creature to Creator is utterly unequal, but it is a mutual one; the soul is conscious of loving God and being loved by Him in return. Like the Vision of Dame Kind, the Vision of Agape is multiple, but it is a multiplicity of persons; like the Vision of Eros, it involves human persons only; like the Vision of God it is of a mutual relation; but unlike any of the others, this relation is a relation between equals.

Not the least puzzling thing about it is that most of the experiences which are closest to it in mode, involving plurality, equality and mutuality of human persons, are clear cases of diabolic possession, as when thousands cheer hysterically for the Man-God, or cry bloodthirstily for the crucifixion of the God-Man. Still, without it, there might be no Church.

VI

The Vision of God

No one could be less qualified than I to discuss what the bulk of these selections are concerned with, the direct encounter of a human soul with God. In the first place because I lead an ordinary sensual worldly life, so that I can scarcely be surprised if I have never seen the God whom no man has seen at any time, a vision which is reserved, the Gospels tell us, for the pure in heart. In the second place, because I am an Anglican. Of all the Christian Churches, not excluding the Roman Catholic, the Anglican Church has laid the most stress upon the institutional aspect of religion. Uniformity of rite has always seemed to her more important than uniformity of doctrine, and the private devotions of her members have been left to their own discretion without much instruction or encouragement from her. Her intellectual temper is summed up in a remark by one of her bishops, "Orthodoxy is reticence," and the frigid welcome she offers to any kind of religious "enthusiasm" in a sentence of C. D. Broad's: "A healthy appetite for righteousness, kept in due control by good manners, is an excellent thing; but to 'hunger and thirst' after it is often merely a symptom of spiritual diabetes."

It would be false to say that she has completely neglected the intellect: in the field of Biblical criticism, in particular, she has done great things, for the freedom of her scholars to

inquire has not been hampered, as it has been sometimes in
the Roman Church, by hierarchical fiats, and the atmosphere of spiritual moderation with which she surrounds her
children has restrained them from the extravagant specula-
tions in which German Protestant scholars have sometimes
indulged.

Nor has she failed to inspire many men and women to a
life of interior prayer. There is, as one can see in the writings of men like George Herbert, Lancelot Andrewes,
Charles Williams, a characteristic Anglican style of piety,
different from both Catholic and Evangelical piety, but
none the less genuinely Christian. At its best, it shows spiritual good manners, a quality no less valuable in the religious life than in social life, though, of course, not the ultimate criterion in either, reverence without religiosity, and
humor (in which last trait it resembles Jewish piety). Like
all styles of piety it becomes detestable when the fire of
love has gone out. It is no insult to say that Anglicanism is
the Christianity of a gentleman, but we know what a tiny
hairsbreadth there is between a gentleman and a genteel
snob.

In every sphere of life, when we read or listen to accounts
of experiences which are completely strange to us, we tend
either to be bored or, if they make us envious, to try and explain them away, and in reading the Christian mystics,
Catholic or Protestant, I have, as a worldly man, to be constantly on my guard about this tendency. Then, as an Anglican with an Anglican's prejudices, I must not pretend
that I do not have them, but I must pray that the evidence
these writers present will refute them.

The first thing which disturbs me is the number of mystics who have suffered from ill-health and various kinds of
psycho-physical disturbances. I am aware, of course, that
many, perhaps the majority, of those whose achievements in
this world, in art, in science, in politics, have earned them

the right to be called great men, have suffered from physical and psychological abnormalities, and that to dismiss their achievements on that account as "sick" is the cheapest kind of philistine envy. I cannot help feeling, however, that there is a fundamental difference between a great man and a mystic. In the case of the latter, what matters, surely, is not what he or she outwardly "achieves"— the vision of God cannot be a "work" like a poem — but what they are. The vision is only granted to those who are far advanced in the practice of the Imitation of Christ. In the Gospels, there is no suggestion that, in his human nature, Christ was anything but physically and psychologically normal, no reports of any mental crisis such as we read of in the life of Mahomet. Even more importantly, since the God-Man is a unique case, the twelve Apostles whom he chose seem to have been equally healthy. The mystics themselves do not seem to have believed their physical and mental sufferings to be a sign of grace, but it is unfortunate that it is precisely physical manifestations which appeal most to the religiosity of the mob. A woman might spend twenty years nursing lepers without having any notice taken of her, but let her once exhibit the stigmata or live for long periods on nothing but the Host and water, and in no time the crowd will be clamoring for her beatification.

Then I am a little disturbed by the sometimes startling resemblances between the accounts of their experiences given by mystics and those given by persons suffering from a manic-depressive pychosis. The differences between them are, of course, obvious too. The inflated egoism of the manic-depressive is always conspicuous, whether, in his elated phase, he thinks that, unlike other folks, he is God, or, in his depressed phase, he thinks that, unlike other folks, he has committed the Sin against the Holy Ghost. The genuine mystics, on the other hand, always interpret their ecstasy as a gratuitous blessing from God which they have done nothing to deserve and their dark night of the soul not as evidence of their extraordinary wickedness, but as a period of trial and purgation. Thus, speaking of the two phases, the Arab mystic Qushayri says:

There are cases of contraction the cause of which is not easily ascertainable by the subject . . . the only remedy for this condition is complete submission to the will of God until the mood passes. . . . Expansion, on the other hand, comes suddenly and strikes the subject unexpectedly, so that he can find no reason for it. It makes him quiver with joy, yet scares him. The way to deal with it is to keep quiet and observe conventional good manners.

A similarity, however, remains. This suggests to me two possibilities. Is it not possible that those who fall into a manic-depressive psychosis are persons with a vocation for the Via Negativa which they are either unaware of or have rejected? In the late Middle Ages there were, no doubt, many persons in monasteries and convents who had no business there and should have been out in the world earning an honest living, but today it may well be that there are many persons trying to earn a living in the world and driven by failure into mental homes whose true home would be the cloister. Secondly, though no one in this life can experience the Vision of God without having, through a life of prayer and self-mortification, reached a high level of spiritual life, is it not possible that certain psycho-physical human types are more likely to have such experiences than others who have reached the same level? Whether this is so or not, both the ecclesiastical authorities and the mystics themselves have always insisted that mystical experience is not necessary to salvation or in itself a proof of sanctity. St. John of the Cross, for instance, says:

All visions, revelations, heavenly feelings, and whatever is greater than these, are not worth the least act of humility, being the fruits of that charity which neither values nor seeks itself, which thinketh well, not of self, but of others. . . . many souls, to whom visions have never come, are incomparably more advanced in the way of perfection than others to whom many have been given.

Certainly, in reading accounts of the early life of those who have chosen the Via Negativa, whether or not their choice was later rewarded by visions, how often one comes across the same kind of character, a man or woman who seems, both by talent and temperament, born to command, to wield power either in the temporal or the spiritual sphere, a person, that is, for whom the Third Temptation of Christ can be, as it cannot for most of us, a real temptation. (If Satan were to promise me all the kingdoms of the earth on condition that I bowed down and worshipped him, I should laugh because I should know that, given my limited capacities, he could not fulfil his promise.) Their rejection of what one would have thought to be their natural destiny may have been occasioned by an awareness that, in their case, their gift for power and domination, if exercised, could only bring disaster to others and themselves. As Goethe, who certainly felt no natural sympathy for the Via Negativa, observed about St. Philip Neri:

Only superior and essentially proud men are capable of choosing on principle to taste the enmity of a world which is always opposed to the good and the great, and empty the bitter cup of experience before it is offered to them.

In this selection of writings by Protestants, practicing or lapsed, I can find little which a Catholic reader will consider alien to his experience or contrary to faith and morals. (He may find Swedenborg rather hard to swallow but so, as a Protestant, do I.) Many of them are concerned with visions of nature, at which level theological doctrine is irrelevant, though it is relevant to any interpretation of their significance. Among those directly concerned with man's

relation to God, more attention is paid, as one would expect, to the Pauline conversion experience than one would
find in a similar collection written by Catholics, for it is this
experience upon which most of the Protestant churches
have based their claims. There are two kinds of conversion,
the conversion from one faith — it may be atheism — to
another, and the transformation of an unthinking traditional faith into a personal conviction. Here we are only
concerned with the second. It would be nonsense to say
either that this experience does not occur among Catholics
or that the Catholic Church, institutionally and theologically, does not pray that it shall occur and welcome it when
it does: she certainly does not desire, and never has, that her
children should go through their lives attending Mass and
going to confession as she prescribes without this ever becoming more than a ritual routine in which they experience
nothing for themselves. But she has been, perhaps, overly
aware, as the Protestant churches have certainly been in-
sufficiently aware, of the spiritual danger implicit in all firsthand experience, the temptation to imagine one is a special
person to whom the common rules do not apply, the temptation intellectually to suppose that since an experience is
new to oneself, it is new to the human race, the thinkers of
the past cannot possibly throw light on it, and one must
construct a new philosophy of one's own.

But, at least during her post-tridentine phase, now hap-
pily over, the Catholic Church seemed more or less to take
the view that the proper place for her protestants, those
who claimed firsthand experience, was the priesthood or the
cloister where she could keep a sharp eye on them, and that
no more could be asked of the laity than obedience to her
rules. The Protestant churches, on the other hand, probably
asked more of the average layman than is, humanly speaking, possible. Kierkegaard, himself a Protestant, put the
difference neatly:

Catholicism has the universal premise that we men are pretty well rascals . . . The Protestant principle is related to a particular premise: a man who sits in the anguish of death, in fear and trembling and much tribulation — and of those there are not many in any one generation.

Aside from this difference in emphasis, the main difference seems to be one of vocabulary. The language of the Catholic mystics shows an acquaintance with a whole tradition of mystical literature, that of the Protestant is derived almost entirely from the Bible. The former, living in monastic orders and, usually, under the spiritual direction of a confessor, have at their disposal a highly developed technical theological language, which the latter, except for the Calvinists, have lacked. Consequently one might say that the Catholic writes like a professional, the Protestant like an amateur.

The virtue of the amateur is freshness and honesty, his defect a clumsiness in expression; the difficulty for a professional is that he may be unaware that the traditional language he has inherited is falsifying what he means to say. One sometimes comes across passages written by Catholic mystics which, taken out of the context of their whole writings and their lives, seem to be not Christian but monist or manichaean, and I think the reason for this is probably the influence on the Catholic vocabulary of certain writers, in particular Plotinus and Pseudo-Dionysius, who were not Christians but Neoplatonists.

VII

Even among the most ignorant, there can be very few Protestants today who still think that Rome is the Scarlet Woman, or Catholics who think, like the officer Goethe met in Italy, that Protestants are allowed to marry their sisters. And among the more thoughtful, there can be few, no matter what church they belong to, who do not regard the series of events in the sixteenth and seventeenth centuries whereby the Western Church became divided into Catholics and Protestants with capital letters, hating and despising each other, as a spiritual tragedy for which all parties concerned must bear some of the blame. Looking back, there seems no *rational* reason why the habits of reading the Bible and family prayers from which Protestants have obviously derived so much strength and refreshment could not have been added to the sacramental habits from which Catholics have, as obviously, derived so much, instead of both parties regarding them as incompatible. There seems no *rational* reason why a return to St. Paul and St. Augustine could not have rescued theology from its sterile debate between Realism and Nominalism without leading to Calvinism and, as a defense reaction, to the adoption by Rome, understandably but still, to my mind, mistakenly, of Thomism as the official Catholic philosophy. But history, of course, is not rational nor repeatable. (For me the most mysterious aspect of the whole affair is not theological or political but cultural. Why was it that the peoples and nations who became Protestant were precisely those who, before Christ was born, had been least influenced by the culture of *pagan* Rome?)

That Protestant and Catholic no longer regard each other as monsters is a reason for thanking God, but also a reason to be ashamed of ourselves that we, as Christians, have contributed so little to this more charitable atmosphere. If we have learned that it is wicked to inflict secular penalties on heresy, to keep people in the faith by terror, we have learned it from sceptical rationalists who felt, like Earl Halifax, that "Most men's anger about religion is as if two men should quarrel for a lady they neither of them care for." Even after the burnings stopped, the religious minority, Catholic or Protestant, still continued to suffer sufficient civil disabilities to ensure that to a great extent religious boundaries would coincide with state boundaries and prevent the average Protestant and Catholic from ever meeting. Defoe says that in the England of his time "there were a hundred thousand fellows ready to fight to the death against popery, without knowing whether popery was a man or a horse," and the situation in Catholic countries can have been no better. Again, the campaign to make the secular authorities grant equal rights to all citizens, irrespective of their religious beliefs, was certainly not headed by Christians. Even when equality in law had been granted, class barriers remained which have only begun to disappear in my own lifetime. Among the English middle classes, thanks to the existence of old Catholic families whose social status was unimpeachable, it might be eccentric or immoral to be a Catholic, but it was not infra dig like being a Dissenter. When I was young, for an Anglican to "go over to Rome" was rather like having an illegitimate baby, an unfortunate event but something which can happen in the best families. But for an Anglican to become a Baptist would have been unthinkable: Baptists were persons who came to the back door, not the front. Once again, the part played by Christians in fighting against social injustice and snobbery has not been a conspicuous one. Lastly, whether we desire it or not, we are being brought closer together by simple physical fear. There are large areas of the globe where it is now a serious worldly disadvantage, and sometimes dangerous, to be a Christian of any kind, and these areas may very well increase.

When all fleshly and worldly circumstances favor a greater mutual understanding, any failure of charity on our part becomes all the more inexcusable. As I write, it is but a few days to Pentecost, the Ecumenical Feast, in what the Pope has proclaimed an Ecumenical Year. As a preliminary we might start by thanking each other, and the modern secular culture against which we both inveigh, for the competition. It is good for Protestant minister and Catholic priest to know that there is a church of another persuasion round the corner and a movie-house across the way from them both, to know that they cannot hold their flocks simply because there is no other place of worship to attend, or because not attending some place of worship will incur social disapproval. I have often observed how much more vital, liturgically, both Catholic and Protestant services become in countries with religiously mixed populations than in countries which are overwhemingly one or the other. Then, after this exchange of compliments, we might reread together the second chapter of Acts. The miracle wrought by the Holy Spirit is generally referred to as a gift of tongues: is it not equally a gift of ears? It is just as miraculous that those in the parts of Libya about Cyrene and strangers from Rome should be able to listen to Galileans, as that Galileans should be able to speak to them. The Curse of Babel is not the diversity of human tongues — diversity is essential to life — but the pride of each of us which makes us think that those who make different verbal noises from our own are incapable of human speech so that discourse with them is out of the question, a pride which, since the speech of no two persons is identical — language is not algebra — must inevitably lead to the conclusion that the gift of human speech is reserved for oneself alone. It is due to this curse that, as Sir William Osler said, "Half of us are blind, few of us feel, and we are all deaf." That we may learn first how to listen and then how to translate are the two gifts of which we stand most urgently in need and for which we should most fervently pray at this time.

W. H. AUDEN

Martin Luther

Founder of the Reformation. Born in 1483, the son of a miner, he was educated at Magdeburg, Eisenach and Erfurt University. In 1505 he became an Augustinian monk. He was ordained priest in 1507 and in 1508 was sent to the newly founded university of Wittenberg as professor of moral philosophy. He visited Rome in 1510. In 1515 he was made Vicar of his order. Anxiety about his salvation led him to give up celebrating Mass and reciting his office, until the so-called "Tower" experience, which was a sudden revelation that faith alone justified without works. In 1517 J. Tetzel promulgated indulgence and Luther drew up his ninety-five theses against them and affixed these to the door of the Wittenberg Stadskapelle. Luther's break with the Church was completed by the censorship of three of his works by a bull in 1520 and he was excommunicated in 1521. Summoned before the Diet of Worms, he was put under the ban of the Empire, but was hidden by the Elector Frederick III of Saxony in the Wartburg Castle for eight months. Here he translated the Bible into German. The Diet of Augsburg, which Luther did not attend owing to being under the ban, approved the Augsburg Confession drawn up by Luther's pupil, Melanchthon. Luther died in 1546.

From PREFACE TO LATIN WRITINGS

Though I lived as a monk without reproach, I felt that I was a sinner before God with an extremely disturbed conscience. I could not believe that he was placated by my satisfaction. I did not love, yes, I hated the righteous God who punishes sinners, and secretly, if not blasphemously, certainly murmuring greatly, I was angry with God and said, "As if, indeed, it is not enough that miserable sinners, eternally lost through original sin, are crushed with every kind of calamity by the law of the decalogue, without having God add pain to pain by the gospel and also by the gospel threatening us with his righteousness and wrath." Thus I raged with a fierce and troubled conscience. Nevertheless, I beat importunately upon Paul at that place, most ardently desiring to know what St. Paul wanted.

At last, by the mercy of God, meditating day and night, I gave heed to the context of the words, namely: "In it the righteousness of God is revealed, as it is written 'he who through faith is righteous shall live." There I began to understand that the righteousness of God is that by which the righteous lives by a gift of God, namely by faith. And this is the meaning: the righteousness of God is revealed by the gospel, namely, the passive righteousness with which merciful God justifies us by faith, as it is written, "He who through faith is righteous shall live." Here I felt that I was altogether born again and had entered Paradise itself through open gates.

John Donne

The celebrated English metaphysical poet and divine was born in 1572. Won the notice of King James I, but was promoted only within the Anglican Church. He entered Anglican orders in 1615, and six years later was appointed Dean of St. Paul's Cathedral. His poetry, uniquely characterized by intellectual audacity and an energy at once erotic and transcendent, has been subject to many vagaries of taste, and owes much of its present eminence to the revival of attention initiated by T. S. Eliot. Best known for a sonnet to Death and *Anniversaries*, two elegies. His sermons are also among the most distinguished in the language. He died in 1631.

From HOLY SONNETS

Holy Sonnet V

I am a little world made cunningly
Of Elements, and an Angelike spright,
But black sinne hath betraid to endlesse night
My worlds both parts, and (oh) both parts must die.
You which beyond that heaven which was most high
Have found new sphears, and of new lands can write,
Powre new seas in mine eyes, that so I might
Drowne my world with my weeping earnestly,
Or wash it, if it must be drown'd no more:
But oh it must be burnt! Alas the fire
Of lust and envie have burnt it heretofore,
And made it fouler; Let their flames retire,
And burne me ô Lord, with a fiery zeale
Oh thee and thy house, which doth in eating heale.

Holy Sonnet VII

At the round earths imagin'd corners, blow
Your trumpets, Angells, and arise, arise
From death, you numberlesse infinities
Of soúles, and to your scattered bodies goe,
All whom the flood did, and fire shall o'erthrow,
All whom warre, dearth, age, agues, tyrannies,
Despaire, law, chance, hath slaine, and you whose eyes,
Shall behold God, and never tast deaths woe.
But let them sleepe, Lord, and mee mourne a space,
For, if above all these, my sinnes abound,
'Tis late to aske abundance of thy grace,
When wee are there; here on this lowly ground,
Teach mee how to repent; for that's as good
As if thou'hadst seal'd my pardon, with thy blood.

Holy Sonnet XIV

Batter my heart, three person'd God; for you
As yet but knocke, breathe, shine, and seeke to mend;
That I may rise, and stand o'erthrow mee, 'and bend
Your force, to breake, blowe, burn and make me new.
I, like an usurpt towne, to'another due,
Labour to'admit you, but Oh, to no end,
Reason your viceroy in mee, mee should defend,
But is captiv'd, and proves weake or untrue.
Yet dearely'I love you, 'and would be loved faine,
But an betroth'd unto your enemie:
Divorce mee, 'untie, or breake that knot againe,
Take mee to you, imprison mee, for I
Except you'enthrall mee, never shall be free,
Nor ever chast, except you ravish mee.

Jakob Boehme

A German Lutheran theosophical writer, Jakob Boehme was born in 1575, the son of a farmer. At first a shepherd, he later became a shoemaker, following this trade from 1599 until 1623. He claimed in his writings to describe only what he learned in person from divine revelation. His first work, *Aurora*, was published in 1612 and aroused opposition from the local Lutheran pastor who obliged the municipal authorities to forbid Boehme to write. Boehme's views on the universe as the manifestation of God, and of evil as God's wrath, were denounced as heretical. Between 1618 and 1623 Boehme wrote a series of devotional treatises called *The Way to Christ*. As his pastor still opposed him, Boehme left his birthplace, Gorlitz, in 1624 and went first to Dresden and later to Silesia. Most of his writings were posthumously published. He had a far-reaching influence on such German romantics as Schelling and Hegel, and on the English Platonist, P. Sterry, and later also on William Law. He died in 1624.

From THE WAY TO CHRIST

20. And as God dwelleth in the world, and filleth all things, and yet possesseth nothing; and as the fire dwelleth in water, and yet possesseth it not; Also, as the light dwelleth in darkness, and yet possesseth not the darkness; as the day is in the night, and the night in the day, time in eternity, and eternity in time; so is man created according to the outward humanity, he is the time, and in the time, and the time is the outward world, and it is also the outward man.

21. The inward man is eternity and the spiritual time and world, which also consisteth of light and darkness, viz.,

of the love of God, as to the eternal light, and of the anger of God as to the eternal darkness; whichsoever of these is manifest in him, his spirit dwelleth in that, be it darkness or light.

22. For light and darkness are both in him, but each of them dwelleth in itself, and neither of them possesseth the other; but if one of them entereth into the other, and will possess it, then that other loseth its right and power.

From THE CONFESSIONS OF JAKOB BOEHME

Men have always been of the opinion that heaven is many hundred, nay, many thousand, miles distant from the face of the earth, and that God dwells only in that heaven.

Some have undertaken to measure this height and distance, and have produced many strange and monstrous devices. Indeed, before my knowledge and revelation of God, I held that only to be the true heaven which, in a round circumference, very azure of a light blue colour, extends itself above the stars; supposing that God had therein his peculiar Being, and did rule only in the power of his Holy Spirit in this world.

But when this had given me many a hard blow and repulse, doubtless from the Spirit, which had a great longing yearning towards me, at last I fell into a very deep melancholy and heavy sadness, when I beheld and contemplated the great Deep of this world, also the sun and stars, the clouds, rain and snow, and considered in my spirit the whole creation of the world.

Wherein then I found, in all things, evil and good, love and anger; in the inanimate creatures, in wood, stones, earth and the elements, as also in men and beasts.

Moreover I considered the little spark of light, man, what

he should be esteemed for with God, in comparison of this great work and fabric of heaven and earth.

And finding that in all things there was evil and good, as well in the elements as in the creatures, and that it went as well in this world with the wicked as with the virtuous, honest and godly; also that the barbarous people had the best countries in their possession, and that they had more prosperity in their ways than the virtuous, honest and godly had; I was thereupon very melancholy, perplexed and exceedingly troubled, no Scripture could comfort or satisfy me though I was very well acquainted with it and versed therein; at which time the Devil would by no means stand idle, but was often beating into me many heathenish thoughts which I will here be silent in.

Yet when in this affliction and trouble I elevated my spirit (which then I understood very little or nothing at all what it was), I earnestly raised it up into God, as with a great storm or onset, wrapping up my whole heart and mind, as also all my thoughts and whole will and resolution, incessantly to wrestle with the Love and Mercy of God, and not to give over unless he blessed me, that is, unless he enlightened me with his Holy Spirit, whereby I might understand his will and be rid of my sadness. And then the Spirit did break through.

But when in my resolved zeal I gave so hard an assault, storm, and onset upon God and upon all the gates of hell, as if I had more reserves of virtue and power ready, with a resolution to hazard my life upon it (which assuredly were not in my ability without the assistance of the Spirit of God), suddenly my spirit did break through the gates of hell, even into the innermost moving of the Deity, and there I was embraced in love as a bridegroom embraces his dearly beloved bride.

The greatness of the triumphing that was in my spirit I cannot express either in speaking or writing; neither can it be compared to any thing but that wherein life is generated in the midst of death. It is like the resurrection from the dead.

In this light my spirit suddenly saw through all, and in and by all, the creatures; even in herbs and grass it knew God, who he is and how he is and what his will is. And suddenly in that light my will was set on by a mighty impulse to describe the Being of God.

But because I could not presently apprehend the deepest movings of God and comprehend them in my reason, there passed almost twelve years before the exact understanding thereof was given me.

And it was with me as with a young tree, which is planted in the ground and at first is young and tender, and flourishing to the eye, especially if it comes on lustily in its growing; but does not bear fruit presently, and though it has blossoms they fall off: also frost and snow and many a cold wind beat upon it before it comes to any growth and bearing of fruit.

So also it went with my spirit: the first fire was but a beginning and not a constant and lasting light; since that time many a cold wind blew upon it, yet never extinguished it.

The tree was also often tempted to try whether it could bear fruit, and showed itself with blossoms; but the blossoms were struck off till this very time, wherein it stands in its fruit.

From this light now it is that I have my knowledge, as also my will, impulse and driving; and therefore I will set down the knowledge in writing according to my gift, and let God work his will. Though I should enrage the whole world, the Devil, and all the gates of hell, I will look on and wait what the Lord intends with it.

For I am too, too weak to know his purpose; and though the Spirit affords in the light some things to be known

which are to come, yet according to the outward man I am
too weak to comprehend them.

The animated or soulish spirit, which unfolds its powers
and unites with God, comprehends it well; but the animal
body attains only a glimpse thereof; just as by a lightning-
flash. This is the state of the innermost moving of the soul,
when it breaks through the outermost in an elevation by
the Holy Ghost. But the outermost presently closes again,
for the wrath of God is stirred up there as fire is struck from
the stone, and holds it captive in its power.

Then the knowledge of the outward man is gone, and he
walks up and down, afflicted and anxious, as a woman with
child who is in her travail, and would willingly bring forth,
but cannot and is full of throes.

Thus it goes also with the animal body when it has once
tasted of the sweetness of God. Then it continually hungers
and thirsts after it; but the Devil in the power of God's
wrath opposes exceedingly, and so a man in such a course
must continually be anxious; and there is nothing but fighting and warring for him.

I write not this for my own glory, but for a comfort to the
reader, so that if perhaps he be minded to walk with me
upon my narrow bridge, he should not suddenly be discouraged, dismayed, and distrustful, when the gates of hell and
God's wrath meet him and present themselves before him.

When we shall come together, over this narrow bridge
of the fleshly working, to be in yonder green meadow to
which the wrath of God does not reach, then we shall be
fully requited for all our damages and hurts we have sus-
tained; though indeed at present the world accounts us for
fools, and we must suffer the Devil to domineer rush, and
roar over us.

Now observe: if thou fixest thy thoughts concerning
heaven, and wouldst willingly conceive in thy mind what it

is and where it is and how it is, thou needst not to cast thy thoughts many thousand miles off, for that place, that heaven, is not thy heaven.

And though indeed that is united with thy heaven as one body, and so together is but the one body of God, yet thou art not become a creature in that very place which is above many hundred thousand miles off, but thou art in the heaven of this world, which contains also in it such a Deep as is not of any human numbering.

The true heaven is everywhere, even in that very place where thou standest and goest; and so when thy spirit presses through the astral and the fleshly, and apprehends the innermost moving of God, then it is clearly in heaven.

But that there is assuredly a pure glorious heaven in all the three movings aloft above the deep of this world, in which God's Being together with that of the holy angels springs up very purely, brightly, beauteously, and joyfully, is undeniable. And he is not born of God that denies it.

Thou must know that this world in its innermost unfolds its properties and powers in union with the heaven aloft above us; and so there is one Heart, one Being, one Will, one God, all in all.

The outermost moving of this world cannot comprehend the outermost moving of heaven aloft above this world, for they are one to the other as life and death, or as a man and a stone are one to the other.

There is a strong firmament dividing the outermost of this world from the outermost of the upper heaven; and that firmament is Death, which rules and reigns everywhere in the outermost in this world, and sets a great gulf between them.

The second moving of this world is in the life; it is the astral, out of which is generated the third and holy moving; and therein love and wrath strive one with the other.

For the second moving stands in the seven fountain spirits of this world, and is in all places and in all the creatures as in man. But the Holy Ghost also rules and reigns in that second, and helps to generate the third, the holy moving.

This, the third, is the clear and holy heaven which unites with the Heart of God, distinct from and above all heavens, as one heart.

Therefore, thou child of man, be not discouraged, be not so timorous and pusillanimous; if thou in thy zeal and earnest sincerity sowest the seed of thy tears, thou dost not sow it in earth but in heaven; for in thy astral moving thou sowest, and in thy soulish moving thou reapest, and in the kingdom of heaven thou possessest and enjoyest it.

If man's eyes were but opened he should see God everywhere in his heaven; for heaven stands in the innermost moving everywhere.

John Amos Komensky

Born in 1592 at Uhersky Brod, in Moravia, he lost his parents young, and was sent to a Moravian Brothers' school. Thence he proceeded to the Unity School at Prerau and the Calvinist University at Herborn, in Nassau, and thereafter to Heidelberg and Amsterdam. In 1616 he was appointed minister of the church at Fulneck. After the battle of the White Mountain in 1620 he fled with his wife and children to Charles, Lord of Zerotin, at Brandeis on the Orlice, but he lost his wife and children on the journey. In a hut at Brandeis he wrote his masterpiece, in Czech, *The Labyrinth of the World and the Paradise of the Heart*. In January 1628, Komensky left Bohemia for Silesia, where he lived for several years as schoolmaster in Lissa. In 1641 he went to England on the invitation of Milton's friend Samuel Hartlie. In 1642, after the Civil War broke out, Komensky went to Sweden. He lived at Elbing from 1642 to 1648 and wrote schoolbooks. He was made Moravian (Unity) Bishop of Lissa in 1648. After war broke out between Poland and the Swedes, first the Swedes, then the Poles, captured Lissa. Komensky's house and library were burned. He went to Amsterdam, where he died on 15 November 1670, and is buried in the church of the French Protestants.

From THE LABYRINTH OF THE WORLD

Chapter XXVI
THE PILGRIM DESIRES TO FLEE FROM THE WORLD

(The Pilgrim beholds the Dying and Dead. The Bottomless Abyss beyond the World.)

3. Looking now about me, I behold the ways of the dying, of whom there were many; and I see a mournful thing

— to wit, that all gave up the ghost with horror, lamentation, fear and trembling, knowing not what would befall them and whither they would go. Although I was afeard, yet wishing ever to acquire more knowledge. I walked through the rows of the dead to the limits of the world and of light. Here, where others, shutting their eyes, blindly cast forth their dead, I threw off the glasses of Falsehood, rubbed my eyes, and leaned forward as far as I dared. And I behold awful darkness and gloom, of which the mind of man can find neither the end nor the ground; and there was here naught but worms, frogs, serpents, scorpions, rottenness, stench, the smell of brimstone and pitch that overwhelmed body and soul, generally unspeakable horror.

(*The Pilgrim falls to the Ground terrified.*)

4. Then my bowels quaked, my whole body trembled, and, terrified, I fell swooning to the ground, and cried mournfully: "Oh, most miserable, wretched, unhappy mankind! this, then, is your last glory! this the conclusion of your many splendid deeds! this the term of your learning and much wisdom over which you glory so greatly! this the rest and repose that you crave after countless labours and struggles! this the immortality for which you ever hope! Oh, that I had never been born, never passed through the gate of life! For after the many vanities of the world; nothing but darkness and horror are my part! O God, God, God! God, if Thou art a God, have mercy on wretched me!"

Chapter XXXVIII
THE PILGRIM RECEIVES CHRIST AS HIS GUEST

(*Our Illumination cometh from on High.*)

Behold, a clear light appeared on high, and raising my eyes towards it, I see the window above me full of brightness, and from out of that brightness there appeared One, in aspect, indeed, similar to a man, but in His splendour truly God. His countenance shone exceedingly, yet could human eyes gaze at it, for it caused not terror; rather had it a loveliness such as I had never seen in the world. He then — kindness itself, friendliness itself — addressed me in these most sweet words:

(Wherein the Source of all Light and
all Joy lieth.)

2. "Welcome, welcome, my son and dear brother." And having said these words, He embraced me, and kissed me kindly. There came forth from Him a most delightful odour, and I was seized by such unspeakable delight that tears flowed from my eyes, and I knew not how to respond to so unexpected a greeting. Only sighing deeply, I gazed at Him with meek eyes. Then He, seeing me overwhelmed with joy, spoke thus further to me: "Where, then, hast thou been, my son? why hast thou tarried so long? by what path hast thou come? what hast thou sought in the world? Joy! where could thou seek it but in God; and where couldst thou seek God, but in His own temple; and what is the temple of the living God, but the living temple that He Himself has fashioned — thine own heart? I saw, my son, that thou wentest astray, but I would see it no longer. I have brought thee to thy own self. I have led thee into thyself. For here have I chosen my palace and my dwelling. If thou wishest here to dwell with me, thou wilt find here, what thou hast vainly sought on earth, rest, comfort, glory, and abundance of all things. This I promise thee, my son, that thou wilt not be deceived here as thou wert there in the world."

(The Pilgrim gives himself over entirely to Jesus.)

3. Hearing such speech, and understanding that He who spake was my Redeemer, Jesus Christ, of whom I had in-

deed heard somewhat in the world, but superficially only, I folded my hands, and then stretched them out, not, as in the world, with fear and doubt, but with full happiness and complete faith; then I said: "I am here, my Lord Jesus; take me to Thee. Thine I wish to be, and to remain for ever. Speak to Thy servant, and permit me to hear Thee; tell me what Thou desirest, and grant that I find pleasure in it; lay on me what burden Thou thinkest fit, and grant that I may bear it; employ me for whatever purpose Thou desirest, and grant me that I may not be found wanting; order me to act according to Thy will, and grant me grace to do so. Let me be nothing, that Thou mayest be everything."

Chapter XXXIX
THEIR BETROTHAL

(God's Wisdom directs even our Errors.)

"I accept this from thee, my son," quoth He. "Hold to this, become, call thyself, and remain mine own. Mine, indeed, thou wert and art from all eternity, but thou knewest it not. I have long prepared for thee that happiness to which I will now lead thee; but thou didst not understand this. I have led thee to thyself through strange paths and by round-about ways; this thou knewest not, nor what I, the ruler of all my chosen ones, intended; neither didst thou perceive by what means I worked on thee. But I was everywhere with thee, and therefore somewhat guided thee through these crooked paths, that I might at last bring thee yet closer to me. Naught could the world, naught thy guides, naught Solomon teach thee. They could by no means enrich thee, content thee, satisfy the desires of thy heart, for they had not that which thou didst seek. But I will teach thee everything, enrich thee, content thee."

*(All Worldly Striving should be
transferred to God.)*

2. "This only I demand of thee, that whatever thou hast seen in the world, and whatever struggles thou hast witnessed among men, thou shouldst transfer it to me, and lay the burden of it on me. This, as long as thou livest, shall be thy work and thy task; of that which men seek there in the world, but find not — to wit, peace and joy — I will give thee abundance."

*(The Pilgrim joins Christ only,
his Eternal Spouse.)*

3. "Thou hast seen in the estate of the married people how those who find pleasure in one another leave everything, that they may belong to each other. Do thus thou also, leave everything, even thyself; give thyself up fully to me, and thou wilt be mine, and it will be well. As long as thou dost not this, thou wilt, I assure thee, obtain no solace for thy soul. For in the world everything changeth; everything beside me for which thy mind and thy desire will strive, will, in one way or another, cause thee toil and discontent; at last it will forsake thee, and the joy that thou hadst found in it will turn to woe. Therefore I faithfully counsel thee, my son, forsake everything and cling to me; be mine, and I thine. Let us shut ourselves up together here in this shrine, and thou wilt feel truer joy than can be found in carnal wedlock. Strive, then, to love me alone; to have me as thy one counsellor, leader, friend, companion, and comrade in all things. And whenever thou speakest to me, say, 'I only and thou, oh, my Lord!' Thou needest not heed any third one. Cling but to me, gaze at me, converse sweetly with me, embrace me, kiss me; expect also all things from me.

George Herbert

Born in 1593, he became, like John Donne, a clergyman of the Church of England. Herbert translated religious experience into a poetry of spiritual autobiography and contemplative drama. This became an expression of his ardent temperament. Herbert assumes the Christian sensibility of his audience, and the dialogue with Christ which is the substance of his finest poems is among the most personal and affecting in the English mystical tradition. Many of his religious poems were published after his death in a volume entitled *The Temple: Sacred Poems and Private Ejaculations* (1652). He died in 1633.

AFFLICTION (1)

When first thou didst entice to thee my heart,
        I thought the service brave:
So many joyes I write down for my part,
        Besides what I might have
Out of my stock of naturall delights,
Augmented with thy gracious benefits.

I looked on thy furniture so fine,
        And made it fine to me:
Thy glorious houshold-stuffe did me entwine,
        And 'tice me unto thee.
Such starres I counted mine: both heav'n and earth
Payd me my wages in a world of mirth.

What pleasures could I want, whose King I served,
        Where joyes my fellows were?

Thus argu'd into hopes, my thoughts reserved
        No place for grief or fear.
Therefore my sudden soul caught at the place,
And made her youth and fiercenesse seek thy face.

At first thou gav'st me milk and sweetnesses;
        I had my wish and way:
My dayes were straw'd with flow'rs and happinesse;
        There was no moneth but May.
But with my yeares sorrow did twist and grow,
And made a partie unawares for wo.

My flesh began unto my soul in pain,
        Sicknesses cleave my bones;
Consuming agues dwell in ev'ry vein,
        And tune my breath to grones.
Sorrow was all my soul; I scarce beleeved,
Till grief did tell me roundly, that I lived.

When I got health, thou took'st away my life,
        And more; for my friends die:
My mirth and edge was lost; a blunted knife
        Was of more use then I.
Thus thinne and lean without a fence or friend,
I was blown through with ev'ry storm and winde.

Whereas my birth and spirit rather took
        The way that takes the town;
Thou didst betray me to a lingring book,
        And wrap me in a gown.
I was entangled in the world of strife,
Before I had the power to change my life.

Yet, for I threatened oft the siege to raise,
        Not simpring all mine age,

Thou often didst with Academick praise
        Melt and dissolve my rage.
I took thy sweetened pill, till I came where
I could not go away, nor persevere.

Yet lest perchance I should too happie be
        In my unhappinesse,
Turning my purge to food, thou throwest me
        Into more sicknesses.
Thus doth thy power crosse-bias me, not making
Thine own gift good, yet me from my wayes taking.

Now I am here, what thou wilt do with me
        None of my books will show:
I reade, and sigh, and wish I were a tree;
        For sure then I should grow
To fruit or shade: at least some bird would trust
Her household to me, and I should be just.

Yet, though thou troublest me, I must be meek;
        In weaknesse must be stout.
Well, I will change the service, and go seek
        Some other master out.
Ah my deare God! though I am clean forgot,
Let me not love thee, if I love thee not.

Samuel Rutherford

Presbyterian clergyman and theologian. Born in 1600 at Nisbet, in Roxburghshire, he went to the University of Edinburgh in 1617, where he got his M.A. in 1621 and became Professor of Humanity in 1623. Settled as pastor of the parish of Anwoth in Kircudbright, in 1627. Banished in 1636 for extreme Calvinism, he was confined during the King's pleasure within the town of Aberdeen. In 1638 he returned quietly to Anwoth. In 1643, he was a deputy to the Westminster Assembly as a commissioner of the Church of Scotland. Professor of Divinity at St. Andrews in 1647, he wrote *Lex Rex* in 1660; this was publicly burnt at the cross of Edinburgh, and he was placed under house arrest and died 20 March 1661.

LETTER V
To the VISCOUNTESS OF KENMURE

My very Honourable and Dear Lady, — Grace, mercy, and peace be to you. I cannot forget your ladyship and that sweet child: I desire to hear what the Lord is doing to you and him. To write to me were charity. I cannot but write to my friends, that Christ hath trysted * me in Aberdeen, and my adversaries have sent me here to be feasted with love-banquets with my royal, high, high, and princely King Jesus. Madam, why should I smother Christ's honesty; I dare not conceal His goodness to my soul; He looked framed† and uncouth-like upon me when I came first here, but I believe Himself better than His looks. I shall not again quarrel

*Met with.
† Strange or alien.

Christ for a gloom, now He hath taken the mask off His face and saith, "Kiss thy fill;" and what can I have more, while* I get great heaven in my little arms, O, how sweet are the sufferings of Christ, for Christ! God forgive them that raise an ill report upon the sweet cross of Christ; it is but our weak and dim eyes that look but to the black side that makes us mistake: those who can take that crabbed tree handsomely upon their back, and fasten it on cannily† shall find it such a burden as wings unto a bird or sails to a ship. Madam, rue not of your having chosen the better part: upon my salvation this is Christ's truth I now suffer for. If I found but cold comfort in my sufferings I would not beguile others, I would have told you plainly; but the truth is, Christ's crown, His sceptre, and the freedom of His kingdom, is that which is now called in question. Because we will not allow that Christ pay tribute and be a vassal to the shields of the earth, therefore the sons of our mother are angry at us: but it becometh not Christ to hold any man's stirrup. It were a sweet and honourable death to die for the honour of that royal and princely King Jesus. His love is a mystery to the world. I would not have believed that there was so much in Christ, as there is; "Come and see," maketh Christ to be known in His excellency and glory. I wish all this nation knew how sweet His breath is; it is little to see Christ in a book, as men do the world in a card;‡ they talk of Christ by the book and the tongue, and no more; but to come nigh Christ and have Him, and embrace Him is another thing.

* Till.
† Gently.
‡ Chart or map.

LETTER CVII
To ROBERT GORDON OF KNOCKBREX

My very worthy and dear Friend, — Grace, mercy, and peace be unto you. Though all Galloway should have forgotten me, I would have expected a letter from you ere now. But I will not expound it to be forgetfulness of me. Now, my dear brother, I cannot show you how matters go betwixt Christ and me. I find my Lord going and coming seven times a day. His visits are short, but they are both frequent and sweet. I dare not for my life think of a challenge of my Lord. I hear ill tales, and hard reports of Christ, from the tempter and my flesh, but love believeth no evil. I may swear that they are liars, and that apprehensions make lies of Christ's honest and unalterable love to me. I dare not say that I am a dry tree, or that I have no room at all in the vineyard; but yet, I often think, that the sparrows are blessed who may resort to the house of God in Anwoth, from which I am banished. Temptations, that I suppose to be stricken dead and laid upon their back, rise again and revive upon me; yea, I see that while I live, temptations will not die. The devil seemeth to brag and boast as much as if he had more court* with Christ than I have, and as if he had charmed and blasted my ministry, that I shall do no more good in public; but his wind shaketh no corn. I will not believe Christ would have made such a mint† to have me to Himself, and have taken so much pains upon me as He hath done, and then slip so easily from possession, and lose the glory of what He had done; nay, since I came to Aberdeen, I have been taken up to see the new land, the fair palace of the Lamb. And will Christ let me see heaven to break my heart, and never give it to me? I shall not think

* Influence.
† Effort.

my Lord Jesus giveth a dumb earnest, or putteth His seals to blank paper, or intendeth to put me off with fair and false promises. I see that now which I never saw well before. 1. I see faith's necessity in a fair day is never known aright; but now I miss nothing so much as faith. Hunger in me runneth to fair and sweet promises; but when I come, I am like a hungry man that wanteth teeth, or a weak stomach having a sharp appetite, that is filled with the very sight of meat; or like one stupified with cold under the water, that would fain come to land, but cannot grip anything casten to him. I can let Christ grip me, but I cannot grip Him. I love to be kissed and to sit on Christ's knee; but I cannot set my feet to the ground, for afflictions bring the cramp upon my faith. All I now do is to hold out a lame faith to Christ, like a beggar holding out a stump, instead of an arm or leg, and cry Lord Jesus, work a miracle. O, what would I give to have hands and arms to grip strongly and fold heartsomely about Christ's neck, and to have my claim made good with real possession! I think my love to Christ hath feet abundance and runneth swiftly to be at Him, but it wanteth hands and fingers to apprehend Him. I think I would give Christ every morning my blessing, to have as much faith as I have love and hunger; at least, I miss faith more than love and hunger. 2. I see mortification, and to be crucified to the world, is not so highly accounted of by us as it should be. O, how heavenly a thing is it to be dead, and dumb, and deaf to this world's sweet music! I confess it hath pleased His Majesty to make me laugh at children who are wooing this world for their match. I see men lying about the world as nobles about a king's court, and I wonder what they are a-doing there. As I am at this present, I would scorn to court such a feckless* and petty princess, or buy this world's kindness with a bow of my knee. I scarce now either hear or see what it is that

* Worthless.

this world offereth me; I know it is little it can take from me, and as little it can give me. I recommend mortification to you above anything. For, alas, we but chase feathers flying in the air, and tire our own spirits for the froth and overgilded clay of a dying life. One sight of what my Lord hath let me see, within this short time, is worth a world of worlds. 3. I thought courage in the time of trouble for Christ's sake a thing that I might take up at my foot: I thought the very remembrance of the honesty of the cause would be enough: but I was a fool in so thinking. I have much ado now to win to one smile; but I see joy groweth up in heaven, and it is above our short arm. Christ will be steward and dispenser Himself, and none else but He. Therefore, now, I count much of one drachm-weight of spiritual joy; one smile of Christ's face is now to me as a kingdom, and yet He is no niggard to me of comforts. Truly, I have no cause to say, that I am pinched with penury, or that the consolations of Christ are dried up; for He hath poured down rivers upon a dry wilderness, the like of me, to my admiration: and in my very swoonings, He holdeth up my head, and "stayeth me with flagons of wine," and "comforteth me with apples." My house and bed are strawed with kisses of love. Praise, praise with me.

Jeremy Taylor

Anglican bishop and writer, Jeremy Taylor was born in 1613, a barber's son. He went to Cambridge, where he was elected a fellow of Caius College in 1633, and was ordained in London to the Anglican ministry. Archbishop Laud made him chaplain to King Charles I in 1635, and in the same year Taylor became a fellow of All Souls College, Oxford. Given the living of Uppingham, he left it to become chaplain to the Royalist forces in 1642. In 1645, he retired to Wales and operated a school, later becoming private chaplain to Lord Carbery at Golden Grove. In 1658 he went to Lisburne in Ireland, and in 1660 became Bishop of Down and Vice-Rector of Dublin University. In 1661 he was also given the see of Dromore. He was harsh both to Presbyterians and Catholics, but his devotional writings are characteristic examples of Anglican spirituality "in their balanced sobriety and their insistence on well-ordered piety." He died in 1667.

From HOLY LIVING

Several Manners of the Divine Presence

The presence of God is understood by us in several manners, and to several purposes.

1. God is present by his essence; which, because it is infinite, cannot be contained within the limits of any place; and because he is of an essential purity and spiritual nature, he cannot be undervalued by being supposed present in the places of unnatural uncleanness; because as the sun, reflecting upon the mud of strands and shores, is unpolluted in its beams, so is God not dishonoured when we suppose

him in every of his creatures, and in every part of every one of them; and is still as unmixt with any unhandsome adherence as is the soul in the bowels of the body.

2. God is every where present by his power. He rolls the orbs of heaven with his hand; he fixes the earth with his foot; he guides all the creatures with his eye, and refreshes them with his influence; he makes the powers of hell to shake with his terrors, and binds the devils with his word, and throws them out with his command; and sends the angels on embassies with his decrees; he hardens the joints of infants, and confirms the bones, when they are fashioned beneath secretly in the earth. He it is that assists at the numerous productions of fishes; and there is not one hollowness in the bottom of the sea, but he shows himself to be Lord of it by sustaining there the creatures that come to dwell in it: and in the wilderness, the bittern and the stork, the dragon and the satyr, the unicorn and the elk, live upon his provisions, and revere his power, and feel the force of his almightiness.

3. God is more specially present, in some places, by the several and more special manifestations of himself to extraordinary purposes. First, by glory. Thus, his seat is in heaven, because there he sits encircled with all the outward demonstrations of his glory, which he is pleased to show to all the inhabitants of those his inward and secret courts. And thus, they that "die in the Lord" may be properly said to be "gone to God"; with whom although they were before, yet now they enter into his courts, into the secret of his tabernacle, into the retinue and splendour of his glory. That is called walking with God, but this is dwelling or being with him. "I desire to be dissolved and to be with Christ"; so said St. Paul. But this manner of the Divine presence is reserved for the elect people of God, and for their portion in their country.

4. God is, by grace and benediction, specially present in

holy places, and in the solemn assemblies of his servants. If holy people meet in grots and dens of the earth, when persecution or a public necessity disturbs the public order, circumstance, and convenience, God fails not to come thither to them: but God is also, by the same or a greater reason, present there, where they meet ordinarily, by order, and public authority; there God is present ordinarily, that is, at every such meeting. God will go out of his way to meet his saints, when themselves are forced out of their way of order by a sad necessity: but else, God's usual way is to be present in those places where his servants are appointed ordinarily to meet. But his presence there signifies nothing but a readiness to hear their prayers, to bless their persons, to accept their offices, and to like even the circumstance of orderly and public meeting. For thither the prayers of consecration, the public authority separating it, and God's love of order, and the reasonable customs of religion, have in ordinary, and in a certain degree, fixed this manner of his presence; and he loves to have it so.

5. God is especially present in the hearts of his people, by his Holy Spirit: and indeed the hearts of holy men are temples in the truth of things, and, in type and shadow, they are heaven itself. For God reigns in the hearts of his servants: there is his kingdom. The power of grace hath subdued all his enemies: there is his power. They serve him night and day, and give him thanks and praise: that is his glory. This is the religion and worship of God in the temple. The temple itself is the heart of man; Christ is the High Priest, who from thence sends up the incense of prayers, and joins them to his own intercession, and presents all together to his Father; and the Holy Ghost, by his dwelling there, hath also consecrated it into a temple"; and God dwells in our hearts by faith, and Christ by his Spirit, and the Spirit by his purities; so that we are also cabinets of the mysterious Trinity; and what is this short of heaven itself,

but as infancy is short of manhood, and letters of words? The same state of life it is, but not the same age. It is heaven in a looking-glass, dark, but yet true, representing the beauties of the soul, and the graces of God, and the images of his eternal glory, by the reality of a special presence.

6. God is especially present in the consciences of all persons, good and bad, by way of testimony and judgment: that is, he is there a remembrancer to call our actions to mind, a witness to bring them to judgment, and a judge to acquit or to condemn. And although this manner of presence is, in this life, after the manner of this life, that is, imperfect, and we forget many actions of our lives; yet the greatest changes of our state of grace or sin, our most considerable actions, are always present, like capital letters to an aged and dim eye: and, at the day of judgment, God shall draw aside the cloud, and manifest this manner of his presence more notoriously, and make it appear that he was an observer of our very thoughts, and that he only laid those things by, which, because we covered with dust and negligence, were not then discerned. But when we are risen from our dust and imperfection, they all appear plain and legible.

Now, the consideration of this great truth is of a very universal use in the whole course of the life of a Christian. All the consequents and effects of it are universal. He that remembers that God stands a witness and a judge, beholding every secrecy, besides his impiety, must have put on impudence, if he be not much restrained in his temptation to sin. "For the greatest part of sin is taken away, if a man have a witness of his conversation: and he is a great despiser of God who sends a boy away, when he is going to commit fornication, and yet will dare to do it though he knows God is present, and cannot be sent off: as if the eye of a little boy were more awful than the all-seeing eye of

God. He is to be feared in public, he is to be feared in private: if you go forth, he spies you; if you go in, he sees you: when you light the candle, he observes you; when you put it out, then also God marks you. Be sure, that while you are in his sight, you behave yourself as becomes so holy a presence." But if you will sin, retire yourself wisely, and go where God cannot see; for no where else can you be safe.

Richard Baxter

Richard Baxter was a Puritan divine. Born in Shropshire in 1615, he was largely self-educated. He studied eventually at Ludlow, and in 1633 went to London. Disgusted by the frivolity of the Court, he quickly returned home. In 1638 he was ordained in the Church of England by the Bishop of Worcester and in 1639 appointed master of the free grammar school at Bridgenorth for two years. At this time, Baxter rejected belief in episcopacy. In 1641 he became curate at Kidderminster where he remained until 1660. He joined the Parliamentary Army, and was at the Battle of Edgehill in 1642. After the Battle of Naseby in 1645 he became chaplain to Colonel Whalley's regiment but in 1647 retired and wrote his most famous book, *The Saint's Everlasting Rest*. He played a part in the recall of Charles II, and later refused the Bishopric of Hereford. In 1661 he participated in the Savoy Conference, and was persecuted by Judge Jeffreys. He took part in the overthrow of James II. Baxter left over two hundred writings and is the author of several well-known hymns. He died in 1691.

From THE SAINTS' EVERLASTING REST

This Rest Defined

Though the sense of the text includes in the word "rest" all that is ease and safety, which a soul, wearied with the burden of sin and suffering, and pursued by law, wrath, and conscience hath with Christ in this life — the Rest of Grace — yet because it chiefly intends the Rest of Eternal Glory, as the end and main part, I shall confine my discourse to this last.

Rest is the end and perfection of motion. The saint's rest here in question is the most happy estate of a Christian, having obtained the end of his course: or, it is the perfect, endless fruition of God, by the perfected saints, according to the measure of their capacity, to which their souls arrive at death; and both soul and body most fully, after the resurrection and final judgement.

I call it the estate of a Christian, (though perfection consists in action, as the philosopher thinks), to note both the active and passive fruition, wherein a Christian's blessedness lies and the established continuance of both. Our title will be perfect, and perfectly cleared; ourselves, and so our capacity, perfected; our possession and security for its perpetuity perfect; our reception of [God] perfect; our motion or action in and upon him perfect: and, therefore our fruition of him, and consequently our happiness, will then be perfect. . . .

I call it the most happy estate, to difference it, not only from all seeming happiness, which is to be found in the enjoyment of creatures, but also from all those beginnings, foretastes, earns, first fruits, and imperfect degrees, which we have here in this life, while we are but in the way. It is the chief good which the world hath so much disputed, yet mistaken or neglected, without which the greatest confluence of all other good leaves a man miserable. . . .

I add that this happiness consists in obtaining the end, where I mean the ultimate and principal end. . . . Not the end of conclusion, in regard of time, for so every man hath his end; but the end of intention, which sets the soul a work, and is its prime motive in all its actions. . . . How much doth our everlasting state depend on our right judgement and estimation of our end!

But it is a great doubt with many, whether the obtainment of this glory may be our end; nay, concluded, that it is mercenary; yea, that to make salvation the end of duty, is to be a legalist, and act under a covenant of works, whose tenour is, "Do this and live." And many that think it may be our end, yet think it may not be our ultimate end, for that should be only the glory of God. I shall answer these particularly, and briefly.

It is properly called mercenary, when we expect it as wages for work done; and so we may not make it our end. Otherwise it is only such a mercenariness as Christ commandeth. For consider what this end is; it is the fruition of God in Christ: and if seeking Christ be mercenary, I desire to be so mercenary.

What This Rest Containeth

I

There is contained in this Rest, a cessation from motion or action; not of all action, but of that which hath the nature of a means, and implies the absence of the end. When we have obtained the haven, we have done sailing; When the workman hath his wages, it is implied he hath done his work; when we are at our journey's end, we have done with the way. All motion ends at the centre, and all means cease when we have the end. Therefore, prophesying ceaseth, tongues fail and knowledge shall be done away; that is, so far as it had the nature of a means and was imperfect. And so faith may be said to cease: not all faith, for how shall we know all things past, which we saw not but by believing? How shall we know the last judgement, the resurrection of the body beforehand, but by believing? How shall we know the life everlasting, the eternity of the joys we possess, but by believing? But all that faith, which, as a means referred to the chief end shall cease. There shall be no more prayer, because no more necessity, but the full enjoyment of what we prayed for. . . . Neither shall we need to fast, and weep, and watch any more, being out of the reach of sin and

temptations. Nor will there be use for instructions and ex-
hortations; preaching is done, the ministry of man ceaseth,
sacraments useless, the labourers called in because the harvest is gathered, the tares burnt, and the work done, the un-
regenerate past hope, the saints past fear, for ever. Much
less shall there be any need of labouring for inferior ends, as
here we do, seeing they will all devolve themselves into the
ocean of the ultimate end and the lesser good be wholly
swallowed up of the greatest.

II

This Rest containeth a perfect freedom from all the evils
that accompanied us through our course, and which necessarily follow our absence from the chief good. . . . As God
will not know the wicked so as to own them; so neither will
heaven know iniquity to receive it: for there entereth nothing that defileth or is unclean; all that remains without.
And doubtless there is not such a thing as grief and sorrow
known there. Nor is there such a thing as a pale face, a lan-
guid body, feeble joints, unable infancy, decrepit age, pec-
cant humours, dolorous sickness, griping fears, consuming
cares nor whatsoever deserves the name of evil. Indeed a
gale of groans and sighs, a stream of tears accompanied us
to the very gates, and there bid us farewell, for ever. We
did weep and lament when the world did rejoice; but our
sorrow is turned to joy, and our joy shall no man take
from us. God were not the chief and perfect good if the full
fruition of him did not free us from all evil. . . .

III

This Rest containeth the highest degree of the saints' personal perfection, both of soul and body. This necessarily
qualifies them to enjoy the glory and thoroughly to partake
of the sweetness of it. Were the glory never so great, and
themselves not made capable by a personal perfection suit-

able thereto, it would be little to them. There is necessary a right disposition of the recipient, to a right rejoicing and affecting. This is one thing that makes the saints' joys there so great. Here eye hath not seen, nor ear heard, nor heart conceived what God hath laid up for them that wait for him. For this eye of flesh is not capable of seeing it, nor this ear of hearing it, nor this heart of understanding it; but there the eye and ear and heart are made capable; else how do they enjoy it?

VI

But O the full, the near, the sweet enjoyment is that of the affections, love and joy; it is near, for love is of the essence of the soul, and love is the essence of God. . . . "God is love, and he that dwelleth in love dwelleth in God, and God in him." . . . Now the poor soul complains, O that I could love Christ more! but I cannot alas, I cannot; yea but thou canst not choose but love him: I had almost said, forbear if thou canst. . . . Now thy salvation is not perfected, not all the mercies purchased, yet given in; but when the top-stone is set on, thou shalt, with shouting, cry "Grace, grace!" Now thy sanctification is imperfect, and thy pardon and justification not so complete as then it shall be; now thou knowest not what thou enjoyest, and therefore lovest the less; but when thou knowest much is forgiven and much bestowed, thou wilt love more. . . . Christians, doth it not now stir up your love, to remember all the experiences of his love; to look back upon a life of mercies? Doth not kindness melt you and the sunshine of divine goodness warm your frozen hearts? What will it do then when you shall live in love, and have all in him, who is All? O the delights of love, of this love; the content that the heart findeth in it; the satisfaction it brings along with it! Surely love is both work and wages!

And if this were all, what a high favour that God will

give us leave to love him; that he will vouchsafe to be embraced by such arms that have embraced lust and sin before him! But this is not all. He returneth love for love; nay a thousand times more; as perfect as we shall be, we cannot reach his measure of love. Christian, thou wilt be then brimful of love; yet love as much as thou canst, thou shalt be ten thousand times more beloved. Dost thou think thou canst over-love him? What! love more than Love itself? Were the arms of the Son of God upon the cross, and an open passage made to his heart by the spear, and will not arms and heart be open to thee in glory; did he begin to love before thou lovedst, and will he not continue now; did he love thee, an enemy, thee a sinner, thee,who even loathest thyself, and own thee when thou didst disclaim thyself, and will he not now immeasurably love thee, a son; thee, a perfect saint; thee, who returnest some love for love? Thou wast wont injuriously to question his love: doubt of it now if thou canst. . . . Is it a small thing in thine eyes to be beloved of God? . . . Christian, believe this and think on it. Thou shalt be eternally embraced in the arms of that love, which was from everlasting, and will extend to everlasting; of that love which brought the Son of God's love from heaven to earth, from the earth to the cross, from the cross to the grave, from the grave to glory; that love which was weary, hungry, tempted, scorned, scourged, buffeted, spit upon, crucified, pierced; which did fast, pray, teach, heal, weep, sweat, bleed, die—that love will eternally embrace thee. When perfect, created love and most perfect, uncreated love meet together, O the blessed meeting! . . . Christ is the powerful, attractive, the effectual Loadstone who draws to it all like itself. . . . Thou hast not now to deal with an inconstant creature, but with him with whom is no varying nor shadow of change, even the immutable God. . . .

What shall we say to these things? Infinite love must

needs be a mystery to a finite capacity. No wonder if angels desire to pry into this mystery: and if it be the study of the saints here, to know the height and breadth and length and depth of this love, though it passeth knowledge. This is the saint's Rest in the fruition of God by love.

v

Another excellent property of our rest will be that *the joys of it are immediately from God.* . . . We shall see God face to face and stand continually in his presence, and consequently derive our life and comfort immediately from him. Whether God will make use of any creatures for our service then, or, if any, what creatures, and what use, is more than I yet know. It seems . . . that the creature shall have a day of deliverance, and that into the glorious liberty of the sons of God; but whether this before, or at the great and full deliverance, or whether to endure to eternity, or to what particular employment they shall be continued, are questions yet too hard for me. When God speaks them plainer, and mine understanding is made clearer, then I may know these: but it is certain that at least our most and great joys will be immediate, if not all. Now we have nothing at all immediately. . . . From the earth, from man, from sun and moon, from the influence of the planets from the ministration of angels, and from the Spirit and Christ; and, doubtless, the further the stream runs from the fountain, the more impure it is. It gathers some defilement from every unclean channel it passes through. . . . Christ is indeed a precious pearl, but oft held forth in leprous hands: and thus do we disgrace the riches of the Gospel when it is the work of our calling to make it honourable in the eyes of men; and we dim the glory of that jewel by our dull and low expressions, whose lustre we do pretend to discover, while the hearers judge of it by our expressions, and not its proper genuine worth. The truth is the best of men do apprehend but little of what God, in his word, expresseth and what they do apprehend they are unable to utter. . . . If an angel from heaven should preach the gospel, yet could he not deliver it according to its glory; much less we, who never saw what they have seen, and keep this treasure in earthen vessels. The comforts that flow through sermons, through sacraments, through reading, and company, and conference, and creatures are but half comforts; and the life that comes by these is but half a life, in comparison of those which the Almighty shall speak with his own mouth and reach forth to us with his own hand. The Christian knows by experience now, that his most immediate joys are his sweetest joys: which have least of man, and are most directly from the Spirit. That is one reason, as I conceive, why Christians who are much in secret prayer, and in meditation and contemplation, rather than they who are more in hearing, reading and conference, are men of greatest life and joy, because they are nearer the well-head, and have all more immediately from God himself. . . . We are not yet come to the time and state where we shall have all from God's immediate hand. As God hath made all creatures, and instituted all ordinances for us, so will he continue our need of all. We must be the content with love-tokens from him, till we come to receive our all in him. . . . There is joy in these remote receivings but the fullness is in his own presence. O Christians! you will then know the difference betwixt the creature and the Creator, and the content that each of them affords. We shall then have light without a candle, and a perpetual day without the sun. . . . We shall then have rest without sleep, for God will be our rest. . . . We shall then have enlightened understandings without a written law: for the Lord will perfect his law in our hearts, and we shall be all perfectly taught of God. His own will shall be our law, and his own face shall be our light for ever. Then shall we have joy, which we drew not from the promises, nor was fetched us home by faith and hope. Beholding and possessing will exclude most of these. We shall then have communion without sacraments, when Christ shall drink with us of the fruit of the vine new; that is, refresh us with the comforting wine of immediate fruition, in the kingdom of his Father. . . . When we shall live in our Father's house and presence and God shall be all and in all; then we are indeed at home in rest.

Henry Vaughan

———•—•———

Known as "the Silurist," he was born in 1622. Welsh by birth
and a country doctor most of his life, he owed much to the preoccu-
pations and example of his metaphysical predecessors, chiefly Herbert, but his gift of song and intuitive response to nature as the
revelation of God's mind and meaning are singularly his own. His
mystical verse appeared largely in the volume *Silex Scintillans* (1650
and 1655). Vaughan influenced such later poets as William Wordsworth. He died in 1695.

THE RETREATE

Happy those early dayes! when I
Shin'd in my Angell-infancy.
Before I understood this place
Appointed for my second race,
Or taught my soul to fancy ought
But a white, Celestiall thought,
When yet I had not walkt above
A mile, or two, from my first love,
And looking back (at that short space,)
Could see a glimpse of his bright-face;
When on some *gilded Cloud*, or *flowre*
My gazing soul would dwell an houre,
And in those weaker glories spy
Some shadows of eternity;
Before I taught my tongue to wound
My Conscience with a sinfull sound,
Or had the black art to dispence

A sev'rall sinne to ev'ry sence,
But felt through all this fleshly dresse
Bright *shootes* of everlastingnesse.
    O how I long to travell back
And tread again that ancient track!
That I might once more reach that plaine,
Where first I left my glorious traine,
From whence th' Inlightned spirit sees
That shady City of Palme trees;
But (ah!) my soul with too much stay
Is drunk, and staggers in the way.
Some men a forward motion love,
But I by backward steps would move,
And when this dust falls to the urn
In that state I came return.

THE WORLD

I saw Eternity the other night
Like a great *Ring* of pure and endless light,
        All calm, as it was bright,
And round beneath it, Time in hours, days, years
        Driv'n by the spheres
Like a vast shadow mov'd, In which the world
        And all her train were hurl'd;
The doting Lover in his queintest strain
        Did their Complain,
Neer him, his Lute, his fancy, and his flights,
        Wits sour delights,
With gloves, and knots the silly snares of pleasure
        Yet his dear Treasure
All scatter'd lay, while he his eys did pour
        Upon a flowr.

2

The darksome States-man hung with weights and woe
Like a thick midnight-fog mov'd there so slow
  He did not stay, nor go;
Condemning thoughts (like sad Eclipses) scowl
    Upon his soul,
And Clouds of crying witnesses without
  Pursued him with one shout.
Yet dig'd the Mole, and lest his ways be found
    Workt under ground,
Where he did Clutch his prey, but one did see
    That policie,
Churches and altars fed him, Perjuries
    Were gnats and flies,
It rain'd about him bloud and tears, but he
  Drank them as free.

3

The fearfull miser on a heap of rust
Sate pining all his life there, did scarce trust
  His own hands with the dust,
Yet would not place one peece above, but lives
    In feare of theeves.
Thousands there were as frantick as himself
  And hug'd each one his pelf,
The down-right Epicure plac'd heav'n in sense
    And scornd pretence
While others slipt into a wide Excesse
    Said little lesse;
The weaker sort slight, triviall wares Inslave
    Who think them brave,
And poor, despised truth sate Counting by
  Their victory.

4

Yet some, who all this while did weep and sing,
And sing, and weep, soar'd up into the *Ring*,
   But most would use no wing.
O fools (said I,) thus to prefer dark night
   Before true light,
To live in grots, and caves, and hate the day
   Because it shews the way,
The way which from this dead and dark abode
   Leads up to God,
A way where you might tread the Sun, and be
   More bright than he.
But as I did their madnes so discusse
   One whisper'd thus,
This Ring the Bride-groome did for none provide
   But for his bride.

George Fox

The founder of the Society of Friends was born in 1624 at Fenny Drayton, in Leicestershire, the son of a Puritan weaver. He became a shoemaker, but at the age of nineteen felt called to give up his family and friends. In 1646 he won a moral victory through reliance on the Inner Light of the living Christ and abandoned the Church of England. In 1647 he began to preach, and in 1649 was imprisoned at Nottingham. In 1652 he made his home at Swarthmore Hall, near Ulverstone, the home of Thomas Fell, Vice-Chancellor of the Duchy of Lancaster. He married Thomas Fell's widow, Margaret (1614-1702), in 1669. He made a missionary journey to Ireland in 1669, and to the West Indies in 1671-1672, and to Holland in 1677-1684. He died on 13 January 1691, and his *Journal* was published in 1694.

From A JOURNAL

After I had received that opening from the Lord, that to be bred at Oxford or Cambridge, was not sufficient to fit a man to be a minister of Christ, I regarded the priests less, and looked more after the dissenting people. Among them I saw there was some tenderness; and many of them came afterwards to be convinced, for they had some openings. But as I had forsaken the priests, so I left the separate preachers also, and those called the most experienced people; for I saw there was none among them all that could speak to my condition. And when all my hopes in them and in all men were gone, so that I had nothing outwardly, to help me, nor could tell what to do; then, O then, I heard a voice which said, "There is one, even Christ Jesus, that can speak to thy condition." When I heard it, my heart did leap for joy. Then the Lord let me see why there was none upon the earth that could speak to my condition, namely, that I might give him all the glory. For all are concluded under sin, and shut up in unbelief, as I had been, that Jesus Christ might have the pre-eminence, who enlightens, and gives grace, faith and power. Thus when God doth work, who shall let it? This I knew experimentally. My desires after the Lord grew stronger, and zeal in the pure knowledge of God, and of Christ alone, without the help of any man, book, or writing. For though I read the scriptures that spake of Christ and of God, yet I knew him not but by revelation, as he who hath the key did open, and as the Father of life drew me to his Son by his Spirit. Then the Lord gently led me along, and let me see his love, which was endless and eternal, surpassing all the knowledge that men have in the natural state, or can get by history or books. That love let me see myself, as I was without him; and I was afraid of all company: for I saw them perfectly, where they were, through the love of God which let me see myself. I had not fellowship with any people, priests, nor professors, nor any sort of separated people, but with Christ who hath the key, and opened the door of light and life unto me. I was afraid of all carnal talk and talkers, for I could see nothing but corruptions, and the life lay under the burden of corruptions. When I was in the deep, under all shut up, I could not believe that I should ever overcome; my troubles, my sorrows, and my temptations were so great, that I often thought I should have despaired, I was so tempted. But when Christ opened to me how he was tempted by the same devil, and had overcome him, and had bruised his head; and that through him and his power, light, grace, and Spirit, I should overcome also, I had confidence in him. So he it was that opened to me when I was shut up, and had neither hope nor faith. Christ, who had enlightened me, gave me his light to believe in, and gave me hope, which is himself revealed in me, and gave me his spirit and grace, which I found sufficient in the deeps and in weakness. Thus in the deepest miseries, in the greatest sorrows and temptations that beset me, the Lord in his mercy did keep me. I found two thirsts in me; the one after the creatures, to have got help and strength there; and the other after the Lord the Creator, and his son Jesus Christ; and I saw all the world could do me no good. If I had had a king's diet, palace and attendance, all would have been as nothing; for nothing gave me comfort but the Lord by his power. I saw professors, priests, and people, were whole and at ease in that condition which was my misery, and they loved that which I would have been rid of. But the Lord did stay my desires upon himself, from whom my help came, and my care was cast upon him alone. Therefore, all wait patiently upon the Lord, whatsoever condition you be in; wait in the grace and truth that comes by Jesus; for if ye so do, there is a promise to you, and the Lord God will fulfil it in you. Blessed are all they indeed that do indeed hunger and thirst after righteousness, they shall be satisfied with it. I have found it so, praised be the Lord who filleth with it, and satisfieth the desires of the hungry soul. O let the house of the spiritual Israel say, His mercy endureth for ever! It is the great love of God, to make a wilderness of that which is pleasant to the outward eye and fleshly mind; and to make a fruitful field of a barren wilderness. This is the great work of God. But while people's minds run in the earthly, after the creatures and changeable things, changeable ways and religions, and changeable uncertain teachers, their minds are in bondage, and they are brittle and changeable, tossed up and down with windy doctrines, thoughts, notions, and things; their minds being out of the unchangeable truth in the inward parts, the light of Jesus Christ, which would keep them to the unchangeable. He is the way to the Father;

who in all my troubles preserved me by his Spirit and power, praised be his holy name for ever!

Again, I heard a voice which said, Thou serpent, thou dost seek to destroy the life, but canst not; for the sword which keepeth the tree of life shall destroy thee. So Christ, the Word of God, that bruised the head of the serpent, the destroyer, preserved me; my mind being joined to his good seed that bruised the head of this serpent, the destroyer. This inward life sprung up in me to answer all the opposing professors and priests, and brought scriptures to my memory to refute them with.

At another time I saw the great love of God, and was filled with admiration at the infiniteness of it. I saw what was cast out from God, and what entered into God's kingdom; and how by Jesus, the opener of the door by his heavenly key, the entrance was given. I saw death, how it had passed upon all men, and oppressed the seed of God in man, and in me; and how I in the seed came forth, and what the promise was to. Yet it was so, that there seemed to be two pleading in me; and questionings arose in my mind about gifts and prophecies, and I was tempted again to despair, as if I had sinned against the Holy Ghost. I was in great perplexity and trouble for many days; yet I gave up myself to the Lord still. One day, when I had been walking solitarily abroad, and was come home, I was taken up in the love of God, so that I could not but admire the greatness of his love; and while I was in that condition, it was opened unto me by the eternal light and power, and I therein clearly saw, That all was done and to be done in and by Christ; and how he conquers and destroys this tempter the devil, and all his works, and is atop of him; and that all these troubles were good for me, and temptations for the trial of my faith, which Christ had given me. The Lord opened me, that I saw through all these troubles and temptations. My living faith was raised, that I saw all was done by Christ the life, and my belief was in him. When at any time my condition was veiled, my secret belief was stayed firm, and hope underneath held me, as an anchor in the bottom of the sea, and anchored my immortal soul to its bishop, causing it to swim above the sea, the world, where all the raging waves, foul weather, tempests and temptations are. But O! then did I see my troubles, trials, and temptations more clearly than ever I had done. As the light appeared, all appeared that is out of the light; darkness, death, temptations, the unrighteous, the ungodly; all was manifest and seen in the light. After this, a pure fire appeared in me: then I saw how he sat as a refiner's fire, and as the fuller's soap. Then the spiritual discerning came into me; by which I discerned my own thoughts, groans, and sighs; and what it was that veiled me, and what it was that opened me. That which could not abide in the patience, nor endure the fire, in the light I found to be the groans of the flesh, that could not give up to the will of God; which had so veiled me, that I could not be patient in all trials, troubles, anguishes, and perplexities; could not give up self to die by the cross, the power of God, that the living and quickened might follow him, and that that which would cloud and veil from the presence of Christ, that which the sword of the Spirit cuts down, and which must die, might not be kept alive. I discerned the groans of the Spirit, which opened me, and made intercession to God: in which Spirit is the true waiting upon God, for the redemption of the body, and of the whole creation. By this true Spirit, in which the true sighing is, I saw over the false sighings and groanings. By this invisible Spirit I discerned all the false hearing, the false seeing, and the false smelling which was above the Spirit quenching and grieving it; and that all that were there were in confusion and deceit, where the false asking and praying is, in deceit and atop, in that nature and tongue that takes God's holy name in vain, wallows in the Egyptian sea, and asketh but hath not; for they hate his light, resist the Holy Ghost, turn the grace into wantonness, rebel against the Spirit, and are erred from the faith they should ask in, and from the Spirit they should pray by. He that knoweth these things in the true Spirit can witness them. The divine light of Christ manifesteth all things, the spiritual fire trieth and severeth all things. . . .

They that walk in this light, come to the mountain of the house of God, established above all mountains, and to God's teaching, who will teach them his ways. These things were opened to me in the light.

I saw also the mountains burning up, and the rubbish, the rough, crooked ways and places made smooth and plain, that the Lord might come into his tabernacle. These things are to be found in man's heart; but to speak of these things being within, seemed strange to the rough, crooked, and mountainous ones. Yet the Lord saith, "O earth, hear the word of the Lord!" The law of the Spirit crosseth the fleshly mind, spirit, and will, which lives in disobedience, and doth not keep within the law of the Spirit. I saw this law was the pure love of God which was upon me and which I must go through, though I was troubled while I was under it; for I could not be dead to the law but through the law, which did judge and condemn that which is to be condemned.

Now was I come up in Spirit, through the flaming sword, into the paradise of God. All things were new; and all the creation gave another smell unto me than before, beyond what words can utter. I knew nothing but pureness, innocency, and righteousness, being renewed up into the image of God by Christ Jesus; so that I was come up to the state of Adam, which he was in before he fell. The creation was opened to me; and it was shewed me, how all things had their names given them, according to their nature and virtue. I was at a stand in my mind, whether I should practice physick for the good of mankind, seeing the nature and virtues of the creatures were so opened to me by the Lord. But I was immediately taken up in Spirit, to see into another or more steadfast state than Adam's in innocency, even into a state in Christ Jesus, that should never fall.

Then passing from thence, I heard of a people in prison at Coventry for religion. As I walked towards the gaol, the word of the Lord came to me saying, MY LOVE WAS ALWAYS TO THEE, AND THOU ART IN MY LOVE. And I was ravished with the sense of the love of God, and greatly strengthened in my inward man. But when I came into the gaol where those prisoners were, a great power of darkness struck at me; and I sat still, having my spirit gathered into the love of God.

John Bunyan

He was born in 1628 at Elstow, near Bedford, the son of a brazier. At seventeen he enlisted in the Parliamentary Army, and served during the campaign of 1645. In 1653 he was received into an Independent Congregation at Bedford and in 1657 he was formally recognized as a preacher. In November 1660 he joined a Baptist society in Bedford, and suffered from the repressive measures of the Royalists. After the Restoration he spent nearly twelve years in jail, convinced that he was divinely set apart. He wrote his autobiography, *Grace Abounding*, in 1666, and his *The Pilgrim's Progress* in 1675, while in jail. The success of the latter book was immediate, and Bunyan became a popular preacher, known as Bishop Bunyan. He died on 31 August 1688.

BUNYAN'S MINISTRY

In my preaching of the word, I took special notice of this one thing, namely, that the Lord did lead me to begin where his word begins with sinners; that is, to condemn all flesh, and to open and allege that the curse of God by the law doth belong to, and lay hold on all men as they come into the world, because of sin.

Now this part of my work I fulfilled with great feeling; for the terrors of the law, and guilt for my transgressions, lay heavy on my conscience: I preached what I felt, what I smartingly did feel; even that under which my poor soul did groan and tremble to astonishment.

Indeed, I have been as one sent to them from the dead; I went myself in chains, to preach to them in chains; and carried that fire in my own conscience, that I persuaded them to be aware of. I can truly say, and that without dissembling, that when I have been to preach, I have gone full of guilt and terror even to the pulpit-door, and there it hath been taken off, and I have been at liberty in my mind until I have done my work; and then immediately, even before I could get down the pulpit-stairs, I have been as bad as I was before; yet God carried me on, but surely with a strong hand, for neither guilt nor hell could take me off my work.

Thus I went on for the space of two years, crying out against men's sins, and their fearful state because of them. After which the Lord came in upon my soul with some sure peace and comfort through Christ; for he did give me many sweet discoveries of his blessed grace through him: wherefore now I altered my preaching — for still I preached what I saw and felt. Now, therefore, I did much labor to hold forth Jesus Christ in all his offices, relations, and benefits unto the world; and did strive also to discover, to condemn, and remove those false supports and props on which the world doth both lean and by them fall and perish. On these things also I staid as long as on the other.

When I have been preaching, I thank God, my heart hath often all the time of this and the other exercise, with great earnestness cried to God that he would make the word effectual to the salvation of the soul; still being grieved lest the enemy should take the word away from the conscience, and so it should become unfruitful: wherefore I have labored so to speak the word, as that thereby, if it were possible, the sin and person guilty might be particularized by it.

And when I have done the exercise, it hath gone to my heart to think the word should now fall as rain on stony places; still wishing from my heart. Oh, that they who have heard me speak this day did but see as I do, what sin,

death, hell, and the curse of God are; and also what the
grace, and love, and mercy of God are, through Christ, to
men in such a case as they are who are yet estranged from
him. And indeed, I did often say in my heart before the
Lord, that if I should be hanged up presently before their
eyes, and it would be a means to awaken them and confirm
them in the truth. I gladly should be contented.

For I have been in my preaching, especially when I
have been engaged in the doctrine of life by Christ without works, as if an angel of God had stood at my back to
encourage me. Oh, it hath been with such power and heavenly evidence upon my own soul, while I have been labor-
ing to unfold it, to demonstrate it, and to fasten it upon the
consciences of others, that I could not be contented with
saying, I believe, and am sure. Methought I was more
than sure — if it be lawful thus to express myself — that
those things which then I asserted were true.

If any of those who were awakened by my ministry did
after that fall back — as sometimes too many did — I can
truly say, their loss hath been more to me than if my own
children, begotten of my body, had been going to their
grave. I think verily I may speak it without any offence to
the Lord, nothing has gone so near me as that; unless it
was the fear of the loss of the salvation of my own soul. I
have counted as if I had goodly buildings and lordships in
those places where my children were born: my heart
hath been so wrapped up in the glory of this excellent work,
that I counted myself more blessed and honored of God by
this, than if he had made me emperor of the Christian
world or the lord of all the glory of the earth without it. Oh
those words. "He that converteth the sinner from the error
of his way, shall save a soul from death." "The fruit of the
righteous is a tree of life; and he that winneth souls is

wise." "They that be wise shall shine as the brightness of the firmament; and they that turn many to righteousness, as the stars forever and ever." "For what is our hope, our joy, our crown of rejoicing? Are not even ye in the presence of our Lord Jesus Christ at his coming? For ye are our glory and joy." These, I say, with many others of a like nature, have been great refreshments to me.

I have observed that a word cast in by the by, hath done more execution in a sermon, than all that was spoken besides: sometimes also, when I have thought I did no good, then I did the most of all; and at other times when I thought I could catch them, I have fished for nothing.

For my descent, it was, as is well known by many, of a low and inconsiderable generation; my father's house being of that rank that is meanest and most despised of all the families of the land. Wherefore I have not, as others, to boast of noble blood and of any high-born estate according to the flesh; though all things considered, I magnify the heavenly Majesty for that by this door he brought me into the world, to partake of the grace and life that is in Christ by the gospel.

What need you, before you have showed one syllable of a reasonable argument in opposition to what I assert, thus trample my person, my gifts, and grace — have I any — so disdainfully under your feet, because of my low descent among men; stigmatizing me for a person of that rank that need not to be heeded. And what, is my rank so mean that the most gracious and godly among you may not duly and soberly consider what I have said? Was it not the act of the false apostles to say thus — to bespatter a man that his doctrine might be disregarded? "Is not this the carpenter?" and, "His bodily presence is weak and his speech contemptible," did not use to be in the mouths of the saints; for they knew the wind blew where it listed. Neither is it high birth, worldly breeding, or wealth; but electing love, grace, and the wisdom that comes from heaven, that those who strive for strictness of order in the things and kingdom of Christ, should have in regard and esteem. Need I read you a lecture? Hath not God chosen the foolish, the weak, the base, yea and even things that are not to bring to naught things that are? Why then do you despise my rank, my state, and quality in the world?

Since you would know by what name I would be distinguished from others, I tell you, I would be, and I hope I am, *a Christian*; and choose, if God should count me worthy, to be called *a Christian, a believer*, or other such name which is approved by the Holy Ghost.

Your artificial, squibbling suggestions to the world about myself, my imprisonment, and the like, I freely bind unto me as an ornament among the rest of my reproaches, till the Lord shall wipe them off at his coming.

Faith and holiness are my professed principles, with an endeavor, so far as in me lieth, to be at peace with all men. What shall I say? Let mine enemies themselves be judges, if any thing in these following doctrines, or if aught that any man hath heard me preach, doth or hath, according to the true intent of my words, savored either of heresy or rebellion. I say again, let them themselves be judges, if aught they find in my writing or preaching doth render me worthy of almost twelve years' imprisonment, or one that deserveth to be hanged or banished for ever, according to their tremendous sentence. Indeed my principles are such as lead me to a denial to communicate in the things of the kingdom of Christ with the ungodly and open profane; neither can I consent that my soul should be governed in any of my approaches to God by the superstitious inventions of this world, because commanded to the contrary, or commended for so refusing. Wherefore, excepting in this one thing — for which I ought not to be rebuked — I shall, I trust, in despite of slander and falsehood, discover myself at all times a peaceable and obedient subject. But if nothing will do, unless I make my conscience a continual butchery or slaughter-shop — unless, putting out mine own eyes, I commit myself to the blind to lead me, as I doubt not is desired by some — I have determined, the Almighty God being my help and shield, yet to suffer, if frail life might continue so long, even till the moss shall grow on mine eyebrows, rather than thus to violate my faith and principles.

From THE PILGRIM'S PROGRESS

Christian then and his companion asked the men to go along with them: so they told them that they would. But, said they, you must obtain it by your own faith. So I saw in my dream, that they went on together till they came in sight of the gate.

Now I further saw, that betwixt them and the gate was a river; but there was no bridge to go over: the river was very deep. At the sight, therefore, of this river the pilgrims were much stunned; but the men that went with them said, You must go through, or you cannot come at the gate.

The pilgrims then began to inquire, if there was no other way to the gate? To which they answered, Yes; but there hath not any, save two, to wit, Enoch and Elijah, been permitted to tread that path since the foundation of the world, nor shall until the last trumpet shall sound. The pilgrims then, especially Christian, began to despond in his mind, and looked this way and that; but no way could be found by them, by which they might escape the river. Then they asked the men if the waters were all of a depth? They said, No; yet they could not help them in that case; for, said they, you shall find it deeper or shallower, as you believe in the King of the place.

They then addressed themselves to the water, and, entering, Christian began to sink, and, crying out to his good friend Hopeful, he said, I sink in deep waters; the billows go over my head; all his waves go over me. Selah.

Then said the other, Be of good cheer, my brother; I feel the bottom, and it is good. Then said Christian, Ah! my friend, the sorrows of death have compassed me about, I shall not see the land that flows with milk and honey. And with that a great darkness and horror fell upon Christian, so that he could not see before him. Also here he in a great measure lost his senses, so that he could neither remember nor orderly talk of any of those sweet refreshments that he had met with in the way of his pilgrimage. But all the words that he spoke still tended to discover that he had horror of mind, and heart-fears that he should die in that river, and never obtain entrance in at the gate. Here also, as they that stood by perceived, he was much in the troublesome thoughts of the sins that he had committed, both since and before he began to be a pilgrim. It was also observed, that he was troubled with apparitions of hobgoblins and evil spirits; for ever and anon he would intimate so much by words.

Hopeful therefore here had much ado to keep his brother's head above water; yea, sometimes he would be quite gone down, and then, ere a while, he would rise up again half dead. Hopeful did also endeavour to comfort him, saying, Brother, I see the gate, and men standing by to receive us; but Christian would answer, 'Tis you, 'tis you they wait for; for you have been hopeful ever since I knew you. And so have you, said he to Christian. Ah, brother, (said he), surely if I was right, He would now arise to help me; but for my sins he hath brought me into the snare, and hath left me. Then said Hopeful, My brother, you have quite forgot the text, where it is said of the wicked, "There are no bands in their death, but their strength is firm: they are not troubled as other men, neither are they plagued like other men." These troubles and distresses that you go through in these waters, are no sign that God hath forsaken you; but are sent to try you, whether you will call to mind that which heretofore you have received of his goodness, and live upon him in your distresses.

Then I saw in my dream, that Christian was in a muse a while. To whom also Hopeful added these words, Be of good cheer, Jesus Christ maketh thee whole. And with that Christian brake out with a loud voice, Oh, I see him again! and he tells me, "When thou passest through the waters, I will be with thee; and through the rivers, they shall not overflow thee." Then they both took courage, and the enemy was after that as still as a stone, until they were gone over. Christian therefore presently found ground to stand upon, and so it followed that the rest of the river was but shallow: thus they got over.

Now, upon the bank of the river, on the other side, they saw the two shining men again, who there waited for them. Wherefore being come out of the river, they saluted them, saying, We are ministering spirits, sent forth to minister for those that shall be heirs of salvation. Thus they went along towards the gate.

Now, you must note, that the City stood upon a mighty hill: but the pilgrims went up that hill with ease, because they had these two men to lead them up by the arms: they had likewise left their mortal garments behind them in the river; for though they went in with them, they came out without them. They therefore went up here with much agility and speed, though the foundation upon which the City was framed was higher than the clouds: they therefore went up through the region of the air, sweetly talking as they went, being comforted, because they safely got over the river, and had such glorious companions to attend them.

The talk that they had with the shining ones was about the glory of the place; who told them, that the beauty and of it was inexpressible. There, said they, is "Mount Zion, the heavenly Jerusalem, the innumerable company of angels, and the spirits of just men made perfect." You are going now, said they, to the paradise of God, wherein you shall see the tree of life, and eat of the never-fading fruits thereof: and when you come there, you shall have white robes given you, and your walk and talk shall be every day with the King, even all the days of eternity. There you shall not see again such things as you saw when you were in the lower region upon the earth; to wit, sorrow, sickness, affliction, and death; "for the former things are passed away." You are going now to Abraham, to Isaac, and Jacob, and to the prophets, men that God hath taken away from the evil to come, and that are now "resting upon their beds, each one walking in his righteousness." The men then asked, What must we do in the holy place? To whom it was answered, You must there receive the comfort of all your toil, and have joy for all your sorrow; you must reap what you have sown, even the fruit of all your prayers, and tears, and sufferings for the King by the way. In that place you must wear crowns of gold, and enjoy the perpetual sight and vision of the Holy One; for "there you shall see him as he is." There also you shall serve him continually with praise, with shouting, and thanksgiving, whom you desired to serve in the world, though with much difficulty, because of the infirmity of your flesh. There your eyes shall be delighted with seeing, and your ears with hearing the pleasant voice of the Mighty One. There you shall enjoy your friends again that are gone thither before you; and there you shall with joy receive even every one that follows into the holy place after you. There also you shall be clothed with glory and majesty, and put into an equipage fit to ride out with the King of Glory. When he shall come with sound of trumpet in the clouds, as upon the wings of the wind, you shall come with him; and, when he shall sit upon the throne of judgment, you shall sit by him; yea, and when he shall pass sentence upon all the workers of iniquity, let them be angels or men, you also shall have a voice in that judgment, because they were his and your enemies. Also, when he shall again return to the City, you shall go too, with sound of trumpet, and be ever with him.

Thomas Traherne

He was born in 1637. After education at Oxford, he took holy orders and spent his life — "simple and devout," we are told, "well read in primitive antiquity and the fathers" — as domestic chaplain to Sir Orlando Bridgeman, Lord Keeper of the Seal. His poems, at first mistakenly ascribed to Henry Vaughan, came to light only at the end of the last century, and share with his prose *Centuries of Meditations* a luminous and contemplative radiance. He died in 1674.

From CENTURIES OF MEDITATIONS

The corn was orient and immortal wheat, which never should be reaped, nor was ever sown. I thought it had stood from everlasting to everlasting. The dust and stones of the street were as precious as gold: the gates were at first the end of the world. The green trees when I saw them first through one of the gates transported and ravished me, their sweetness and unusual beauty made my heart to leap, and almost mad with ecstasy, they were such strange and wonderful things! The Men! O what venerable and reverend creatures did the aged seem! Immortal Cherubims! And young men glittering and sparkling Angels, and maids strange seraphic pieces of life and beauty! Boys and girls tumbling in the street, and playing, were moving jewels. I knew not that they were born or should die; but all things abided eternally as they within their proper places. Eternity was manifest in the Light of the Day, and something infinite behind everything appeared: which talked with my expectation and moved my desire. The city seemed to stand in Eden, or to be built in Heaven. The streets were mine, the temple was mine, the people were mine, their clothes and gold and silver were mine, as much as their sparkling eyes, fair skins and ruddy faces. The skies were mine, and so were the sun and moon and stars, and all the World was mine; and I the only spectator and enjoyer of it. I knew no churlish proprieties, nor bounds, nor divisions: but all proprieties and divisions were mine: all treasures and the possessors of them. So that with much ado I was corrupted, and made to learn the dirty devices of this world. Which now I unlearn, and become, as it were, a little child again that I may enter into the Kingdom of God. *1 0 2 / 8 6*

. . . This, my dear friends, this was my blessed case;
For nothing spoke to me but the fair face
Of Heaven and Earth, before myself could speak,
I then my Bliss did, when my silence, break.
My non-intelligence of human words
Ten thousand pleasures unto me affords;
For while I knew not what they to me said,
Before their souls were into mine conveyed,
Before that living vehicle of wind
Could breathe into me their infected mind. . . .
Then did I dwell within a world of light,
Distinct and separate from all men's sight,
Where I did feel strange thoughts, and such things see
That were, or seemed, only revealed to me,
There I saw all the world enjoyed by one;
There I was in the world myself alone;
No business serious seemed but one; no work
But one was found; and that did in me lurk.
    D'ye ask me what? It was with clearer eyes
To see all creatures full of Deities;
Especially one's self: And to admire
The satisfaction of all true desire. . . .
To reign in silence, and to sing alone,
To see, love, covet, have, enjoy and praise, in one.

Charles Marshall

A distinguished early English Quaker, he was born at Bristol in June 1637. While still a young man, he joined a company of penitents in prayer and fasting, but did not become a Quaker until 1654. Marshall is remembered as a physician, chemist and apothecary, a man of great charity and gentleness, who dispensed free service to the poor. Married in 1662 to Hannah Prince, he settled in Wiltshire, and eight years later sacrificed many of his professional advantages to the call of preaching. Marshall spent the years 1670-1680 "running through the nation," a period in which he attended about four hundred meetings.

Marshall and his wife were heavily persecuted by the Church of England for their Quaker convictions, and in 1682 he was committed to a London prison. While there, he wrote *A Tender Visitation in the Love of God to All People Everywhere, Particularly unto the Inhabitants of Wiltshire, Gloucestershire and Bristol*. On his release, Marshall remained in London, where he died of consumption on 15 November 1698. *The Way of Life Revealed and the Way of Death Discovered* was first published by the Society of Friends at London in 1772.

From THE JOURNAL OF CHARLES MARSHALL

About the eleventh and twelfth years of my life, I not only longed to know the true and living God, but also sought after him, and loved and esteemed sober, honest people, who feared the Lord.

I went with my mother to the Independents' meetings, in the days of that people's tenderness and sincerity; and sometimes I went to the Baptists' meeting, and in public, to hear those men who were esteemed most zealous in their day. Among those people, and in those assemblies, there were awakenings inwardly, through the stirrings and strivings of the gift of God, under the sense of which, living pantings and breathings were in many of their souls, after the true, spiritual knowledge of God who is a Spirit. But they went out from that [state,] into a profession of the saints' words, works and enjoyments, and left this pure principle of light, life and truth behind. Now, as I advanced in years, I grew more and more dissatisfied with lifeless, empty professions and professors, feeling the burden of the nature of sin, which lay on my spirit; in the sense whereof, I became like the solitary desert, and mourned like a dove without a mate. And seeing I could not find the living among the dead professions, I spent much time in retirements alone, in the fields and woods, and by springs of water, which I delighted to lie by and drink of. And in those days of retirement, strong, great, and many were my cries unto the Lord; and sometimes being retired into places free from passengers, to ease my heart, I did cry aloud, because of disquietness of spirit. And I had openings of the miserable fall and inexpressible degeneration of mankind, and the captivity and bondage which my soul lay in; in the sense of which state of bondage and thraldom, I cried out, Oh, that my soul might be eased from these heavy burdens and loads of death and darkness! that out of this state of gross Egyptian darkness I might be saved, and from the land of drought, a land of anguish, a land of horrible darkness! Oh, undeclarable fall! said my soul; oh, inexpressible wall of partition and separation! Oh, gulf unutterable! For the fallen and undone state of the sons and daughters of men was opened unto me, beyond all words to demonstrate. And in those days, as I walked and beheld the creation of God Almighty, every thing testified against me, heaven and earth, the day and the night, the sun, moon,

and stars, yea, the watercourses and springs of the great
deep, keeping in their respective places; the grass and flowers of the field, the fish of the sea and fowls of the air, keeping their order; but man alone, the chief of the work of
God's hand, [I saw was] degenerated. Then cried I out
bitterly, — Man's state in the fall is worse than [that of]
the beast that perisheth; for "the ox knoweth his owner,
and the ass his master's crib," but man, in this state, is ignorant of God his maker, and is become a stranger unto him,
walking in enmity and disobedience, serving and obeying
the devil, who neither created any thing, nor can preserve
any living thing; and from the beginning, his appearance
against God hath been mere enmity, altogether evil; a
destroyer and a murderer. And such is the inexpressibly
thick darkness that over mankind is come and spread, that
they give up themselves in body, soul and spirit, to be led
by him. Oh, thick darkness! that thus is come over the families of the earth! Here could I set my seal to the truth of
that scripture, "darkness covers the earth, and gross darkness the people."

So in a deep sense of man's miserable state, and particularly the sense of my own captivity, and share in this inexpressible state of darkness, death, bondage, misery, sorrow
and amazement, I fell to the ground, and cried unto God
for deliverance and redemption out of this state; and, although the witness of God thus stirred, and was the discov-
erer of this miserable state, yet I saw not, neither had a
clear knowledge of that which thus discovered.

So was I brought into great dread, fear and awe of God
eternal, and had great esteem of, and regard to God's mes-
sengers, who brought the acceptable tidings of life and salvation. Through them doctrine dropped as the dew, and
was received; and as their words were gracious words, so
was there a great estimation in my soul of every word, and

a fear of rebelling against any part of that counsel I received from them, either by word or writing. A long travail I saw, through the ministration of condemnation, which indeed was glorious in its time: and as I kept down to the judgment of the Lord in my heart, the operation whereof was as a sword, fire, and hammer, and the evil nature, in some measure, came to be overcome, then something of divine refreshing streamed in, and love flowed, which refreshed me in my travails. But now began the old subtle enemy to lay snares, and hunt after my soul, which was in some measure rescued out of the jaws of death; so that when I had precious, refreshing openings of the way of truth, through which a secret hope and joy sprang, the enemy led me out from sinking down into a sweet enjoyment and treasuring up, to spend my own bread in disputes for truth, against opposers; and to declare of it unto those who had some love for it. But so it was, that after I had given and spent my own bread, which was given me only to strengthen my own soul, that when I came home and communed with my own heart, and came to stillness, then I saw myself quite empty, having leaked out that which was given for my refreshment and consolation. My beloved was withdrawn; then distress took hold on me beyond all expression, and I was greatly bowed down; and having an understanding of the cause, I was ready to promise and covenant, that if I came to my former peace and refreshment and feeding again, I would not run out prodigally again, nor spend my portion, through which that inward trouble and barrenness came over my spirit. But in time the Lord helped me through and over this exercise, and I came rather to stand as a fool, and to sit in silence before the Lord among his people, than to wrong my condition and grieve the Spirit of God. And when I thus kept obedient to Wisdom's directings, a secret joy would spring, and pure peace and inward ease; yet when I came to inward peace, and felt life and joy, for that the light of the Lord shined on my tabernacle, for want of keeping low in humility, where the growth in the truth is, the enemy wrought subtly again, to persuade that there was not that need of such a severe watch and inward exercise, as formerly; through which he sometimes prevailed, to lead into a liberty, inward and outward, that had a tendency to lead again into inward bondage: and I, through often refreshings, openings, prophecies and promises, was ready to conclude my mountain was immoveable. But soon I found a withdrawing again of the Lord; then I knew a winter again, and the storms of the enemy; and not having yet learned the state of being contented in want, as well as in aboundings, I not only fell into a poor, wanting, murmuring state, but also into great trouble, in a sense of this change, and fears and doubts were ready to enter: I toiled in this night, but could catch nothing which administered any comfort that was lasting. Here I was willing and running and striving, being in great fear and sorrow; and the more I toiled and laboured, kindling sparks of my own, the more my sorrow was increased; for as yet I had not learned the state of resignation. And now, I was brought very low; and having mourned many days, in the sense of the withdrawings of the presence, love and power of my God, being in deep distress and amazement, Israel's travels in the wilderness were opened unto me; how the Lord tried them with want of bread and water, and that their happiness stood in their being content and resigned up to the will of God, and in the belief of the Lord's faithfulness, to have endured the trial. But they murmured and repined, and thereby grieved the Spirit of God; so did I: yet through the loving kindness of God, the state of resignation was opened unto me, in which man stood before he fell through transgression, into his own workings and willings. Now, when my understanding was thus opened, my soul cried unto the Lord my God,

— Oh! preserve me in pure patience and passiveness, and in living, acceptable obedience, and I will trust in thee.

And as I believed in the light of the Lord, and thereby and therein was comprehended and resigned, his pure power, love and life broke in as formerly, which greatly refreshed; then the sun shined upon my tabernacle, and I bowed before the Lord, blessing and praising his holy, glorious name; then he instructed me, and *his pure Spirit and power opened in me the way of preservation, and that was, to centre down into true humility.* So then my soul began to be as the dove that found a place for the soles of her feet. Yet did the enemy continue to tempt by his allurements, and so laid his baits and snares, that if at any time I was drawn to look abroad, and went out to view, as Dinah did, I was in great danger of being defiled: for I found, if at any time I went out from this pure, preserving power of God, that had wrought in my soul through inexpressible travail, and let in the spirit of the world and reasoned, and thereby beheld a beauty in any fruit but what was brought forth by the Tree of Life, then came over me a wound, a stain and defilement. And if at any time the enemy prevailed in the inward ground, to cause any cleaving to his temptations, through the lusts of the flesh, or lusts of the eye, then was I afraid, because of horror and inward wrath; and then the power of the Lord, in love to my soul, wrought mightily, to sanctify and cleanse it again. This inward exercise I passed through, when no friend nor intimate acquaintance knew thereof. Oh! I remember the nights of bitter sorrow that I passed through, when no defilement could be discerned by any, I walking blamelessly among men. For such was the great love of God to my soul all along, in those days of inward travail and exercise, that judgment followed presently upon the outgoing of my mind.

Pierre Poiret

———•———

"Pierre Poiret is the only mystic of the French Reformed Church," wrote Ernest Ott. Poiret was born 15 April 1646 of Protestant parents at Metz. He intended to be a painter, but read Descartes and determined to become a philosopher. He studied theology at Basle and in 1668 became a preacher at Heidelberg. In 1672 he read Tauler and à Kempis and Antoinette Bourignon, a contemporary mystic living in Hamburg. Poiret went there to meet her, and studied mysticism with her for eight years. Forced to leave owing to disapproval of his opinions by the local pastors, he retired to Rhynsburg where he died on 21 May 1719. He left many translations, adaptations, biographies of pious people, and philosophical works, among which the most important are the seven volumes of his *L'économie divine*. He has been called the father of the German romantic mystics, and certainly had an immense influence on them.

From LA PAIX DES BONNES AMES

Letter II

Of what does prayer consist? Of regular prayers and exercises and of their utility and of continual prayer, its nature, its absolute necessity in order to conquer our exterior and interior enemies, and in order to obtain God's grace and arrive at perfection.

My DEAR FRIEND,

Since you have resolved to renounce yourself and no longer to follow your sensual nature, you must pray continually in order to bring your good intention to fulfilment. Because once the Devil has obtained power over a person, and has caused him to love and to follow his own sensuali-

ties, he does not let go easily, not wishing to quit the fortress of which he once was ruler; but he remains there per-
force and against the will of the person who wishes to get rid
of him; so his force must be met by force. It is of similar
devils that Jesus Christ said that they "do not come out
except by prayer and fasting." It was not that Jesus Christ
and the apostles would not have had enough grace to chase
the devils, but when they have once acquired power over
a man's will and he has consented to all the demon's suggestions, he will not be able to get out of the situation except by prayer and fasting, since the devil has got hold of
his soul by dint of accepted sensualities and negligences in
prayer.

So, from the very beginning, I exhort you to continual
prayer, in order to conquer this enemy of your soul, and to
chase him away by your intercession.

But I must tell you what prayer is, so you may learn how
to do it well, because often a person takes for prayer a few
fine phrases read or heard from someone, just as in some
places one has the habit of singing psalms or hymns when
one wishes to pray — others recite a specified number of
Pater Nosters or Ave Marias or other prayers written in
certain books where one learns by heart the words one
wishes to pray. None of this can be called prayer, for these
words and psalms can perfectly well be said without making any prayer to God. Indeed, to pray while saying such
psalms, one must have the same desires as their authors
and one must say the same words with the same desires
they had when saying them, otherwise, there can be no
prayer, but only idle words that are no use. Indeed often
such words are insulting to God, if by mouthing them one
lies.

For example, those who say those Psalms David made
when he was penitent, when he fasted and prayed and wet
his couch with tears, are often themselves full of wine and

good food, and spend their nights in voluptuousness and sin. Is not such behaviour a mockery of God and a lie before him? So too are those who say the Pater or any other prayers without desiring those things the prayer requires. Such men will say God is their father, without wishing to obey Him like children. *Hallowed be thy name,* they will say when in reality they despise and dishonor Him preferring their own honor and will to that of God. Thy Kingdom come, they say, when all they wish is to reign in this world where they always wish to live as though God had given it to them in perpetuity. They say *Thy will be done in earth as it is in Heaven* while refusing to give way in anything to the love of God. And while praying for their daily bread they scrabble and struggle to get more for themselves than they have prayed for. They pray that He forgive them their trespasses while they love these and daily commit more. And that He will deliver them from temptation when they seek out its occasions.

Such prayers as these I would not have you say, but to pray without ceasing. Such prayer must come from the heart. For since you have continually need of God's assistance, so also you need continual prayer. So you must begin it and never cease. For the devil does not get worried by the prayers that are said morning or evening or before or after meals, for he then retires only briefly and comes back with the more zest, as a lover who absents himself for a time from his beloved, and returns from his journey the more fervent. I do not wish to discredit morning or evening prayers nor grace at table, because for worldly people there are good — if they did not say them they might say no prayers at all. But for God's children and those who seek Christian perfection, they should pray continually without ceasing, now to implore heaven's help, now to give thanks, and always to praise and bless God. So there should be no moment of the day without its prayer.

I don't want your mind ordinarily engaged in prayer, for then your head would soon be exhausted, and would invent a thousand unnecessary imaginations. But I would have you ask for one particular grace, that of continual prayer.

And that you may know what is prayer, and that it is not difficult but that on the contrary nothing is sweeter or pleasanter, remember it is not in vocal phrases, nor in meditations nor mental aspirations that it is to be found. True prayer consists in a spiritual conversation between man and God. And this elevation of mind or colloquy with God is the true prayer, compared with which none other is valid.

God never asks the impossible from man. If one had always to be at church, man would die for lack of the necessities of life; and were one obliged to be always on one's knees, the body could not bear this constant fatigue. And if one had always to meditate with one's head one would break down for one could neither eat, drink nor sleep. But God asks only for this conversation to continue always between Himself and the soul, and it can continue when you are working, eating, drinking, writing, even sleeping. So you see it is perfectly possible to pray without ceasing, as Jesus Christ taught us. For myself, I could not live without this continual prayer, and I would prefer death to being without it for an hour, for all pleasures other than this conversation bore me and are, indeed, mortal afflictions to me. That is why I keep always in this prayer, and I do not think you have ever seen me leave this conversation to enjoy any other pleasure. From this you can see that it is perfectly possible and good and pleasant always to pray for anyone who is in such continual prayer is never melancholy. Do not therefore try and speculate upon the mysteries of God nor His relations with man but just talk continually to Him. . . . All the religions in the world cannot give us union with God: we must find it for ourselves.

Johannes Kelpius

He was born probably in 1673 at Denndorf and was graduated from the University of Altdorf. Inspired by Jacob Boehme, he came to America with Jane Leade, head of a group of English mystics called the Philadelphists, and settled near Germantown, Pennsylvania. Kelpius sought out a wilderness along the Wissahickon where he lived an austere and ascetic existence. Kelpius was known as the Magister, and lived at first in a cave, later in a hut. Died in 1708, at the age of thirty-five, in his garden, surrounded by pupils and disciples. His only book *A Short Easy and Comprehensive Method of Prayer* was published in 1761, over fifty years after his death.

From A METHOD OF PRAYER

For as much as internal prayer is so weighty a point that one may call it the only means to attain perfection in this life and to kindle the pure and disinterested love in our hearts, and as all Christians (who will indeed be such) are called to this state of pure love and perfection, and will, by the power of this call, have the necessary grace offered to them to attain such a state: so this inward prayer suits all persons, even the most simple and ignorant, who are also capable of performing this order or manner of prayer.

This brings us soonest to the union with and conformity to the Will of God: so that by the resignation to, the union with, and the change of our wills into the Will of God — after many vicissitudes, trials and purifyings in and after this life — we shall find ourselves so settled and established that we shall not find any more self-love in us, but that we will only what God wills, and the Will of God is become wholly our will.

The Inward Prayer That Never Ends

Now remains only to show that there is a prayer which may be performed at all times and in all places, which by nothing can be interrupted but by sin and unfaithfulness.

This inward prayer is performed in the spirit of the inward man through faith and love, and therefore is justly called the Prayer of Faith and Love.

This Prayer of Faith is simple, pure, universal, and obscure, without observing or distinguishing plainly the affections, words, or what one prays for; and as nothing can put bounds to its vast extent, so is nothing able to interrupt it or to make it cease. And so the Prayer of the Will, or the Prayer of Divine Love, which consists in the entire inclination of the heart towards the Supreme Good, which is God, can be as little or rather less interrupted, since the heart is never weary of loving.

This incessant prayer now consists in an everlasting inclination of the heart to God, which inclination flows from Love. This love draws the presence of God into us; so that, as by the operation of divine grace the love to God is generated in us, so is also the presence of grace increased by this love, that such prayer is performed in us, without us, or our cogitation. It is the same as with a person living in the air and drawing it in with his breath without thinking that by it he lives and breathes, because he does not reflect upon it. Wherefore this way is called a Mystical Way — that is, a secret and incomprehensible way. In one word, the prayer of the heart may be performed at all times, though the heart cannot think or speak at all times.

The Kindling and the Burning

Besides this never-ceasing Prayer of the Heart, there is another more expressive and more particular prayer which is performed at certain times appointed for that purpose:

then the soul is solely engaged with God and all other occupation put off. This particular prayer is performed either at the appointed times when we are in an active state, or at such times which are indicated by the drawing of the inward spirit when we find ourselves in a passive state.

It is a delusion to imagine that, since we enjoy the Presence of God the whole day, we need take no other time for the performance of the inward prayer. The Presence of God is the fruit and farther propagation or increase of this inward prayer, and those who omit the performance of it at certain times, under whatever pretense it may be, will not long retain the divine presence in their daily occupations.

I know very well that it is not always necessary to pray at a certain regular hour, if we are hindered by unavoidable accidents. But we must, however, take some time daily to perform this prayer. We give nourishment to our bodies; therefore let us also give nourishment to our souls. We spend so much time idly; let us dedicate a part of it to God, which part alone will be called time not lost.

Now the soul that will perform this inward prayer has in the beginning only two exercises to use towards her excitation. First, the representation of the Presence of God. And since it is a truth belonging to the Christian faith that the infinite majesty of God and the whole adorable trinity fills all things, so must the soul undertake an inward exercise of this faith and stir herself up, firmly believing this truth, that God the Father, the Son and Holy Ghost is in her, as well as in the place where she is, and in all places truly present.

Secondly, after this exercise of faith and stirring-up, the soul must practice a resigned committing herself into His fatherly hands, most sincerely resolving to dedicate herself, her inward and outward man, with all her faculties and performances, to His most holy Will; that with regard to her He may direct and order everything according to this His good Will, in her prayer and out of it, in Time and Eternity.

Thus it is necessary in the beginning to kindle the fire by working; but afterwards, when once it is kindled, to let it burn.

When this is done, then the soul has no more to do the whole time of prayer but to remain in Peace and Silence, endeavoring to continue in this loving remembrance of God, who is so truly present in her as He is in Heaven.

There are times wherein the Prayer of the Heart, the internal exercise of prayer, becomes toilsome and painful to us, because the loving inclinations of the heart are more hidden and less sensible. We must either stir up the will by some elevation of the mind to love, confidence, resignation, and turning inwardly, or remain quite resigned to God, performing at such times a Prayer of Patience, according to the degrees of the soul's attainment, and to suffer, as the Scripture saith, that comfort tarries and is delayed, that so our life may grow and be renewed.

But you will say and object, I perform nothing by my prayer, for I am within quite dry and scattered. God will hereby do something for you if you are faithful, if your scatterings are not wilful and against your inclination.

William Law

He was born at King's Cliffe, Northamptonshire, in 1686 and in 1711 was elected a fellow of Emmanuel College, Cambridge and was ordained. He stayed there until George I became King, when conscience forbade him to take the oath of allegiance to the new King and abjure the Stuarts. He was suspended from his fellowships for his loyalty and was deprived of his living. In 1727 he became tutor to Edward Gibbon's son in Putney (this son became the father of the historian). Law went to Cambridge with Gibbon and remained there three years with him, then went back to Putney and became a religious guide to Gibbon's family. Among other of his disciples were John and Charles Wesley, and John Byrom, the poet. In 1740, Law retired to King's Cliffe, where his father had left him a small property. He died in 1761. Law was a follower of Jakob Boehme and his most famous work is *A Serious Call to a Devout and Holy Life*, which influenced the English Evangelical revival.

From THE WAY TO
DIVINE KNOWLEDGE

For nothing leads or carries you anywhere, nothing generates either life or death in you but the working of your mind, will, and desire. If your will is angelic, you are an angel and angelic happiness must be yours. If your will is with God you work with God; God is then the life of your soul, and you will have your life with God to all eternity. If you follow an earthly will, every step you take is a departure from God, till you become as incapable of God and the life of God as the animals of this world. If your will worketh in pride and self-exaltation, in envy and wrath, in hatred and

ill-will, in deceit, hypocrisy, and falseness, you work with
the devil, you are generating his nature within you and
making yourself ready for the kingdom of hell. And thus it
is that our works follow us, and that everyone will be rewarded according to his works, and none can reap anything
else but that which he hath sown. And the seed of everything that can grow in us is our will. The will maketh the
beginning, the middle, and the end of everything; it is the
only workman in nature, and everything is its work. It has
all power, its works cannot be hindered, it carries all before
it, it creates as it goes and all things are possible to it. It
enters wherever it wills and finds everything that it seeks,
for its seeking is its finding. The will overrules all nature,
because nature is its offspring and born of it; for all the
properties of nature, whether they be good or evil, in darkness or in light, in love or in hatred, in wrath or in meekness, in pride or humility, in trouble or joy, are all of them
the offspring or birth of the will; as that liveth, so they live,
and as that changeth, so they change. So that whatever
you are, or whatever you feel, is all owing to the working
and creating power of your own will. This is your God or
your Devil, your Heaven or your hell, and you have only
so much of one or the other as your will, which is the first
mover, is either given up to the one or to the other.

For where the will of man is not, there he hath nothing,
and where his will is, there is all that something which
he hath, be it of what kind it will, and it is inseparable from
him till his will worketh contrary to it.

Academicus. Whence hath the will of man this mighty
power that it can have nothing but that which itself hath
willed?

Theophilus. You might as well ask why a circle must be
perfectly round, or a straight line free from every degree of
crookedness. For as it is not a circle till it is perfectly
round, nor a straight line till it is free from crookedness, so

the will is not in being but so far as it is free, is its own mover, and can have nothing but that which it willeth. Secondly, the will is not a made thing, which is made out of something or that came out of some different state into the state of a will. But the free will of man is a true and real birth from the free, eternal, uncreated will of God, which willed to have a creaturely offspring of itself or to see itself in a creaturely state. And therefore the will of man hath the nature of divine freedom, hath the nature of eternity and the nature of omnipotence in it, because it is what it is and hath what it hath as a spark, a ray, a genuine birth of the eternal, free, omnipotent will of God. And therefore, as the will of God is superior to and ruleth over all nature, so the will of man, derived from the will of God, is superior to and ruleth over all his own nature. And thence it is that, as to itself and so far as its own nature reacheth, it hath the freedom and omnipotence of that will from which it is descended, and can have or receive nothing but what itself doth and worketh in and to itself.

And herein consisteth the infinite goodness of God, in the birth of all intelligent creatures, and also the exceeding height, perfection, and happiness of their created state: they are descended from God, full of divine power; they can will and work with God and partake of the divine happiness. They can receive no injustice, hurt, or violence either from nature or creature, but must be only that which they generate, and have no evil or hurt but that which they do in and to themselves. All things stand in the will, and everything, animate or inanimate, is the effect and produce of that will, which worketh in it and formeth it to be that which it is. And every will, wherever found, is the birth and effect of some antecedent will, for will can only proceed from will, till you come to the first working will, which is God Himself.

From THE SPIRIT OF PRAYER

PART THE FIRST
Chapter I

The greatest part of mankind — nay, of Christians —
may be said to be asleep, and that particular way of life
which takes up each man's mind, thoughts, and actions
may be very well called his particular dream. This degree of
vanity is equally visible in every form and order of life. The
learned and the ignorant, the rich and the poor, are all in
the same state of slumber, only passing away a short life in
a different kind of dream. But why so? It is because man
has an eternity within him, is born into this world, not for
the sake of living here, not for anything this world can give
him, but only to have time and place to become either an
eternal partaker of a divine life with God or to have an hellish eternity among fallen angels. And therefore, every man
who has not his eye, his heart, and his hands continually
governed by this twofold eternity may be justly said to be
fast asleep — to have no awakened sensibility of himself.
And a life devoted to the interests and enjoyments of this
world, spent and wasted in the slavery of earthly desires,
may be truly called a dream, as having all the shortness,
vanity, and delusion of a dream; only with this great difference, that when a dream is over nothing is lost but fictions
and fancies; but when the dream of life is ended only by
death, all that eternity is lost, for which we were brought
into being. Now, there is no misery in this world, nothing
that makes either the life or death of man to be full of
calamity, but this blindness and insensibility of his state,
into which he so willingly — nay, obstinately — plunges
himself. Everything that has the nature of evil and distress
in it takes its rise from hence. Do but suppose a man to

know himself that he comes into this world on no other errand but to rise out of the vanity of time into the riches of eternity; do but suppose him to govern his inward thoughts and outward actions by this view of himself, and then to him every day has lost all its evil; prosperity and adversity have no difference, because he receives and uses them both in the same spirit; life and death are equally welcome, because equally parts of his way to eternity. For poor and miserable as this life is, we have all of us free access to all that is great, and good, and happy, and carry within ourselves a key to all the treasures that heaven has to bestow upon us. We starve in the midst of plenty, groan under infirmities, with the remedy in our own hand; live and die without knowing and feeling anything of the One only Good, whilst we have it in our power to know and enjoy it in as great a reality as we know and feel the power of this world over us; for Heaven is as near to our souls as this world is to our bodies; and we are created, we are redeemed, to have our conversation in it. God, the only good of all intelligent natures, is not an absent or distant god, but is more present in and to our souls than our own bodies; and we are strangers to Heaven and without God in the world for this only reason, because we are void of that spirit of prayer which alone can and never fails to unite us with the One only Good, and to open Heaven and the kingdom of God within us. A root set in the finest soil, in the best climate, and blessed with all that sun, and air, and rain can do for it, is not in so sure a way of its growth to perfection as every man may be whose spirit aspires after all that which God is ready and infinitely desirous to give him. For the sun meets not the springing bud that stretches towards him with half that certainty as God, the source of all good, communicates Himself to the soul that longs to partake of Him.

We are all of us by birth the offspring of God — more

nearly related to Him than we are to one another, for in Him we live, and move, and have our being. The first man that was brought forth from God had the breath and Spirit of Father, Son, and Holy Ghost breathed into him, and so he became a living soul.

He made the creature for this sole end, to receive good. The first motive towards the creature is unchangeable; it takes its rise from God's desire to communicate good, and it is an eternal impossibility that anything can ever come from God as His will and purpose towards the creature but that same love and goodness which first created it; He must always will that to it which He willed at the creation of it. This is the amiable nature of God. He is the Good, the unchangeable, overflowing fountain of good that sends forth nothing but good to all eternity. He is the Love itself, the unmixed, unmeasurable Love, doing nothing but from love, giving nothing but gifts of love to everything that He has made; requiring nothing of all his creatures but the spirit and fruits of that love which brought them into being. Oh, how sweet is this contemplation of the height and depth of the riches of Divine Love! With what attraction must it draw every thoughtful man to return love for love to this overflowing fountain of boundless goodness! What charms has that religion which discovers to us our existence in, relation to, and dependence upon this ocean of Divine Love! View every part of our redemption, from Adam's first sin to the resurrection of the dead, and you will find nothing but successive mysteries of that first love which created angels and men. All the mysteries of the Gospel are only so many marks and proofs of God's desiring to make His love triumph in the removal of sin and disorder from all nature and creature. . . .

See here the deep ground and absolute necessity of that new birth of Word, Son, and Spirit of God which the Scripture speaks so much of. It is because our soul, as fallen, is quite dead to and separate from the kingdom of Heaven by having lost the light and Spirit of God in itself; and therefore it is and must be incapable of entering into Heaven till by this new birth the soul gets again its first heavenly nature. . . .

Poor sinner! consider the treasure thou hast within thee; the Saviour of the world, the eternal Word of God lies hid in thee, as a spark of the divine nature which is to overcome sin and death and hell within thee, and generate the life of Heaven again in thy soul. Turn to thy heart, and thy heart will find its Saviour, its God within itself. Thou seest, hearest, and feelest nothing of God, because thou seekest for Him abroad with thy outward eyes, thou seekest for Him in books, in controversies, in the church, and outward exercises, but there thou wilt not find Him till thou hast first found Him in thy heart. Seek for Him in thy heart, and thou wilt never seek in vain, for there He dwells, there is the seat of His Light and holy Spirit.

For this turning to the light and Spirit of God within thee is thy only true turning unto God; there is no other way of finding Him but in that place where He dwelleth in thee. For though God be everywhere present, yet He is only present to thee in the deepest and most central part of thy soul. Thy natural senses cannot possess God or unite thee to Him; nay, thy inward faculties of understanding, will, and memory, can only reach after God, but cannot be the place of His habitation in thee. But there is a root or depth in thee from whence all these faculties come forth, as lines from a centre or as branches from the body of the tree. This depth is called the centre, the *fund* or bottom of the soul. This depth is the unity, the eternity, I had almost said the infinity of thy soul; for it is so infinite that nothing can satisfy it or give it any rest but the infinity of God. In this depth of the soul the Holy Trinity brought forth its own living image in the first created man, bearing in himself a living representation of Father, Son, and Holy Ghost, and this was his dwelling in God and God in him. This was the kingdom of God within him, and made Paradise without him. But the day that Adam did eat of the forbidden earthly tree, in that day he absolutely died to this kingdom of God within him. This depth or centre of his soul having lost its God, was shut up in death and darkness and became a prisoner in an earthly animal that only excelled its brethren, the beasts, in an upright form and serpentine subtlety. Thus ended the fall of man. But from that moment that the God of mercy inspoke into Adam the Bruiser of the Serpent, from that moment all the riches and treasures of the divine nature came again into man, as a seed of salvation sown into the centre of the soul, and only lies hidden there in every man till he desires to rise from his fallen state and to be born again from above.

Awake, then, thou that sleepest, and Christ, who from all eternity has been espoused to thy soul, shall give thee light. Begin to search and dig in thine own field for this pearl of eternity that lies hidden in it; it cannot cost thee too much, nor canst thou buy it too dear, for it is *all*; and when thou has found it thou wilt know that all which thou hast sold or given away for it is as mere a nothing as a bubble upon the water.

But if thou turnest from this heavenly pearl or tramplest it under thy feet for the sake of being rich or great, either in Church or State; if death finds thee in this success, thou canst not then say that though the pearl is lost yet something has been gained instead of it. For in that parting moment the things and the sounds of this world will be exactly alike; to have had an estate or only to have heard of it, to have lived at Lambeth twenty years or only to have twenty times passed by the palace will be the same good or the same nothing to thee.

Ask what God is? His name is love; He is the good, the perfection, the peace, the joy, the glory, and blessing of every life. Ask what Christ is? He is the universal remedy of all evil broken forth in nature and creature. He is the destruction of misery, sin, darkness, death, and hell. He is the resurrection and life of all fallen nature. He is the unwearied compassion, the long-suffering pity, the never-ceasing mercifulness of God to every want and infirmity of human nature.

He is the breathing forth of the heart, life, and Spirit of God into all the dead race of Adam. He is the seeker, the finder, the restorer of all that was lost and dead to the life of God. He is the love that, from Cain to the end of time, prays for all its murderers; the love that willingly suffers and dies among thieves, that thieves may have a life with Him in Paradise; the love that visits publicans, harlots, and sinners and wants and seeks to forgive where most is to be forgiven. O, my friends, let us surround and encompass Humanus with these flames of love till he cannot make his escape from them, but must become a willing victim to their power. For the universal God is universal love; all is love but that which is hellish and earthly. All religion is the spirit of love; all its gifts and graces are the gifts and graces of love; it has no breath, no life but the life of love. Nothing exalts, nothing purifies but the fire of love; nothing changes death into life, earth into Heaven, men into angels but love alone. Love breathes the Spirit of God; its words and works are the inspiration of God. It speaketh not of itself, but the Word, the eternal Word of God speaketh in it; for all that love speaketh, that God speaketh, because love is God. Love is Heaven revealed in the soul; it is light and truth; it is infallible; it has no errors, for all errors are the want of love. Love has no more of pride than light has of darkness; it stands and bears all its fruits from a depth and root of humility. Love is of no sect or party; it neither makes nor admits of any bounds; you may as easily enclose the light or shut up the air of the world into one place as confine love to a sect or party. It lives in the liberty, the universality, the impartiality of Heaven. It believes in one holy, catholic God, the God of all spirits; it unites and joins with the catholic Spirit of the one God, who unites with all that is good, and is meek, patient, well-wishing, and long-suffering over all the evil that is in nature and creature. Love, like the Spirit of God, rideth upon the wings of the wind, and is in union and communion with all the saints that are in Heaven and on earth. Love is quite pure; it has no by-ends; it seeks not its own; it has but one will, and that is to give itself into everything and overcome all evil with good. Lastly, love is the Christ of God; it comes down from Heaven; it regenerates the soul from above; it blots out all transgressions; it takes from death its sting, from the devil his power, and from the serpent his poison. It heals all the infirmities of our earthly birth; it gives eyes to the blind, ears to the deaf, and makes the dumb to speak; it cleanses the lepers and casts out devils, and puts man in Paradise before he dies. It lives wholly to the will of Him of whom it is born; its meat and drink is to do the will of God. It is the resurrection and life of every divine virtue, a fruitful mother of true humility, boundless benevolence, unwearied patience, and bowels of compassion.

What life is so much to be dreaded as a life of worldly ease and prosperity? What a misery, nay, what a curse is there in everything that gratifies and nourishes our self-love, self-esteem, and self-seeking! On the other hand, what happiness is there in all inward and outward troubles and

vexations when they force us to feel and know the hell that
is hidden within us and the vanity of everything without
us, when they turn all our self-love into self-abhorrence and
force us to call upon God to save us from ourselves, to give
us a new life, new light, and new spirit in Christ Jesus.

"O happy famine," might the poor Prodigal have well
said, "which, by reducing me to the necessity of asking to
eat husks with swine, brought me to myself and caused my
return to my first happiness in my father's house."

Now, I will suppose your distressed state to be as you
represent it: inwardly, darkness, heaviness, and confusion
of thoughts and passions; outwardly, ill usage from friends,
relations, and all the world, unable to strike up the least
spark of light or comfort by any thought or reasoning of
your own.

O happy famine, which leaves you not so much as the
husk of one human comfort to feed upon! For this is the
time and place for all that good and life and salvation to
happen to you which happened to the Prodigal Son. Your
way is as short and your success as certain as his was. You
have no more to do than he had; you need not call out for
books or methods of devotion; for in your present state
much reading and borrowed prayers are not your best
method. All that you are to offer to God, all that is to help
you to find Him to be your Saviour and Redeemer, is best
taught and expressed by the distressed state of your heart.

Only let your present and past distress make you feel and
acknowledge this twofold great truth: first, that in and of
yourself you are nothing but darkness, vanity, and misery;
secondly, that of yourself you can no more help yourself to
light and comfort than you can create an angel.

Would you have done with error, scruple and delusion?
Consider the Deity to be the greatest love, the greatest
meekness, the greatest sweetness, the eternal, unchangeable

will to be a good and blessing to every creature; and that all the misery, darkness, and death of fallen angels and fallen men consist in their having lost their likeness to this divine nature. Consider yourself and all the fallen world as having nothing to seek or wish for, but by the spirit of prayer to draw into the life of your soul rays and sparks of this divine, meek, loving, tender nature of God. Consider the holy Jesus as the gift of God to your soul, to begin and finish the birth of God and Heaven within you, in spite of every inward or outward enemy. These three infallible truths, heartily embraced and made the nourishment of your soul, shorten and secure the way to Heaven and leave no room for error, scruple, or delusion. . . .

Reading is good, hearing is good, conversation and meditation are good; but then, they are only good at times and occasions, in a certain degree, and must be used and governed with such caution as we eat and drink and refresh ourselves, or they will bring forth in us the fruits of intemperance. But the spirit of prayer is for all times and all occasions; it is a lamp that is to be always burning, a light to be ever shining; everything calls for it, everything is to be done in it and governed by it, because it is and means and wills nothing else but the whole totality of the soul, not doing this or that, but wholly, incessantly given up to God to be where and what and how He pleases.

For if every desire is in itself, in its own essence, the kindling of fire, then we are taught this great practical lesson, that our own desire is the kindler of our own fire, the former and raiser of that life which leads us. What our desire kindles, that becomes the fire of our life, and fits us either for the majestic glories of the Kingdom of God or the dark horrors of hell. So that our desire is all, it does all, and governs all, and all that we have and are must arise from it, and therefore it is that the Scripture saith, "Keep thy heart with all diligence, for out of it are the issues of life."

We are apt to think that our imaginations and desires may be played with, that they rise and fall away as nothing, because they do not always bring forth outward and visible effects. But, indeed, they are the greatest reality we have and are the true formers and raiser of all that is real and solid in us. All outward power that we exercise in the things about us is but as a shadow in comparison of that inward power that resides in our will, imagination and desires; these communicate with eternity and kindle a life which always reaches either Heaven or hell. This strength of the inward man makes all that is the angel and all that is the devil in us, and we are neither good nor bad, but according to the working of that which is spiritual and invisible in us. Now, our desire is not only thus powerful and productive of real effects, but it is always alive, always working and creating in us — I say creating, for it has no less power, it perpetually generates either life or death in us. And here lies the ground of the great efficacy of prayer, which when it is the prayer of the heart, the prayer of faith, has a kindling and creating power, and forms and transforms the soul into everything that its desires reach after: it has the key to the Kingdom of Heaven and unlocks all its treasures, it opens, extends and moves that in us which has its being and motion in and with the divine nature, and so brings us into real union and communion with God.

Emanuel Swedenborg

The celebrated Swedish scientist and mystical philosopher was born in 1688, the son of the professor of philosophy at Uppsala who was also Bishop of Skara. Swedenborg was influenced by Henry More, the Cambridge Platonist, and by John Locke and Isaac Newton. Appointed by Charles XII to the Swedish Board of Mines, he anticipated the nebular theory, the magnetic theory, the machine gun and the airplane, and has been claimed as the founder of crystallography. In 1743 he became conscious of direct control by angels, not only in dreams but also in waking, and felt the Lord wanted him to make known His doctrines. In 1747 he resigned his position on order to study the Scriptures and spent the rest of his life in Sweden, London and Holland. He wrote many books, of which perhaps the best known are *Arcana Coelestia* (8 vols., 1756) and *Divine Love and Wisdom* (1763). He died in London on 29 March 1772, and his remains were reinterred at Uppsala in 1908.

From SPIRITUAL DIARY

That I was raised into an interior Sphere, but with Variation, as often as I prayed the Lord's Prayer.

As often as I said the prayer of the Lord, morning and evening, I was raised, almost every time with variety, into an interior sphere, and, indeed, so perceptibly, together with the change or variation, that nothing could be more so; and this experience I have now had upwards of two years. Interior explications of the prayer were then opened to my mind with very much variety. But when the prayer was finished, I came again into my ordinary sphere [or state].

That there are tranquil Spheres, which are to be
called the Spheres of Ignorance in the
ultimate Heaven.

This morning I was led into some spheres, so called, of the ultimate heaven, and indeed into the inmost part; for every heaven has its inmost, its interior, and its exterior; spirits, who are recently taken out of the pit, are said to remain there a short time; a tranquillity was there, nor was anything sad perceived, wherefore, here is the tranquillity which, in an interior degree, corresponds to peace in the inmost. Afterwards, being surrounded, as it were, by a column [of spirits], I was led into other spheres of the exterior heaven, and indeed into the heaven of ignorance; (each heaven can be distinguished into its own heavens); here nothing was heard; but there was tranquillity; at length I came into another heaven of ignorance, of such as were unconcerned about heresies, and who neither affirmed nor denied anything, saying, that every one might entertain his own opinion; here, however, it was not so tranquil; it was as though somebody was striking the wall with a hammer, whom every one said he feared, lest he should at length break in upon them. These heavens are separated and well guarded: thus, in the heavens, there is nothing indistinct; except according to the appearance in the inferior heaven, which is no longer to be called an exterior, but an inferior heaven, for there is the crew of inferior spirits above hell, who act licentiously. 1747, Nov. 21, o. s. — Obs. The heaven of *ignorance*, in the exterior heaven, corresponds to *innocence* in the interior and inmost heavens. These are the habitations, or the mansions of heaven, of which God Messiah speaks (John xiv); they are here called spheres.

*That the Understanding of Things, especially of
interior Things, was taken away [from me].*

This I can also solemnly testify, that the understanding of things, especially of interior things, has been frequently, and so manifestly taken away from me, and also changed into another [or into the understanding of something else], and thus so often changed, that I cannot say how often. From so much experience it can be sufficiently concluded, that a man can understand nothing else (especially when he considers the interior things of faith) than those which God Messiah permits and in mercy grants [him to understand]. Sometimes the contention and objurgation with those spirits who took away the understanding of interior things, or changed it into another [or into the understanding of something else], were such as I cannot describe. 1747, Oct. 22, *o. s.*

*That it has been permitted me to communicate,
as it were, heavenly Delight to the good
Souls in Captivity.*

(For several years back I have been permitted manifestly to experience heavenly delights in various ways, so many and of such a quality that I can in no wise describe them; which were of such a nature, that a man could by no means believe and understand them if I were to attempt to describe them. And also this day I was permitted to enjoy heavenly delights which were inexpressible, and which also it was granted to me, as it were of myself (although it was not from myself), to transfer to the souls in captivity; which delights they said they could feel, from which also they received consolation. They are also [sometimes] called sheep, which is likewise a great comfort to them. In what manner they ascend from captivity into a sort of liberty both of speaking, understanding, perceiving, and seeing, cannot be described, although it was granted me to perceive it with a manifest or lively sensation. 1747, Oct. 24, o. s.)

How Representations descend from the Heavens.

I saw a certain garden of large extent and embellished with shaded walks, in which the trees, as I was informed, were adorned with leaves, but without fruits. I inquired how the spirits could produce these and similar representations which are so frequent among them.

I perceived that the angels of the interior heaven, while they are in their ideas, and, as it were, in parables, have inserted into these ideas corresponding objects or scenery, by which their ideas are aided. These things, when they are conveyed down among spirits, are immediately formed by them, according to their fantasies, into new representations on a larger scale, retaining, however, the idea of the angelic society, though modified by their own. Thus the [original] idea grows into a representation.

A similar process of growth or expansion takes place when an idea passes from a more interior (*intimiori*) to a more exterior (*interius*) heaven,* although unconsciously to the recipients, for in the exterior (*interiori*) heaven are certain natural elements, to which their ideas adhere, and which govern their form. In the heaven of spirits, or the spiritual world, the same things become material.

Concerning the interior Heaven.

I was in the interior heaven, and certain spirits were at the same time with me in their own world; and although being in heaven, yet I was not in any peculiar ec-

---

* It is important to remark in reference to these terms that in this and many other passages of the Diary, Swedenborg uses *interior*, *intimior*, which in order to be clearly intelligible to the English reader, we are obliged to express by *exterior* and *interior*; inasmuch as by the Latin *interior*, *interius*, he means that which is relatively or comparatively exterior. — TR.

static idea, but in the body, for the kingdom of the Lord is in man, and everywhere, or in every place, so that at the Lord's good pleasure a man may be conducted into heaven, and yet not be in an ecstatic idea. I was then just as I am at this present writing, but my interior man was [developed] in the exterior, which was the reason of my being associated with spirits in their world, for our ratiocination and our cupidities are in the world of spirits; sensual things in the body correspond to them.

The interior heaven is therefore in degree within the world of spirits, for the world of spirits is separated from heaven, because the world of spirits derive what pertains to them from corporeal things, consequently they are conjoined with things corporeal and worldly, or rather [I may say] the world of spirits stands related to corporeal things as does the crasser atmospheric world to the terraqueous; wherefore the world of spirits occupies the interiors of corporeal things.

The interior heaven, however, is, in relation to the world of spirits, in an interior degree, for what spirits did in particular, that I could feel, and could hear, and thus distinctly perceive, but not what occurred in heaven, except so far as they operate in common.

A State of mental Quiet; concerning celestial States in general.

A state of peace is in a higher degree, a state of mental quiet in a lower. To-day, from an early hour in the morning, it was given me to learn from experience the nature of a state of mental quiet, and indeed, by a species of attraction or subtraction towards the interiors, and towards spirits who were in this quiet state, and that, too, for a whole night, the state continuing till morning, and afterwards for more than an hour. It was thus given to know how sweet the state is, and how indefinite are the states of joy in heaven. It was also given me, in that state, to reflect upon those who desire to live in cares and solicitudes pertaining to corporeal and worldly things, how miserable they are, though they imagine they are in their fullest delight. It was given also to reflect how this state [of quiet] might be supplanted by a state of solicitude, which are like clouds in a serene sky. States of this kind, however, together with many others which are peculiar to the celestials, cannot be perceived [by every one], for they are unknown to the unknowing; neither can they be so expressed in words as to be credible. A certain degree of knowledge may contribute something towards credence, but I can affirm that the states of joy are indefinite as to all things that are pleasant and delightful in the heavens, which yet no one, as a mere man [on the earth] can apprehend, but which still are such that, if one had a sense of them, even of the least, he would never more desire to be in the body, or in corporeal or worldly cares. — 1748, May 9.

Concerning the fallacies of the senses, that they are to be removed in things that are to be believed.

(((I have spoken sometimes with spirits, as also now, who were present with me, (to the effect) that they are not near me, although they seem to themselves to be near, yea sometimes very often (to be) so near as to touch (and) move me, operate to the touch, within me, at the side, at the head, when yet experience is most certain that they cannot be here, but sometimes 10, 100, 1000, 3000 miles distant; yea that it is similar with spirits of other earths. But because spirits from the appearance, entirely as if it were so, that they were near and next to me, do not wish to believe it, because it was wholly contrary to appearance, it was given to tell them that experience is constant and certain, and it is not to be doubted, and least from that cause that it appears so, and that they cannot perceive it from any cause because they have not perceived the cause.

It was granted to elucidate this before them, (and) to say that when experience is clear and certain, there should be no doubt, because the appearance is other, and because they do not know causes; in like manner very many similar things are given in nature which are evident from experience, and nevertheless because true it is to be believed: for instance that they can sail around the globe (globo telluris) and from the opposite part from (a point) opposite our feet. This is certain because experience shows it. Should any one in the world doubt concerning it, because it appeared otherwise, and because he did not know the cause, then there would be innumerable similar things in the nature of things which he would not believe when yet they are such.)))

From MEMORABILIA OF SWEDENBORG

Spirits enjoy vision, inasmuch as they live in light, which with good spirits, angelic spirits, and angels, is so bright, that the mid-day light of this world can hardly be compared with it; concerning the light in which they live and see, by the Divine Mercy of the Lord, in what follows. They enjoy the faculty of hearing also, and that so exquisite, as beyond comparison to exceed what they enjoyed in the body: they have conversed with me now for some years almost continually; but concerning their speech also, by the Divine Mercy of the Lord, in the things which follow. They enjoy likewise the faculty of smelling, which, by the Divine Mercy of the Lord, will be further described in what follows. They have besides a most exquisite sense of touch, whence the pains and torments in hell; for all sensations have relation to the touch, and are only diversities and varieties of touch. They have moreover desires and affections, to which those which they possessed during the life of the body cannot be compared; of which, by the Divine Mercy of the Lord, more heareafter. They think with much more perspicuity and distinctness than they thought in the life of the body; in a single idea of thought they involve more than in a thousand, when they thought in the life of the body. They converse with each other so acutely, with so much penetration, sagacity, and distinctness, that if a man had the least perception thereof, he would be amazed. In short, they have lost nothing, but are still, though more perfect, like men in all respects, except as to bones and flesh, and the imperfections thence. They acknowledge and perceive, that whilst they lived in the body, it was the spirit which had sensation; that although this appeared in the body, yet still it was not of the body; wherefore on the rejection of the body, the sensations live in a much more exquisite and perfect state: life consists in sense, for without sense, there can be no life, and such as the sense is, such is the life, which every one may know.

In another life it is given to perceive clearly what opinions people have entertained whilst they lived in the body, concerning the soul, or spirit, and concerning a life after death; for when they are kept in a state, as if they were in the body, they then think in like manner, and their thoughts are communicated as plainly as if they spoke them aloud. From one person, not long after his decease, I perceived, as he himself confessed, that he had believed indeed in the existence of the spirit, but imagined that it must live after death an obscure kind of life, by reason that, on the removal of the life of the body, there would remain something obscure: for he placed life in the body; wherefore his idea of a spirit was as of a ghost; and he confirmed himself herein from this, that he saw brutes also have life, almost as men; he now wondered, seeing that spirits and angels live in the highest degrees of light, of intelligence, of wisdom, and of happiness, with such a clearness of perception, as can scarcely be described: consequently that their life, so far from being obscure, was most perfectly clear and distinct.

A certain spirit, soon after his decease, on hearing me speak concerning the spirit, said, What is a spirit? supposing himself to be a man: and when I told him that there is a spirit in every man, and that every man, in respect to life, is a spirit, and that the body only serves him to live on the earth, and that bone and flesh, or the body, do in nowise live and think; and when he hesitated, I asked him whether he had ever heard respecting the soul? He replied, "What is the soul? I know not what it is." It was then given me to acquaint him, that he was now a soul, or spirit, as he might know from this, that he was over my head, and did not stand on the earth, whether or not he could perceive this; then he fled away in terror, exclaiming, "I am a spirit, I am a spirit." A certain Jew fully supposed himself to be still living in the body, so that it was with difficult he was persuaded otherwise; and when it was shown him that he was a spirit, he still persisted in declaring that he was a man, because he saw and heard. Such are they who during their abode in the world were corporeal. Many other cases might be adduced; but these are merely to confirm the truth, that it is the spirit in man which has sensation, and not the body.

I have conversed with many after their decease, with whom I was acquainted during their life in the body; and such conversation has been of long continuance, sometimes for months, sometimes for a whole year; and with as clear and distinct a voice, but internal, as with friends in the world. The subject of our discourse has sometimes turned on the state of man after death; and they have greatly wondered that no one in the life of the body knows or believes that he is to live in such a manner after the life of the body;

when nevertheless it is a continuation of life, and that of such a nature, that the deceased passes from an obscure life into a clear and distinct one; and they who are in faith towards the Lord, into a life more and more clear and distinct. They have desired me to acquaint their friends on earth that they were alive, and to write to them an account of their states, as I have often told them many things respecting their friends: but my reply was, that if I should speak to them or write to them, they would not believe, but would call my information mere fancy, and would ridicule it, asking for signs or miracles before they should believe; and thus I should be exposed to their derision: and that the things here declared are true, few perhaps will believe, for men deny in their hearts the existence of spirits; and they who do not deny such existence, are yet very unwilling to hear that any one can converse with spirits. Such a faith respecting spirits did not at all prevail in ancient times, but does at this day, when men wish by reasoning of the brain to explore what spirits are, whom, by definitions and suppositions, they deprive of every sense; and the more learned they wish to be, the more they do this.

This I can assert, that a spirit has much more exquisite sight than a man in the body, and also hearing, and what will seem surprising, more exquisite sense of smell, and especially sense of touch, for they see each other, hear each other, and touch each other. This also he who believes a life after death, might conclude from this, that no life can be given without sense, and that the quality of the life is according to the quality of the sense; yea, that the intellectual is nothing but an exquisite sense of interior things, and the superior intellectual of spiritual things; hence also the things which are of the intellectual and of its perceptions are called the internal senses. With the sensitive of man immediately after death, the case is this. As soon as man dies, and the corporeal things with him grow cold, he is raised up into life, and thus into the state of all sensations, insomuch that at first he scarcely knows otherwise than that he is still in the body; for the sensations in which he is, lead him so to believe. But when he perceives that he has more exquisite sensations, and this especially when he begins to speak with other spirits, he then takes notice that he is in another life, and that the death of his body was the continuation of the life of his spirit. I have spoken with two with whom I had been acquainted, on the same day that they were buried, and with one who saw through my eyes his own coffin and bier, and inasmuch as he was in every sensation in which he had been in the world, he talked with me about the obsequies while I was following his funeral, and also about his body, saying, that they reject it because he himself lives.*

* One of the cases to which Swedenborg here alludes is undoubtedly that of his friend Polhem, recorded in the "Spiritual Diary," in an article bearing the following title: — *Concerning a certain Person* (Polhem) *Resuscitated shortly after Death, and beholding his own Burial.*

"Polhem died on Monday; he spake with me on Thursday, when attending his funeral, to which I had been invited. He saw the corpse, the obsequies, the procession, and also when he was laid in the grave. In the mean time he conversed with me as to why they should bury him when he was yet alive; and so also when the priest said that he should be raised at the last judgment, when yet he would then have been long since raised; and he wondered that such a belief should exist, as that men should rise at the last judgment, when he was already alive; and that the body should rise, when yet he perceived himself to be in a body; besides more of like nature."

Gerhard Tersteegen

A German Protestant writer, he was born in 1697 at Moers, near Düsseldorf, and at the age of twenty was converted to a Pietist circle and dedicated himself to God. He retired into solitude and earned his living by weaving ribbons. In 1728 he became a director of souls and arranged devotional meetings. He translated the works of the French Quietists and wrote *The Compendium of True Godliness*, *The Hidden Life with Christ in God*, *The Pious Lottery* and *The Spiritual Flower Garden*. He also wrote biographies of Catholic mystics. He died on 3 April 1769.

From THE LIFE AND CHARACTER OF GERHARD TERSTEEGEN

I have at present to inform you, that it has pleased the Lord to visit me with sickness. In the beginning of my disorder, I lay and sat as if stupefied, without feeling, and even almost without any recollection of God, or of my own soul. At present my mind is led with silent pleasure, to contemplate the existence of God, his goodness, wisdom, power, holiness, &c. all which infinite perfections are in the highest degree lovely and adorable; so that it is therefore true, that God, and what is in him, and all his works and ways, is the proper food and happiness of a created spirit. In him is all my treasure. *1st February, 1746.*

We know that God is alone supremely good — that he bears with his creatures and children in Christ — prepares them for the enjoyment of himself with incomprehensible condescension — and loves them with peculiar tenderness. We are, nevertheless, so much inclined to rest in ourselves, and to return to ourselves, that I have often been astonished at my own weakness. I have gone to school so long to the best of teachers, and am already employed to give others their lessons, and yet I continue myself such an helpless infant. At present, to all appearance, I can, with singleness of heart, commit myself and all I have to the Lord. I can let every thing go, and still feel composed. I am poor, yet in a wealthy place. I am weak, but contented.

As long as union with God is sensible, the communication is only made through the senses. I find myself so weak and destitute, that with regard to myself, I would rather write nothing respecting the state of my soul. But it is nevertheless true, that I occasionally seem to experience something of a divine communication, which is exceedingly precious, but which lasts only a few moments. We must seek to do nothing and to retain nothing, but resign ourselves and all we have and are into the Lord's hands. Every good thing cometh from him, and he can give or take it away of his good pleasure. I sometimes think that which is really good, would not appear to me to be so, were it in my own possession; but I am infinitely well pleased, that the Lord alone is good. In this, I say perhaps too much of myself, but it is not my intention to do so, nor dare I trouble myself on that account; the Lord however enables me to cast myself and all I am and have quietly into his hands. May he be loved and glorified to all eternity! Amen. *4th November, 1742.*

I wish you much grace, to enable you, with a child-like spirit, to forget and forsake yourself, in order that you may be received in and by the Lord, and be kept until the end. Yes, my dear sister, in the Lord alone is our salvation and our glory. Do you not feel it to be so? What does he require more of his handmaid, than that she resign herself, just as she is, into his hands, and in future regard herself as little, as something which has once been given who goes to work with a great degree of light and certainty. I am entirely without any knowledge of my way, and know not that I ever read of anything similar. I do not feel so much on committing an evident mistake, as I do on a single consideration of my own state, when caring for myself, or when attempting to help myself. On such occasions nothing but reproof and uneasiness ensue; but when I forget myself, and continue to live simply on the grace of God, I am instantaneously as quiet and contented, as one who is at his post. It even seems as if something great and excellent were at hand — a strength in weakness, a knowledge in ignorance, an unity in variety. I am well aware that some of the saints have passed through states, in which they would perhaps have expressed themselves in a similar manner; but this is not the case with me. I am not only wretched but exceedingly so, and this the Lord well knows. I should be terrified, were I to compare my state with that of these holy men; and whilst I write this, I really fear, dear sister, that you may conceive too exalted ideas of my state. Is it not wonderful to see things, so different in themselves, and apparently at variance, in one and the same person? What will you make of it, or how will you explain it? I must therefore only close the account with saying, 'God is a perfect all; the creature a poor nothing,' and return to that which I recognise as the best, and productive of the greatest peace of mind — that is, forgetting myself as much as I can, and continuing to live simply on the grace of God. 11th October, 1746.

All that is within me, inclines to retirement, tranquility, dormancy of imagination, and unity in and with God. To be able so to live, is life indeed. This, methinks, is my station, my food, the object of my calling — to live retired, be emptied of every thing, to be alone with God in the Spirit, and separated from the world, at rest and in silence, giving place to God and things divine; from which alone results truth, and strength, and life, and salvation. How dear to me are the moments which I can spare for that purpose! But it appears as if they will not suffer me to enjoy my food in peace and quietness. Whilst I give, or rather seem to give to others, I imagine I occasionally receive a few crumbs myself. I am well aware that the will of God can and ought to be my food; but when do I possess the will of God? I mean to say, I do not always know what is the will of God; on the contrary, the thought often occurs to me, where a creature does right, in giving his time so much to others. But I am already tired of complaining, and hope to induce you by this means, to offer me up, so much the more, in your prayers to God, that I may but please him in all things, for I desire nothing else — yea, I repeat it, I desire nothing else than to please him, to be his, and to live to him, in time and in eternity. And this I prefer, with every attendant burden, pain, and inconvenience, to living to myself, in the possession of every pleasure and gratification, if such a thing were possible. In this matter, I do not inquire whether this determination be entirely pure and sincere, or whether something very different does not lie at the bottom of it. I leave it all to God, from whom alone is my salvation; and my spirit rejoices, that my soul's salvation and glory is alone from him and in him. O then, let us go forward, relying solely on his grace, with the simplicity of little children, and doing to the Lord what our hand findeth to do, without having much regard to ourselves or our own doings. *5th October, 1748.*

I continue to live internally on divine grace. I feel I must do nothing, and desire nothing, and letting God do as seemeth him good, be as a child, contented. The view of myself makes me confused, unless the Lord lead me to it.

It is strange that we can be so miserable and good-for-nothing, and yet be able to trust in such a manner upon God. O what a benevolent being! O what substantial goodness! Whilst loving us, he regards not what we are in ourselves; and in loving him, it is his will that we should forget ourselves. He is all that can make us peaceful and happy.

ON INWARD PRAYER

Inward or spiritual prayer is an approach of the soul to God, in the name of Jesus, and an abiding in his presence.

God is essentially present with us, in a manner which is incomprehensible to us. He fills heaven and earth; in him we live, and move, and have our being. He is also near our most secret thoughts, inclinations, desires, and intentions — all our inmost soul lays open in his presence. But God, as a Spirit, is more especially near to our spirits, and to the most secret recesses of the heart. This spirit of ours does not belong to this world, nor to temporal objects; it was created for God alone, and therefore capable of enjoying true fellowship with him. It may, and it ought to be the temple and sacred residence of the Deity. Its occupation is, to contemplate, love, and enjoy this beneficent Being, and to repose in him; for this end it was created; for this it possesses capacity. God, as a Spirit, is near our spirits, and can alone be sought and found there.

This lovely and adorable Being, is not only present with us as God, but also as *our* God in Christ Jesus, as God with us, as our Redeemer, Saviour, and our soul's true friend, who careth for us, who remembers us in love, who, by his drawing, attracts us to himself, who is willing to dwell in us, and abide with us eternally, irrespective of our unworthiness and wretchedness, if we only open and surrender our hearts to him. This is a great, evangelical, fundamental truth, which we ought deeply to impress upon our mind, and never suffer ourselves to be deprived of it, because it includes in it the entire foundation of our redemption and salvation.

Now in this approaching or drawing near, true spiritual prayer consists. I do not here allude to the first approach of a repenting sinner to God, at his primary conversion, in which he turns, in a general way, to God, and devotes himself to him, with the sincere determination to live henceforward alone unto him, who died for him, and rose again. This preliminary happy step, I necessarily presuppose, and do not speak of it here, but I refer to the persevering continuance of that approach, in a soul devoted to God.

Those, who are in reality drawn by him, and devoted to him, cannot possibly rest satisfied with the general dedication of themselves, which they made at their first awakening; and although they acknowledge this first conversion, when it has been genuine, as an eternal memorial of the infinite mercy of God, yet they cannot be contented with it, but observe, in process of time, a latent inclination, by which they are more completely drawn away from all other things, and led and exhorted to set their affections upon God. They perceive that something noble, entire, and complete is required of them — their hearts tell them from God, that he desires to have them solely and wholly for himself. In some, this feeling is found to be distinct and powerful; in others, weak, obscure, and general, according as the state of the mind is settled or confused. Happy is the soul, that recognises within her this divine and holy calling, and surrenders herself to it, childlike, and unconditionally!

This latent inclination, above alluded to, arises from the immediate proximity of God to us, in the name of Jesus. For God, who is love itself, touches our spirits with his love, as a magnet attracts iron. He draws us to himself, and hence it is, that our spirits feel such an impulse and tendency, that they cannot rest satisfied with anything short of God. If we pay due attention to this, and continue inwardly collected, removing every obstacle out of the way of the spirit, by the exercise of self-denial, and follow this impulse, by committing ourselves entirely into the hands of God, this principle, like an impelling power, leads, by love, the soul to God; even as a stream flows towards the ocean, and as a stone, pendant in the air, sinks down to the earth, which is its center of attraction. The exercise of inward prayer, is the abiding by this fundamental inclination, and by this means, approaching and committing ourselves to God in Christ Jesus, whilst denying and forsaking every thing besides.

Our spirits then become the temples, in which the glory of God, as in the Holiest of Holies, is near unto us. The altar is the name of Jesus; the sacrifice, our heart, our will, our all. The love of God which inflames our desires after him, by means of his secret operation, is the eternal fire, the flames of which are truth and sincerity. As much of the world, of corruption, and of self remain in us, so much moisture is there still in the wood and the offering, which is gradually dried up by the flame. This flame is that which I previously denominated an affectionate fundamental inclination; it manifests itself in the souls of beginners, and of those who walk through the gloomy paths of suffering and contrition, by profound sighs and groans. If the soul is obedient, it manifests itself by a gentle Abba, Father! or by something else of a familiar nature, that ascends like a grateful odour; at length it forms the basis of an abiding peace, by which the heart and mind are kept in Christ Jesus. As long as much moisture remains, the fire burns fiercely, and occasions much smoke. Afterwards it burns clearer and less intensely, until it becomes an inwardly calm, and delightful divine heat.

Jonathan Edwards

An American Calvinist preacher and philosopher, he was born in 1703 and from an early age was influenced by John Locke. In 1727 had an experience of conversion and was ordained to the ministry of the Congregational Church at Northampton, Massachusetts. He struggled with the drift against Arminianism, and his labors led to a religious revival. Removed from Northampton in 1749, he embarked on mission work in Stockbridge. He died in 1758. He was a master of the "hell-fire" sermon, his most famous being *Sinners in the Hands of an Angry God* (1741). His autobiography, *Personal Narrative*, contains mystical passages.

From THE LIFE AND CHARACTER OF MR. JONATHAN EDWARDS

SECTION IV
An account of his CONVERSION, EXPERIENCES *and* RELIGIOUS EXERCISES, *given by himself.*

"I had a variety of concerns and exercises about my soul from childhood; but had two more remarkable seasons of awakening before I met with that change by which I was brought to those new dispositions, and that new sense of things that I have since had. The first time was when I was a boy, some years before I went to college, at a time of remarkable awakening in my father's congregation. I was then very much affected for many months, and concerned about the things of religion, and my soul's salvation; and was abundant in duties. I used to pray five times a day in secret, and to spend much time in religious talk with other boys, and used to meet with them to pray together. I experienced I know not what kind of delight in religion. My mind was much engaged in it, and had much self-righteous pleasure, and it was my delight to abound in religious duties. I, with some of my school-mates joined together, and built a booth in a swamp, in a very secret and retired place, for a place of prayer. And besides, I had particular secret places of my own in the woods, where I used to retire by myself; and used to be from time to time much affected. My affections seemed to be lively and easily moved, and I seemed to be in my element when I engaged in religious duties. And I am ready to think, many are deceived with such affections, and such a kind of delight, as I then had in religion, and mistake it for grace.

"But, in process of time, my convictions and affections wore off, and I entirely lost all those affections and delights, and left off secret prayer, at least as to any constant performance of it, and returned like a dog to his vomit, and went on in ways of sin.

"Indeed I was at sometimes very uneasy, especially towards the latter part of the time of my being at college, till it pleased God, in my last year at college, at a time when I was in the midst of many uneasy thoughts about the state of my soul, to seize me with a pleurisy; in which He brought me nigh to the grave, and shook me over the pit of hell.

"But yet it was not long after my recovery, before I fell again into my old ways of sin. But God would not suffer me to go on with any quietness, but I had great and violent inward struggles; until after many conflicts with wicked inclinations, and repeated resolutions, and bonds that I laid myself under by a kind of vows to God, I was brought wholly to break off all former wicked ways, and all ways of known outward sin, and to apply myself to seek my salvation, and practise the duties of religion; but without that

kind of affection and delight that I had formerly experienced. My concern now wrought more by inward struggles
and conflicts, and self-reflections. I made seeking my salvation the main business of my life. But yet it seems to me,
I sought after a miserable manner, which has made me
sometimes since to question, whether ever it issued in that
which was saving; being ready to doubt, whether such miserable seeking was ever succeeded. But yet I was brought to
seek salvation in a manner that I never was before. I felt a
spirit to part with all things in the world for an interest in
Christ. My concern continued and prevailed, with many
exercising thoughts and inward struggles; but yet it never
seemed to be proper to express my concern that I had by
the name of terror.

"From my childhood up, my mind had been wont to be
full of objections against the doctrine of God's sovereignty,
in choosing whom he would to eternal life, and rejecting
whom he pleased, leaving them eternally to perish, and be
everlastingly tormented in hell. It used to appear like a horrible doctrine to me. But I remember the time very well,
when I seemed to be convinced, and fully satisfied, as to
this sovereignty of God, and his justice in thus eternally dis-
posing of men, according to his sovereign pleasure. But
never could give an account, how, or by what means, I was
thus convinced; not in the least imagining, in the time of
it, nor a long time after, that there was any extraordinary
influence of God's Spirit in it; but only that now I saw
further, and my reason apprehended the justice and reason-
ableness of it. However, my mind rested in it, and it put an
end to all those cavils and objections that had till then
abode with me all the preceding part of my life. And there
has been a wonderful alteration in my mind, with respect
to the doctrine of God's sovereignty, from that day to this,
so that I scarce ever have found so much as the rising of
an objection against God's sovereignty, in the most abso-

lute sense, in showing mercy to whom he will show mercy, and hardening and eternally damning whom he will. God's absolute sovereignty and justice, with respect to salvation and damnation, is what my mind seems to rest assured of, as much as of any thing that I see with my eyes; at least it is so at times. But I have often times since that first conviction, had quite another kind of sense of God's sovereignty than I had then. I have often since, not only had conviction, but a *delightful* conviction. The doctrine of God's sovereignty has very often appeared, an exceeding pleasant, bright, and sweet doctrine to me: and absolute sovereignty is what I love to ascribe to God. But my first conviction was not with this.

"The first that I remember that ever I found any thing of that sort of inward, sweet delight in God and divine things, that I have lived much in since, was on reading those words, 1 Tim. i. 17. *Now unto the King eternal, immortal, invisible, the only wise God, be honour and glory for ever, and ever, Amen.* As I read the words, there came into my soul, and was as it were diffused through it, a sense of the glory of the Divine Being, a new sense, quite different from any thing I ever experienced before. Never any words of scripture seemed to me as these words did. I thought with myself, how excellent a Being that was, and how happy I should be if I might enjoy that God, and be wrapt up to God in heaven, and be as it were swallowed up in him. I kept saying, and as it were singing over these words of scripture to myself; and went to prayer, to pray to God that I might enjoy him, and prayed in a manner quite different from what I used to do, with a new sort of affection. But it never came into my thought, that there was any thing spiritual, or of a saving nature in this.

"From about that time, I began to have a new kind of apprehensions and ideas of Christ, and the work of redemption, and the glorious way of salvation by him. I had an inward, sweet sense of these things, that at times came into my heart; and my soul was led away in pleasant views and contemplations of them. And my mind was greatly engaged to spend my time in reading and meditating on Christ, and the beauty and excellency of his person, and the lovely way of salvation by free grace in him. I found no books so delightful to me as those that treated of these subjects. Those words, Cant. ii. 1, used to be abundantly with me, *I am the Rose of Sharon, and the Lily of the valleys.* The words seemed to me, sweetly to represent the loveliness and beauty of Jesus Christ. And the whole book of Canticles used to be pleasant to me; and I used to be much in reading it about that time; and found, from time to time, an inward sweetness, that used, as it were, to carry me away in my contemplations; in what I know not how to express otherwise, than by a calm, sweet abstraction of soul from all the concerns of this world; and a kind of vision, or fixed ideas and imaginations, of being alone in the mountains, or some solitary wilderness, far from all mankind, sweetly conversing with Christ, and wrapt and swallowed up in God. The sense I had of divine things, would often of a sudden, as it were, kindle up a sweet burning in my heart; an ardour of my soul, that I know not how to express.

"Not long after I first began to experience these things, I gave an account to my father of some things that had passed in my mind. I was pretty much affected by the discourse we had together; and when the discourse was ended, I walked abroad alone, in a solitary place in my father's pasture, for contemplation. And as I was walking there, and looked up on the sky and clouds, there came into my mind, so sweet a sense of the glorious majesty and grace of God, that I know not how to express. — I seemed to see them both in a sweet conjunction: majesty and meekness joined together: it was a sweet and gentle, and holy majesty; and

also a majestic meekness; an awful sweetness; a high, and
great, and holy gentleness.

"After this my sense of divine things gradually increased,
and became more and more lively, and had more of that inward sweetness. The appearance of every thing was altered,
there seemed to be, as it were a calm, sweet cast, or appearance of divine glory, in almost everything. God's excellency,
his wisdom, his purity and love, seemed to appear in every
thing; in the sun, moon, and stars; in the clouds, and blue
sky; in the grass, flowers, trees; in the water, and all nature;
which used greatly to fix my mind. I often used to sit and
view the moon for a long time; and so in the day-time,
spent much time in viewing the clouds and sky, to behold
the sweet glory of God in these things; in the mean time
singing forth, with a low voice, my contemplations of the
Creator and Redeemer. And scarce any thing, among all
the works of nature, was so sweet to me as thunder and
lightning: formerly, nothing had been so terrible to me. I
used to be a person uncommonly terrified with thunder, and
it used to strike me with terror when I saw a thunder-storm
rising. But now, on the contrary, it rejoiced me. I felt God
at the first appearance of a thunder-storm; and used to take
the opportunity, at such times, to fix myself to view the
clouds, and see the lightnings play, and hear the majestic
and awful voice of God's thunder, which often times was
exceeding entertaining, leading me to sweet contemplations
of my great and glorious God; and while I viewed, used to
spend my time, as it always seemed natural to me, to sing
or chant forth my meditations; to speak my thoughts in
soliloquies, and speak with a singing voice.

"I felt then a great satisfaction as to my good estate; but
that did not content me. I had vehement longings of soul
after God and Christ, and after more holiness, wherewith
my heart seemed to be full, and ready to break; which often brought to my mind the words of the Psalmist, Psal.

cxix. 28. *My soul breaketh for the longing it hath.* I often felt a mourning and lamenting in my heart, that I had not turned to God sooner, that I might have had more time to grow in grace. My mind was greatly fixed on divine things; I was almost perpetually in the contemplation of them. Spent most of my time in thinking of divine things, year after year; and used to spend abundance of my time in walking alone in the woods, and solitary places, for meditation, soliloquy, and prayer, and converse with God: and it was always my manner at such times to sing forth my contemplations; and was almost constantly in ejaculatory prayer wherever I was. Prayer seemed to be natural to me, as the breath by which the inward burnings of my heart had vent.

"The delights which I now felt in things of religion, were of an exceeding different kind from those forementioned, that I had when I was a boy. They were totally of another kind; and what I then had no more notion or idea of, than one born blind has of pleasant and beautiful colours. They were of a more inward, pure, soul-animating, and refreshing nature. Those former delights never reached the heart, and did not arise from any sight of the divine excellency of the things of God, or any taste of the soul-satisfying and life-giving good there is in them.

"My sense of divine things seemed gradually to increase, until I went to preach at New York, which was about a year and a half after they began. While I was there, I felt them very sensibly, in a much higher degree than I had done before. My longings after God and holiness were much increased. Pure and humble, holy and heavenly Christianity, appeared exceeding amiable to me. I felt in me a burning desire to be in every thing a complete Christian; and conformed to the blessed image of Christ: and that I might live in all things, according to the pure, sweet, and blessed rules of the gospel. I had an eager thirsting after progress in these things. My longings after it, put me upon pursuing and pressing after them. It was my continual strife day and night, and constant inquiry, how I should be more holy, and live more holily, and more becoming a child of God and disciple of Christ. I sought an increase of grace and holiness, and that I might live an holy life, with vastly more earnestness than ever I sought grace, before I had it. I used to be continually examining myself, and studying and contriving for likely ways and means, how I should live holily, with far greater diligence and earnestness than ever I pursued any thing in my life, but with too great a dependence on my own strength; which afterwards proved a great damage to me. My experience had not then taught me, as it has done since, my extreme feebleness and impotence, every manner of way; and the innumerable and bottomless depths of secret corruption and deceit that there was in my heart. However, I went on with my eager pursuit after more holiness, and sweet conformity to Christ.

"The heaven I desired was a heaven of holiness; to be with God, and to spend my eternity in divine love, and holy communion with Christ. My mind was very much taken up with contemplations on heaven, and the enjoyments of those there; and living there in perfect holiness, humility, and love. And it used at that time to appear a great part of the happiness of heaven, that there the saints could express their love to Christ. It appeared to me a great clog, and hindrance, and burden to me, that what I felt within, I could not express to God, and give vent to, as I desired. The inward ardour of my soul, seemed to be hindred and pent up, and could not freely flame out as it would. I used often to think, how in heaven, this sweet principle should freely and fully vent and express itself. Heaven appeared to me exceeding delightful as a world of love. It appeared to me, that all happiness consisted in living in pure, humble, heavenly, divine love.

"I remember the thoughts I used then to have of holiness. I remember I then said sometimes to myself, I do certainly know that I love holiness, such as the gospel prescribes. It appeared to me, there was nothing in it but what was ravishingly lovely. It appeared to me, to be the highest beauty and amiableness, above all other beauties, that it was a *divine* beauty, far purer than any thing here upon earth, and that every thing else was like mire, filth, and defilement, in comparison of it.

"Holiness, as I then wrote down some of my contemplations on it, appeared to me to be of a sweet, pleasant, charming, serene, calm nature. It seemed to me, it brought an inexpressible purity, brightness, peacefulness, and ravishment to the soul; and that it made the soul like a field or garden of God, with all manner of pleasant flowers; that is all pleasant, delightful, and undisturbed; enjoying a sweet calm, and the gently vivifying beams of the sun. The soul of a true Christian, as I then wrote my meditations, appeared like such a little white flower, as we see in the spring of the year, low, and humble on the ground, opening its bosom to receive the pleasant beams of the sun's glory; rejoicing as it were in a calm rapture; diffusing around a sweet fragrancy; standing peacefully and lovingly, in the midst of other flowers round about; all in like manner opening their bosoms, to drink in the light of the sun.

"There was no part of creature-holiness, that I then, and at other times, had so great a sense of the loveliness of, as humility, brokenness of heart, and poverty of spirit: and there was nothing that I had such a spirit to long for. My heart, as it were, panted after this, to lie low before God, and in the dust; that I might be nothing, and that God might be all; that I might become as a little child.

"While I was there at New York, I sometimes was much affected with reflections on my past life, considering how late it was before I began to be truly religious, and how wickedly I had lived till then: and once so as to weep abundantly, and for a considerable time together.

"On *Jan.* 12. 1722-3. I made a solemn dedication of myself to God, and wrote it down; giving up myself and all that I had to God, to be for the future in no respect my own, to act as one that had no right to himself, in any respect. And solemnly vowed to take God for my whole portion and felicity, looking on nothing else as any part of my happiness, nor acting as if it were, and his law for the constant rule of my obedience; engaging to fight with all my might against the world; the flesh, and the devil, to the end of my life. But have reason to be infinitely humbled, when I consider, how much I have failed of answering my obligation.

"I had then abundance of sweet religious conversation in the family where I lived, with Mr John Smith, and his pious mother. My heart was knit in affection to those, in whom were appearances of true piety; and I could bear the thoughts of no other companions, but such as were holy, and the disciples of the blessed Jesus.

"I had great longings for the advancement of Christ's kingdom in the world. My sacred prayer used to be in great part taken up in praying for it. If I heard the least hint of any thing that happened in any part of the world, that appeared to me, in some respect or other, to have a favourable aspect on the interest of Christ's kingdom, my soul eagerly catched at it; and it would much animate and refresh me. I used to be earnest to read public news-letters, mainly for that end; to see if I could not find some news favourable to the interest of religion in the world.

"I very frequently used to retire into a solitary place, on the banks of Hudson's River, at some distance from the city, for contemplation on divine things, and secret converse with God; and had many sweet hours there. Sometimes Mr Smith and I walked there together, to converse of the things of God; and our conversation used much to turn on the advancement of Christ's kingdom in the world, and the glorious things that God would accomplish for his church in the latter days.

"I had then, and at other times, the greatest delight in the holy scriptures, of any book whatsoever. Oftentimes in reading it, every word seemed to touch my heart. I felt a harmony between something in my heart, and those sweet and powerful words. I seemed often to see so much light exhibited by every sentence, and such a refreshing ravishing food communicated, that I could not get along in reading. Used oftentimes to dwell long on one sentence, to see the wonders contained in it; and yet almost every sentence seemed to be full of wonders.

"I came away from New York in the month of April 1723. and had a most bitter parting with Madam Smith and her son. My heart seemed to sink within me, at leaving the family and city where I had enjoyed so many sweet and pleasant days. I went from New-York to Weathersfield by water. As I sailed away, I kept sight of the city as long as I could; and when I was out of sight of it, it would affect me much to look that way, with a kind of melancholy mixed with sweetness. However, that night, after this sorrowful parting, I was greatly comforted in God at Westchester, where we went ashore to lodge; and had a pleasant time of it all the voyage to Saybrook. It was sweet to me to think of meeting dear Christians in heaven, where we should never part more. At Saybrook we went ashore to lodge on Saturday, and there kept Sabbath; where I had a sweet and refreshing season, walking alone in the fields.

"After I came home to Windsor, remained much in a like frame of mind as I had been in at New-York, but only sometimes felt my heart ready to sink with the thoughts of my friends at New-York. And my refuge and support was in contemplations on the heavenly state; as I find in my Diary of May 1. 1723. It was my comfort to think of that state, where there is fulness of joy; where reigns heavenly, sweet, calm, and delightful love, without alloy; where there are continually the dearest expressions of this love; where is the enjoyment of the persons loved, without ever parting; where these persons that appear so lovely in this world, will really be inexpressibly more lovely, and full of love to us. And how sweetly will the mutual lovers join together to sing the praises of God and the Lamb! How full will it fill us with joy to think that this enjoyment, these sweet exercises, will never cease or come to an end, but will last to all eternity!

"Continued much in the same frame in the general that I had been in at New-York, till I went to New-Haven, to live there as Tutor of the College; having one special season of uncommon sweetness; particularly once at Bolton, in a journey from Boston, walking out alone in the fields. After I went to New-Haven I sunk in religion; my mind being diverted from my eager and violent pursuits after holiness, by some affairs that greatly perplexed and distracted my mind.

"In Sep. 1725, was taken ill at New-Haven; and endeavouring to go home to Windsor, was so ill at the North Village that I could go no further; where I lay sick for about a quarter of a year. And, in this sickness God was pleased to visit me again with the sweet influences of his Spirit. My mind was greatly engaged there on divine, pleasant contemplations, and longings of soul. I observed that those who watched with me, would often be looking out for the morning, and seemed to wish for it; which brought to my mind those words of the Psalmist, which my soul with sweetness made its own language, *My soul waiteth for the Lord, more than they that watch for the morning, I say, more than they that watch for the morning.* And when the light of the morning came, and the beams of the sun came in at the windows, it refreshed my soul from one morning to another. It seemed to me to be some image of the sweet light of God's glory.

"I remember, about that time, I used greatly to long for the conversion of some that I was concerned with. It seemed to me, I could gladly honour them, and with delight be a servant to them, and lie at their feet, if they were but truly holy.

"But, some time after this, I was again greatly diverted in my mind, with some temporal concerns, that exceedingly took up my thoughts, greatly to the wounding of my soul; and went on through various exercises, that it would be tedious to relate, that gave me much more experience of my own heart than ever I had before.

JOHN WESLEY   17

John Wesley

He was born in 1709, the son of the rector of Epworth. Educated
at Oxford, he became a fellow there and later curate to his father.
He was the leader of a group of religious young men. For a time he
served as a missionary to Georgia, but returned in a few years to
England. During much of this time he was allied with the Moravians. He and his brother Charles (1707-1788) founded the Metho-
dist Society, of which George Whitefield also was a founding
member. Both brothers wrote many hymns, and both wrote journals.
John Wesley died in 1791; and his life was written by Robert
Southey.

From THE JOURNAL OF JOHN WESLEY

"I Felt my Heart Strangely Warmed"

[24 May 1738]. In the evening I went very unwillingly
to a society in Aldersgate-street, where one was reading
Luther's preface to the Epistle to the Romans. About a
quarter before nine, while he was describing the change
which God works in the heart through faith in Christ, I
felt my heart strangely warmed. I felt I did trust in Christ,
Christ alone, for salvation; and an assurance was given me
that He had taken away my sins, even mine, and saved me
from the law of sin and death.

I began to pray with all my might for those who had in
a more especial manner despitefully used me and persecuted
me. I then testified openly to all there what I now first felt
in my heart. But it was not long before the enemy sug-

gested, "This cannot be faith; for where is thy joy?" Then was I taught that peace and victory over sin are essential to faith in the Captain of our salvation; but that, as to the transports of joy that usually attend the beginning of it, especially in those who had mourned deeply, God sometimes giveth, sometimes withholdeth them, according to the counsels of his own will.

After my return home, I was much buffeted with temptations; but cried out, and they fled away. They returned again and again. I as often lifted up my eyes, and He "sent me help from his holy place." And herein I found the difference between this and my former state chiefly consisted. I was striving, yea, fighting with all my might under the law, as well as under grace. But then I was sometimes, if not often, conquered; now, I was always conqueror.

Thur. 25. — The moment I awaked, "Jesus, Master," was in my heart and in my mouth; and I found all my strength lay in keeping my eye fixed upon him, and my soul waiting on him continually. Being again at St. Paul's in the afternoon, I could taste the good word of God in the anthem, which began, "My song shall be always of the loving-kindness of the Lord: with my mouth will I ever be showing forth thy truth from one generation to another." Yet the enemy injected a fear, "If thou dost believe, why is there not a more sensible change?" I answered (yet not I), "That I know not. But this I know, I have 'now peace with God.' And I sin not to-day, and Jesus my Master has forbid me to take thought for the morrow."

Wed. June 7. — I determined, if God should permit, to retire for a short time into Germany. I had fully proposed, before I left Georgia, so to do, if it should please God to bring me back to Europe. And I now early saw the time was come. My weak mind could not bear to be thus sawn asunder. And I hoped the conversing with those holy men who were themselves living witnesses of the full power of faith, and yet able to bear with those that are weak, would be a means, under God, of so establishing my soul, that I might go on from faith to faith, and from strength to strength."

The Voyage to England

We had a thorough storm, which obliged us to shut all close; the sea breaking over the ship continually. I was at first afraid; but cried to God, and was strengthened. Before ten, I lay down: I bless God, without fear. About midnight we were awaked by a confused noise of seas and wind and men's voices, the like to which I had never heard before. The sound of the sea breaking over and against the sides of the ship, I could compare to nothing but large cannon, or American thunder. The rebounding, starting, quivering motion of the ship much resembled what is said of earthquakes.

The captain was upon deck in an instant. But his men could not hear what he said. It blew a proper hurricane; which beginning at south-west, then went west, north-west, north, and, in a quarter an hour, round by the east to the south-west point again. At the same time the sea running, as they term it, mountain-high, and that from many different points at once, the ship would not obey the helm; nor indeed could the steersman, through the violent rain, see the compass. So he was forced to let her run before the wind, and in half an hour the stress of the storm was over.

Tues. 24. — We spoke with two ships, outward-bound, from whom we had the welcome news of our wanting but one hundred and sixty leagues of the Land's-end. My mind was now full of thought; part of which I writ down as follows:

"I went to America, to convert the Indians; but O! who shall convert me? who, what is he that will deliver me from this evil heart of mischief? I have a fair summer religion. I can talk well; nay, and believe myself, while no danger is near; but let death look me in the face, and my spirit is troubled. Nor can I say, 'To die is gain!'

'I have a sin of fear, that when I've spun
My last thread, I shall perish on the shore!'

"I think, verily, if the Gospel be true, I am safe: for I not only have given, and do give, all my goods to feed the poor; I not only give my body to be burned, drowned, or whatever God shall appoint for me; but I follow after charity (though not as I ought, yet as I can), if haply I may attain it. I now believe the Gospel is true. 'I show my faith by my works,' by staking my all upon it. I would do so again and again a thousand times, if the choice were still to make.

"Whoever sees me, sees I would be a Christian. Therefore 'are my ways not like other men's ways.' Therefore I have been, I am, I am content to be, 'a by-word, a proverb of reproach.' But in a storm I think, 'What, if the Gospel be not true? Then thou art of all men most foolish. For what hast thou given thy goods, thy ease, thy friends, thy reputation, thy country, thy life? For what art thou wandering over the face of the earth? — A dream! a cunningly-devised fable!'

"O! who will deliver me from this fear of death? What shall I do? Where shall I fly from it? Should I fight against it by thinking, or by not thinking of it? A wise man advised me some time since, 'Be still and go on.' Perhaps this is best, to look upon it as my cross; when it comes, to let it humble me, and quicken all my good resolutions, especially that of praying without ceasing; and at other times, to take no thought about it, but quietly to go on 'in the work of the Lord.' "

Useless Doctors

[12 May 1759]. Reflecting to-day on the case of a poor woman who had continual pain in her stomach, I could not but remark the inexcusable negligence of most physicians in cases of this nature. They prescribe drug upon drug, without knowing a jot of the matter concerning the root of the disorder. And without knowing this, they cannot cure, though they can murder, the patient. Whence came this woman's pain? (which she would never have told, had she never been questioned about it) — from fretting for the death of her son. And what availed medicines, while that fretting continued? Why then do not all physicians consider how far bodily disorders are caused or influenced by the mind; and in those cases, which are utterly out of their sphere, call in the assistance of a minister; as ministers, when they find the mind disordered by the body, call in the assistance of a physician? But why are these cases out of their sphere? Because they know not God. It follows, no man can be a thorough physician without being an experienced Christian.

[3 July 1764]. (Leeds). — I was reflecting on an odd circumstance, which I cannot account for. I never relish a tune at first hearing, not till I have almost learned to sing it; and as I learn it more perfectly, I gradually lose my relish for it. I observe something similar in poetry; yea, in all the objects of imagination. I seldom relish verses at first hearing; till I have heard them over and over, they give me no pleasure; and they give me next to none when I have heard them a few times more, so as to be quite familiar. Just so a face or a picture, which does not strike me at first, becomes more pleasing as I grow more acquainted with it; but only to a certain point: for when I am too much acquainted, it is no longer pleasing. O, how imperfectly do we understand even the machine which we carry about us!

David Brainerd

——◆——

He was born 20 April 1718 at Haddam, near Hartford, Connecticut. His father died when Brainerd was nine; his grandfather was a justice of the peace for the colony. His mother, Dorothy Hobart, was the daughter of a minister. David became a missionary to the Indians and pastor of a church for Christian Indians in New Jersey. He died in 1747. Jonathan Edwards wrote his biography, including selections from Brainerd's diary.

From THE LIFE OF
MR. DAVID BRAINERD

Wednesday, *Septemb.* 8 [1742]. Felt very sweetly, when I first rose in the Morning. In Family-Prayer, had some Enlargement, but not much Spirituality, 'till Eternity came up before me and look'd near; I found some Sweetness in the Thoughts of bidding a dying Farewell to this tiresom World: Tho' sometime ago I reckon'd upon seeing my dear Friends at *Commencement,* yet being now denied the Opportunity, for fear of Imprisonment, I felt totally resign'd, and as contented to spend this Day alone in the Woods, as I could have done, if I had been allowed to go to Town. Felt exceedingly wean'd from the World to Day. — In the Afternoon discussed something on some divine Things with a dear Christian Friend, whereby we were both refreshed. Then I pray'd, with a sweet Sense of the Blessedness of Communion with GOD: I think, I scarce ever enjoyed more of GOD in any one Prayer. O it was a blessed Season indeed to my Soul! I knew not that ever I saw so much of my own

Nothingness in my Life; never wondered so, that God allowed me to preach his Word; never was so astonished as now. — This has been a sweet and comfortable Day to my Soul: Blessed be God. — Pray'd again with my dear Friend, with something of the divine Presence. — I long to be wholly conformed to God, and transformed into his Image.

Thursday, *Septemb.* 9. Spent much of the Day alone: Enjoyed the Presence of God in some comfortable Degree: was visited by some dear Friends, and pray'd with them: Wrote sundry Letters to Friends; felt Religion in my Soul while writing. Enjoyed some sweet Meditations on some Scriptures. — In the evening, went very privately into Town, from the Place of my residence at the Farms, and conversed with some dear Friends; felt sweetly in singing Hymns with them; and made my Escape to the Farms again, without being discovered by any one as I knew of. Thus the Lord preserves me continually.

Friday, *September* 10. Longed with intense Desire after GOD: my whole Soul seem'd impatient to be Conformed to him, and to become *Holy, as he is Holy.* — In the Afternoon, pray'd with a dear Friend privately, and had the Presence of God with us; our Souls united together to reach after a blessed Immortality, to be unclothed of *the Body* of *Sin and Death,* and to enter the blessed World, where *no unclean Thing enters.* O, with what intense Desire did our Souls long for that blessed Day, that we might be freed from Sin, and forever live *to* and *in* our GOD! — In the Evening, took leave of that House; But first kneel'd down and prayed; *The Lord was of a Truth in the midst of us;* 'twas a sweet parting Season; felt in my self much Sweetness and Affection in the Things of God. Blessed be God for every such divine Gale of his Spirit, to speed me on in my Way to the *New-Jerusalem!* — Felt some Sweetness afterwards, and spent the Evening in Conversation with Friends, and pray'd with some Life, and retired to Rest very late.

Thursday, *September* 16. At Night, felt exceeding sweetly: Enjoyed much of God in secret Prayer: Felt an uncommon Resignation, to *be* and *do* what God pleased. Some Days past, I felt *great Perplexity* on Account of my past Conduct: *My Bitterness*, and Want of Christian Kindness and Love, has been *very distressing* to my Soul: The Lord forgive me my *unchristian Warmth*, and want of a Spirit of Meekness.

Lord's-Day, *May* 1 [1743]. Was at *Stockbridge* to Day. In the Forenoon had some Relief and Assistance; tho' not so much as usual. In the Afternoon, felt poorly in Body and Soul; while I was preaching, seemed to be rehearsing idle Tales, without the least Life, Fervour, Sense, or Comfort: and especially afterwards, at the Sacrament, my Soul was filled with Confusion, and the utmost Anguish that ever I endured, under the Feeling of my inexpressible Vileness and Meanness: It was a most bitter and distressing Season to me, by Reason of the View I had of my own Heart, and the secret Abominations that lurk there: I tho't the Eyes of all in the House were upon me, and I dared not look any One in the Face; for it verily seem'd as if they saw the Vileness of my Heart, and all the Sins I had ever been guilty of. And if I had been banished from the Presence of all Mankind, never to be seen any more, or so much as thought of, still I should have been distressed with Shame; and I should have been ashamed to see the most barbarous People on Earth, because I was viler, and seemingly more brutishly ignorant than they. — *I am made to possess the Sins of my Youth.*

Tuesday, *May* 10. Was in the same State, as to my Mind, that I have been in for some Time, extremely press'd with a Sense of Guilt, Pollution, Blindness: *The Iniquity of my Heels have compassed me about*; the *Sins of my Youth have been set in order before me; they have gone over my Head, as an heavy Burden, too heavy for me to bear*. Almost all the Actions of my Life past seem to be cover'd over with Sin and Guilt; and those of them that I performed in the most conscientious Manner, now fill me with Shame & Confusion, that I cannot hold up my Face. Oh, the *Pride, Selfishness, Hypocrisy, Ignorance, Bitterness, Party-Zeal,* & the *Want* of Love, Candour, Meekness and Gentleness, that have attended my Attempts to promote Religion and Vertue; and this when I had Reason to hope I had real Assistance from above, and some sweet Intercourse with Heaven! But alas, what *corrupt Mixtures* attended my best Duties!

Wednesday, *May* 18. My Circumstances are such that I have no Comfort, of any Kind, but what I have in God. I live in the most lonesom Wilderness; have but one single Person to Converse with, that can speak *English:* Most of the Talk I hear, is either *Highland-Scotch* or *Indian*. I have no Fellow-Christian to whom I might unbosom my self, and lay open my spiritual Sorrows, and with whom I might take sweet Counsel in Conversation about heavenly Things, and join in social Prayer. I live poorly with Regard to the Comforts of Life: most of my Diet, consists of boil'd Corn, Hasty-Pudding, &c. I lodge on a Bundle of Straw, and my Labour is hard and extremely difficult; and I have little Appearance of Success, to comfort me. The *Indians* Affairs are very difficult; having no Land to live on, but what the *Dutch* People lay Claim to, and threaten to drive them off from; they have no Regard to the Souls of the poor *Indians*; and, by what I can learn, they hate me, because I come to preach to 'em. — But that which makes all my Difficulties grievous to be born, is, that *God hides his Face from me*.

Monday, *Aug.* 1. Was still busy in further Labours on my House. — Felt a little of the Sweetness of Religion, and thought it was worth the while to *follow after God* thro' a Thousand Snares, Desarts and Death it self. O that I might always *follow after Holiness*, that I may be fully conformed to God. Had some Degree of Sweetness, in secret Prayer, tho' I had much Sorrow.

Wednesday, *Aug.* 3. Spent most of the Day in Writing. Enjoyed some Sense of Religion. Thro' divine Goodness I am now uninterruptedly alone; and find my Retirement comfortable. I have enjoyed more Sense of divine Things within a few Days last past, than for some Time before. I longed after Holiness, Humility & Meekness: O that God would enable me to *pass the Time of my sojourning here in his Fear*, and always *live to him.*

Thursday, *Aug.* 4. Was enabled to pray much, thro' the whole Day; and thro' divine Goodness found some Intenseness of Soul in the Duty, as I used to do, and some Ability to persevere in my Supplications: Had some Apprehensions of divine Things, that were engaging, and that gave me some Courage and Resolution. 'Tis good, I find, to *persevere in Attempts* to pray, if I can't *pray with Perseverance*, i.e. continue long in my Addresses to the divine Being. I have generally found, that the more I do in secret Prayer, the more I have delighted to do, and have enjoyed more of a Spirit of Prayer: and frequently have found the contrary, when with Journeying or otherwise, I have been much deprived of Retirement. A seasonable steady Performance of secret Duties in their proper Hours, & a careful Improvement of all Time, filling up every Hour with some profitable Labour, either of Heart, Head, or Hands, are excellent Means of spiritual Peace and Boldness before God. *Christ* indeed is *our Peace*, and *by him we have Boldness of Access to God;* but a *good Conscience, void of Offence,* is an excellent Preparation for an Approach into the divine

Presence. There is Difference between *Self-Confidence* and a *Self-righteous pleasing ourselves* (with our own Duties, Attainments, and spiritual Enjoyments) which godly Souls sometimes are guilty of, and that *holy Confidence* arising from the Testimony of a good Conscience, which good *Hezekiah* had when he says, *Remember, O Lord, I beseech Thee, how I have walked before thee in Truth and with a perfect Heart.* Then (says the holy Psalmist) *shall I not be ashamed, when I have Respect to all thy Commandments.* Filling up our Time *with* and *for* God is the Way to rise up and lie down in Peace.

John Woolman

He was born in Burlington County, New Jersey, on 19 October 1720 of "religious parents" and sailed in 1772 for London, to visit Quakers in Yorkshire. He wrote and spoke against slavery, and induced many Friends to set their slaves free. In 1760 during the yearly meeting at Newport, Rhode Island, he urged the submission to the legislature of a petition he had drafted against the slave trade. In 1763, he went to preach to the Indians at Wyalusing on the Susquehanna. His most famous book is his *Journal* (published in 1774), which he began at the age of thirty-six and continued until his death of smallpox in York on 7 October 1772.

From THE JOURNAL OF JOHN WOOLMAN

I have often felt a Motion of Love to leave some Hints in Writing of my Experience of the Goodness of God; and now, in the thirty-sixth Year of my Age, I begin this Work.

I was born in Northampton, in Burlington County, West-Jersey, in the Year 1720; and before I was seven years old, I began to be acquainted with the Operations of divine Love. Through the Care of my Parents, I was taught to read nearly as soon as I was capable of it; and, as I went from School one seventh Day, I remember, while my Companions went to play by the Way, I went forward out of Sight, and, sitting down, I read the 22d Chapter of the Revelations: "He shewed me a pure River of Water of Life, clear as Chrystal, proceeding out of the Throne of God and of the Lamb, etc." and, in reading it, my Mind was drawn to seek after that pure Habitation, which, I then believed, God had prepared for his Servants. The Place where I sat, and the Sweetness that attended my Mind, remain fresh in my Memory.

A Thing remarkable in my Childhood was, that once, going to a Neighbour's House, I saw, on the Way, a Robin sitting on her Nest, and as I came near she went off, but, having young ones, flew about, and with many Cries expressed her Concern for them; I stood and threw Stones at her, till, one striking her, she fell down dead: At first I was pleased with the Exploit, but after a few Minutes was seized with Horror, as having, in a sportive Way, killed an innocent Creature while she was careful for her Young: I beheld her lying dead, and thought these young ones, for which she was so careful, must now perish for want of their Dam to nourish them; and, after some painful Considerations on the Subject, I climbed up the Tree, took all the young Birds, and killed them; supposing that better than to leave them to pine away and die miserably: And believed, in this Case, that Scripture-proverb was fulfilled, "The tender Mercies of the Wicked are cruel." I then went on my Errand, but for some Hours, could think of little else but the Cruelties I had committed, and was much troubled. Thus he, whose tender Mercies are over all his Works, hath placed a Principle in the human Mind, which incited to exercise Goodness towards every living Creature; and this being singly attended to, People become tender hearted and sympathizing; but being frequently and totally rejected, the Mind becomes shut up in a contrary Disposition.

Thus Time passed on: My Heart was replenished with Mirth and Wantonness, and pleasing Scenes of Vanity were presented to my Imagination, till I attained the Age of eighteen Years; near which Time I felt the Judgments of God, in my Soul, like a consuming Fire; and, looking over my past Life, the Prospect was moving. I was often sad, and longed to be delivered from those Vanities; then again, my Heart was strongly inclined to them, and there was in me a sore Conflict: At Times I turned to Folly, and then again, Sorrow and Confusion took hold of me. In a while, I resolved totally to leave off some of my Vanities; but there was a secret Reserve, in my Heart, of the more refined Part of them, and I was not low enough to find true Peace. Thus, for some Months, I had great Troubles; there remaining in me an unsubjected Will, which rendered my Labours fruitless, till at length, through the merciful Continuance of heavenly Visitations, I was made to bow down in Spirit before the Lord. I remember one Evening I had spent some Time in reading a pious Author; and walking out alone, I humbly prayed to the Lord for his Help, that I might be delivered from all those Vanities which so ensnared me. Thus, being brought low, he helped me; and, as I learned to bear the Cross, I felt Refreshment to come from his Presence; but, not keeping in that Strength which gave Victory, I lost Ground again; the Sense of which greatly affected me; and I sought Desarts and lonely Places, and there, with Tears, did confess my Sins to God, and humbly craved Help of him.

In a time of sickness with the pleurisy, a little upward of two years and a half ago, I was brought so near the gates of death, that I forgot my name: being then desirous to know who I was, I saw a mass of matter of a dull gloomy color, between the south and the east; and was informed, that this mass was human beings in as great misery as they could be, and live; and that I was mixed in with them, and that henceforth I might not consider myself as a distinct or separate being. In this state I remained several hours. I then heard a soft melodious voice, more pure and harmonious than any I had heard before. I believed it was the voice of an angel, who spake to the other angels, and the words were these, "John Woolman is dead." I soon remembered that I once was John Woolman; and being assured that I was alive in the body, I greatly wondered what that heavenly voice could mean.

I believed beyond doubting that it was the voice of an holy angel; but as yet it was a mystery to me.

I was then carried in spirit to the mines, where poor oppressed people were digging rich treasures for those called Christians; and I heard them blaspheme the name of Christ, at which I was grieved; for his name to me was precious.

Then I was informed, that these heathens were told, that those who oppressed them were the followers of Christ; and they said amongst themselves, If Christ directed them to use us in this sort, then Christ is a cruel tyrant.

All this time the song of the angel remained a mystery; and in the morning, my dear wife and some others coming to my bed-side, I asked them if they knew who I was; and they telling me I was John Woolman, thought I was light-headed: for I told them not what the angel said, nor was I disposed to talk much to any one; but was very desirous to get so deep, that I might understand this mystery.

My tongue was often so dry, that I could not speak till I had moved it about and gathered some moisture, and as I lay still for a time, at length I felt Divine power prepare my mouth that I could speak; and then I said, "I am crucified with Christ, nevertheless I live; yet not I, but Christ liveth in me; and the life which I now live in the flesh, I live by the faith of the Son of God, who loved me, and gave himself for me."

Then the mystery was opened; and I perceived there was joy in heaven over a sinner who had repented; and that that language (John Woolman is dead) meant no more than the death of my own will.

Johann Wolfgang von Goethe

German philosopher, scientist, dramatist, poet and novelist, is perhaps the greatest figure in the whole of German literature. He was born at Frankfurt in 1749. In 1765 Goethe went to Leipzig. He studied both law and medicine. In 1775 he went to Weimar at the invitation of Prince Karl August, where he remained until his death except for brief travels in Switzerland and Italy. He wrote dramas, odes, novels, lyrics, and, finally, *Faust* which has been called the "Divine Comedy of eighteenth century humanism." He died in 1832.

From DICHTUNG UND WARHEIT

It will be taken for granted, that we children had among our other lessons a continued and progressive instruction in religion. But the Church-Protestantism imparted to us was, properly speaking, nothing but a kind of dry morality: ingenious exposition was not thought of, and the doctrine appealed neither to the understanding nor to the heart. For that reason, there were various secessions from the Established Church. Separatists, Pietists, Herrnhuter (Moravians), Quiet-in-the-Land, and others differently named and characterized, sprang up, all of whom are animated by the same purpose of approaching the Deity, especially through Christ, more closely than seemed to them possible under the forms of the established religion.

The boy heard these opinions and sentiments constantly spoken of, for the clergy as well as the laity divided themselves into *pro* and *con*. The minority were composed of

those who dissented more or less broadly; but their modes
of thinking attracted by originality, heartiness, perseverance, and independence. All sorts of stories were told of
their virtues, and of the way in which they were mani-
fested. The reply of a pious master-tinman was especially
noted, who, when one of his craft attempted to shame him
by asking, "Who is really your confessor?" answered with
great cheerfulness, and confidence in the goodness of his
cause, "I have a famous one, — no less than the confessor
of King David."

Things of this sort naturally made an impression on the
boy, and led him into similar states of mind. In fact, he
came to the thought that he might immediately approach
the great God of nature, the Creator and Preserver of
heaven and earth, whose earlier manifestations of wrath
had been long forgotten in the beauty of the world, and the
manifold blessings in which we participate while upon it.
The way he took to accomplish this was very curious.

The boy had chiefly kept to the first article of belief. The
God who stands in immediate connection with nature, and
owns and loves it as his work, seemed to him the proper
God, who might be brought into closer relationship with
man, as with every thing else, and who would take care of
him, as of the motion of the stars, the days and seasons,
the animals and plants. There were texts of the Gospels
which explicitly stated this. The boy could ascribe no form
to this Being: he therefore sought him in his works, and
would, in the good Old-Testament fashion, build him an
altar. Natural productions were set forth as images of the
world, over which a flame was to burn, signifying the aspirations of man's heart towards his Maker. He brought out
of the collection of natural objects which he possessed, and
which had been increased as chance directed, the best ores
and other specimens. But the next difficulty was, as to how
they should be arranged and raised into a pile. His father

possessed a beautiful red-lacquered music-stand, ornamented with gilt flowers, in the form of a four-sided pyramid, with different elevations, which had been found convenient for quartets, but lately was not much in use. The boy laid hands on this, and built up his representatives of nature one above the other in steps; so that it all looked quite pretty and at the same time sufficiently significant. On an early sunrise his first worship of God was to be celebrated, but the young priest had not yet settled how to produce a flame which should at the same time emit an agreeable odor. At last it occurred to him to combine the two, as he possessed a few fumigating pastils, which diffused a pleasant fragrance with a glimmer, if not with a flame. Nay, this soft burning and exhalation seemed a better representation of what passes in the heart, than an open flame. The sun had already risen for a long time, but the neighboring houses concealed the east. At last it glittered above the roofs: a burning-glass was at once taken up and applied to the pastils, which were fixed on the summit in a fine porcelain saucer. Every thing succeeded according to the wish, and the devotion was perfect. The altar remained as a peculiar ornament of the room which had been assigned him in the new house. Every one regarded it only as a well-arranged collection of natural curiosities. The boy knew better, but concealed his knowledge. He longed for a repetition of the solemnity. But unfortunately, just as the most opportune sun arose, the porcelain cup was not at hand: he placed the pastils immediately on the upper surface of the stand; they were kindled: and so great was the devotion of the priest, that he did not observe, until it was too late, the mischief his sacrifice was doing. The pastils had burned mercilessly into the red lacquer and beautiful gold flowers, and, as if some evil spirit had disappeared, had left their black, ineffaceable footprints. By this the young priest was thrown into the most extreme perplexity. The mischief could be covered up, it was true, with the larger pieces of his

show materials; but the spirit for new offerings was gone, and
the accident might almost be considered a hint and warning
of the danger there always is in wishing to approach the
Deity in such a way.

From FAUST

The throb of life returns, with pulses beating
Soft to ethereal dawn. O steadfast earth,
True through the night, you waited for my greeting,
Breathing beneath my feet in glad new birth,
And, clothing me afresh in joy of living,
In high resolve that banishes misgiving,
You stir my soul to prove life's utmost worth. —
In gold of dawn the quickened world lies gleaming,
The forest is alive with myriad voices,
Through dell and dale the misty shapes are teeming,
But nature's deepest heart in light rejoices;
Now burgeon, freshly quivering, frond and bough,
Sprung from the fragrant breath where they lay dreaming;
On flower and blade hang trembling pearls, and now
Each colour stands out clear, in glad device,
And all the region is my Paradise,
    Look up on high! — The giant peaks that stand
In joy of light above the mountain-brow,
Are heralds of the solemn hour at hand,
That brings the blessing down upon our land.
Already, down the soft eternal stair,
The shine has reached the lower Alpine sward,
Where clarity and brilliance are restored,
As downward, step by step, the light is poured —
The dazzling sun strides forth, and fills the air.
I turn, from greater power than eyes can bear.
    And thus it is, when hope with earnest striving

Has toiled in aims as high as man may dare,
Fulfilment's open gates give promise fair,
But from those everlasting depths comes driving
A fiery blast that takes us unaware:
We thought to light life's torch, but now, depriving
Our highest hope, a sea of fire surrounds us.
Such fire! Of love? Or the fierce glow of hate?
The blend of joy and sorrow that confounds us,
Sends us to earth: to veil our troubled state,
For benefice of Spring we supplicate.

    And so I turn, the sun upon my shoulders,
To watch the water-fall, with heart elate,
The cataract pouring, crashing from the boulders,
Split and rejoined a thousand times in spate;
The thundrous water seethes in fleecy spume,
Lifted on high in many a flying plume.
Above the spray-drenched air. And then how splendid
To see the rainbow rising from this rage,
Now clear, now dimmed, in cool sweet vapour blended.
So strive the figures on our mortal stage.
This ponder well, the mystery closer seeing;
In mirrored hues we have our life and being.

William Blake

English poet, artist, engraver and mystic, he was born in London
in 1757. His father, a hosier, encouraged his son's drawing. In 1771
William was apprenticed to an engraver. At the age of twenty-one,
he set up on his own as an engraver, and earned his living thus for
twenty years. Blake began writing poetry at twelve. His output of
color prints and of verse was tremendous. From 1800 on he had no
respite from the visions which crowded ceaselessly upon him. He
wrote mystical poetry of great power. In his last years he became
friends with John Linnel the painter, and became the center of a
circle of young artists who admired him. His *Songs of Innocence* and
Songs of Experience are among the best loved poems in English,
and he is now regarded as one of the greatest figures in English
poetry and art. He died in 1827.

TO THOMAS BUTTS

Felpham, *Octr. 2d 1800*

Friend of Religion & Order,

I thank you for your very beautiful & encouraging Verses,
which I account a Crown of Laurels & I also thank you for
your reprehension of follies by me foster'd. Your prediction
will, I hope, be fulfilled in me, & in future I am the determined advocate of Religion & Humility, the two bands of
Society. Having been so full of the Business of Settling the
stick & feathers of my nest, I have not got any forwarder
with "the three Marys" or with any other of your commis-
sions; but hope, now I have commenced a new life of in-
dustry, to do credit to that new life by Improved Works.
Receive from me a return of verses, such as Felpham pro-

duces by me, tho' not such as she produces by her Eldest
Son; however, such as they are, I cannot resist the temptation to send them to you.

> To my Friend Butts I write
> My first Vision of Light,
> On the yellow sands sitting.
> The Sun was Emitting
> His Glorious beams
> From Heaven's high Streams.
> Over Sea, over Land
> My Eyes did Expand
> Into regions of air
> Away from all Care,
> Into regions of fire
> Remote from Desire;
> The Light of the Morning
> Heaven's Mountains adorning:
> In particles bright
> The jewels of Light
> Distinct shone & clear.
> Amaz'd & in fear
> I each particle gazed,
> Astonish'd, Amazed;
> For each was a Man
> Human-form'd. Swift I ran,
> For they beckon'd to me
> Remote by the Sea,
> Saying: "Each grain of Sand,
> Every Stone on the Land,
> Each rock & each hill,
> Each fountain & rill,
> Each herb & each tree,
> Mountain, hill, earth & sea,
> Cloud, Meteor & Star,

Are Men seen Afar."
I stood in the Streams
Of Heaven's bright beams,
And Saw Felpham sweet
Beneath my bright feet
In soft Female charms;
And in her fair arms
My Shadow I knew
And my wife's shadow too,
And My Sister & Friend.
We like Infants descend
In our Shadows on Earth,
Like a weak mortal birth.
My Eyes more and more
Like a Sea without shore
Continue Expanding,
The Heavens commanding,
Till the Jewels of Light,
Heavenly Men beaming bright,
Appear'd as One Man,
Who complacent began
My limbs to infold
In his beams of bright gold;
Like dross purg'd away
All my mire & my clay.
Soft consum'd in delight
In his bosom Sun bright
I remain'd. Soft he smil'd,
And I heard his voice Mild
Saying: "This is My Fold,
O thou Ram horn'd with gold,
Who awakest from Sleep
On the Sides of the Deep.
On the Mountains around
The roarings resound

Of the lion & wolf,
The loud Sea & deep gulf.
These are guards of My Fold,
O thou Ram horn'd with gold!"
And the voice faded mild.
I remain'd as a Child;
All I ever had known
Before me bright Shone.
I saw you & your wife
By the fountains of Life.
Such the Vision to me
Appear'd on the sea.

TO THOMAS BUTTS

. . . I will bore you more with some Verses which My
Wife desires me to Copy out & send you with her kind love
& Respect; they were Composed above a twelvemonth ago,
while walking from Felpham to Lavant to meet my Sister:

With happiness stretch'd across the hills
In a cloud that dewy sweetness distills,
With a blue sky spread over with wings
And a mild sun that mounts & sings,
With trees & fields full of Fairy elves
And little devils who fight for themselves —
Rememb'ring the Verses that Hayley sung
When my heart knock'd against the root of my tongue —
With Angels planted in Hawthorn bowers
And God himself in the passing hours,
With Silver Angels across my way
And Golden Demons that none can stay,
With my Father hovering upon the wind
And my Brother Robert just behind

And my Brother John, the evil one,
In a black cloud making his mone;
Tho' dead, they appear upon my path,
Notwithstanding my terrible wrath:
They beg, they intreat, they drop their tears,
Fill'd full of hopes, fill'd full of fears —
With a thousand Angels upon the Wind
Pouring disconsolate from behind
To drive them off, & before my way
A frowning Thistle implores my stay.
What to others a trifle appears
Fills me full of smiles or tears;
For double the vision my Eyes do see,
And a double vision is always with me.
With my inward Eye 'tis an old Man grey;
With my outward, a Thistle across my way.
"If thou goest back," the thistle said,
"Thou art to endless woe betray'd;
For here does Theotormon lower
And here is Enitharmon's bower
And Los the terrible thus hath sworn,
Because thou backward dost return,
Poverty, Envy, old age & fear
Shall bring thy Wife upon a bier;
And Butts shall give what Fuseli gave,
A dark black Rock & a gloomy Cave."

I struck the Thistle with my foot,
And broke him up from his delving root:
"Must the duties of life each other cross?
Must every joy be dung & dross?
Must my dear Butts feel cold neglect
Because I give Hayley his due respect?
Must Flaxman look upon me as wild,
And all my friends be with doubts beguil'd?

Must my Wife live in my Sister's bane,
Or my Sister survive on my Love's pain?
The curses of Los, the terrible shade,
And his dismal terrors make me afraid."

So I spoke & struck in my wrath
The old man weltering upon my path.
Then Los appear'd in all his power:
In the Sun he appear'd, descending before
My face in fierce flames; in my double sight
'Twas outward a Sun, inward Los in his might.

"My hands are labour'd day & night,
And Ease comes never in my sight.
My Wife has no indulgence given
Except what comes to her from heaven.
We eat little, we drink less;
This Earth breeds not our happiness.
Another Sun feeds our life's streams,
We are not warmed with thy beams;
Thou measurest not the Time to me,
Nor yet the Space that I do see;
My Mind is not with thy light array'd,
Thy terrors shall not make me afraid."

When I had my Defiance given,
The Sun stood trembling in heaven;
The Moon that glow'd remote below,
Became leprous & white as snow;
And every soul of men on the Earth
Felt affliction & sorrow & sickness & dearth.
Los flam'd in my path, & the Sun was hot
With the bows of my Mind & the Arrows of Thought —
My bowstring fierce with Ardour breathes,
My arrows glow in their golden sheaves;

My brother & father march before;
The heavens drop with human gore.

Now I a fourfold vision see,
And a fourfold vision is given to me;
'Tis fourfold in my supreme delight
And threefold in soft Beulah's night
And twofold Always. May God us keep
From Single vision & Newton's sleep!

From JERUSALEM

[All Are Men in Eternity]

For all are Men in Eternity, Rivers, Mountains, Cities, Vil-
lages,
All are Human, & when you enter into their Bosoms you
walk
In Heavens & Earths, as in your own Bosom you bear your
Heaven
And Earth & all you behold; tho' it appears Without, it is
Within,
In your Imagination, of which this World of Mortality is
but a Shadow.

[Spectre and Imagination]

The Spectre is the Reasoning Power in Man, & when
separated
From Imagination and closing itself as in steel in a Ratio
Of the Things of Memory, It thence frames Laws & Mo-
ralities
To destroy Imagination, the Divine Body, by Martyrdoms &
Wars.

Teach me, O holy Spirit, the Testimony of Jesus! let me
Comprehend wonderous things out of the Divine Law!
I behold Babylon in the opening Street of London. I behold
Jerusalem in ruins wandering about from house to house.
This I behold: the shudderings of death attend my steps.
I walk up and down in Six Thousand Years: their Events are
    present before me
To tell how Los in grief & anger, whirling round his Ham-
    mer on high,
Drave the Sons & Daughters of Albion from their ancient
    mountains.

Johann Christian Friedrich Hölderlin

He was born 20 March 1770 at Lauffen on the Neckar and studied theology at Tübingen. He was introduced to Schiller, who published some of his early writings in magazines and got him a job as tutor. In 1796, he became tutor to the family of a banker, J. F. Gothard in Frankfurt-on-Main, and he fell deeply in love with Gothard's wife, Susette. She was the "Diotima" of *Hyperion* and other poems. After her death in 1802, Hölderlin traveled through France on foot "completely destitute and mentally deranged, in an advanced stage of schizophrenia." In 1804 a friend got him a sinecure post as a librarian and took care of Hölderlin for a while. Hölderlin died on 4 June 1843.

MEMORIES

The Northeast blows,
The dearest among the winds
To me, because of the fiery spirit
It promises, bearing good voyage to the sailors.
But go now and greet
The beautiful Garonne
And the gardens of Bordeaux
There where along the precipitous bank
The pathway runs, and into the river
The brook plunges; but over against it
Watches forever a noble pair
Of oaks and silver poplars;
Still it comes back to me well, and how

The elm forest, inclining, sways
The widespread summits above the mill;
In the courtyard, meanwhile, a fig tree grows.
There it is that on feast days go
The swarthy women
Upon silken ground,
At the time of March
When night is equal with day,
And over slow passes,
Heavy with golden dreams,
Drift wild airs bringing sleep.

But let one hand me,
Full of the dark light,
The fragrant cup,
That I might rest; for sweet
Sleep would be, under shadows.
It is not good
Soulless to be, with mortal
Thoughts. Yet good
Is converse, and to say
The heart's meaning, to hear much
Of days of love,
And events, the doing of deeds.

But where are the friends? Bellarmin
With the companion? Many a one
Bears shyness, timid to go to the source;
The beginning of riches is truly
In the sea. They, the seafarers,
Like painters, assemble
The beautiful of the earth, and do not disdain
Winged war, and suffer
To live alone, yearlong, under
The leafless mast, where the night is not lit up

With the glow-lamps of the town's feast days,
Nor the playing of strings nor innate dancing.
But now to Indians
The men are gone;
Deserted is the airy peak
On mountains of vines from which the descending
Dordogne comes,
And together with the magnificent
Garonne, great as a sea,
The river goes out. The sea, though,
Takes and gives recollection,
And love, too, fixes the eyes intently.
What endures, however, poets create.

TRANSLATED BY VERNON WATKINS

PATMOS

Near is God
And hard to apprehend.
But where danger is, there
Arises salvation also.
In darkness dwell
The eagles, and fearless across the abyss
Go the sons of the Alps
On lightly built bridges.
Therefore, since all round are upheaped
The summits of time,
And those that dwell nearest in love
Must languish on uttermost mountains,
Give us then innocent water,
O pinions give us, to pass
Over with constant minds and again return.

So I spoke, when swifter
Than I had fancied, and far,
Whither I never had thought to come,
A Genius bore me away
From my house. In the twilight
The shadowy woods darkened as I went
And the yearning brooks of my home;
No more did I know these lands.

Yet soon in fresh radiance,
Mysterious
In the golden smoke,
Swiftly sprung up
With the tread of the sun,

Asia bloomed out before me,
Fragrant with a thousand peaks, and dazzled
I sought one that I knew, for I was
A stranger to the broad streets
Where the gold-flecked Pactolus
Rushes down from Tmolus,
And Taurus stands and Messogis,
And full of flowers the garden,
A quiet fire. But high in the light
Blossoms the silver snow,
And, witness to life everlasting,
On attainless walls
The immemorial ivy grows, and upborne
Upon living columns of cedars and laurels
Are the solemn,
The divinely built palaces.

But about Asia's portals,
Running hither and thither

In hazardous wastes of sea
Ripple shadowless ways enough,
Yet the seaman knoweth the isles.
And when I heard
That one of those close-lying
Was Patmos,
I longed greatly
To turn in there and approach
The dark grotto there.
For not wondrous, like Cyprus,
The rich in fountains, or
One of the others,
Does Patmos abide.

Yet bountiful
In the needier house
Is she nonetheless.
And when out of shipwreck or in
Lament for his home
Or the departed friend,
One of the strangers
Draws near to her, she hears it with joy,
And her children,
The voices of the warm glade
And the rock-dwelling breezes
And the rocks too, they hear him, and lovingly
The echo rings out to the lament of the man.
So once
Did she foster the Beloved of God,
The Seer, who in blissful youth
Was gone with
The Son of the Most High, inseparable;
For the Storm Bearer loved
The simplicity of the disciple,
And the watchful man viewed well

The face of the god
As, at the mystery of the vine,
They sat together, at the hour of the banquet,
And quietly prescient in his great soul
The Lord spake death and the last love;
For never enough
Had he of words for telling of kindness
At that time, and gladdening,
When he saw it, the wrath of the world.
For all things are good. Therefore he died. Of that
There were much to be said. And the friends saw
How he gazed forth victorious,
The most joyful of all, at the last.

Yet they mourned, as now
It was grown evening, astounded,
For in their souls the men weighed
A mighty decision, but they loved
Life under the sun, and they would not leave
The face of the Lord and their homeland.
Inwrought was that
As fire in the iron, and at their side
Went the shadow of the Beloved.
Therefore he sent them
The Spirit, and the house trembled,
And the storm of God
Rolled far-thundering over their fateful heads,
Where brooding
Were gathered the heroes of death
Now as he, in departure,
Once more appeared before them.
For now was put out
The day of the sun, the kingly one,
And himself, divinely suffering,
Shattered the straight-rayed scepter,

For it shall come again
At the proper time. No good
Had it been later, cleaving abruptly
And truthless, the work of man, and it was joy
From now on
To dwell in loving night and maintain
Steadfast in simple eyes
Abysses of wisdom. And deep
On the mountains too
Living images flourish.

Yet it is dreadful how far and wide
God endlessly scatters the living.
Dreadful it is to leave
The face of dear friends and to wander
Far over the mountains alone,
When the Heavenly Spirit,
Known before in communion,
Was single in meaning; and thought it was never foretold
    them,
Yet by their very
Hair did it seize them,
As, hastening away into the distance,
God of a sudden looked back, and conjuring
Him to remain, naming the evil,
Bounden henceforth as with golden cords,
They gave one another their hands.

But when there died
Him upon whom most beauty
Clung, so that a miracle
Was on his figure and the heavenly ones
Pointed to him, and when, eternally
A riddle to one another, they could not
Understand one another, who lived together

In remembrance; and not the sand only
And the meadows were taken away
And the temples uprooted; when the glory
Of the half-god and his people decays
And even the Most High
Turneth aside his countenance
Up above, so that nowhere
Aught immortal is any more to be seen
In the heavens or on
The green earth, what then is this?

It is the cast of the Sower, as he seizes
The wheat with his spade
And flings across to the clear grain,
Driving it over the threshing floor.
The husks fall at his feet,
But in the end cometh the corn.
And so evil it is if something
Is lost and the living sound
Fades from our speech,
For heavenly labor is like to our own.
The Highest would not have
All at one time.
So long as the pit bear iron,
And Etna glittering resin,
So I have riches
To fashion an image and see in the semblance
Christ as he had been.

But when one spurred himself on,
And sadly speaking on the way where I was weaponless,
Overpowered me, so that I marveled and an impostor
Would be moulding an image of God —
Visible in anger did I once
See the sovereigns of heaven. Not that I were

To become anything, but to learn.
Kindly they are, but most
Hateful to them as long as they reign
Is falsehood, as there dwells
Humanity then no more among men.
For they do not reign, rather Fate
Reigns more immortally,
And their work goes on of itself
And runs hasteningly to an end.
And when ascends higher
The heavenly pageant of triumph,
The exulting Son of the Most High,
Like to the sun itself, is named by the mighty

An emblem, and here is the staff
Of song signaling down,
For nothing is common. It wakens the dead
Who are not yet caught by the rawness of death.
But many shy eyes
Wait to behold the light. They would not
Blossom forth in the sharp radiance,
Though the golden bridle guideth their courage.
But when,
As from swelling eyebrows
Forgetful of the world,
Quietly shining strength falls
From the Holy Scriptures,
Rejoicing in grace
They yield themselves to calm vision.

And if the heavenly ones now,
As I believe, so love me,
How much more You,
For one thing I know,
That the will of the eternal Father

Lies much with you. Quiet is his sign
In the thunderous sky. And One stands beneath it
His life long. For Christ lives yet.
But the heroes, his sons,
All are come and the Holy Scriptures
From him, and the deeds of the earth
Have illumined the lightning till now,
A contest unwaning. But he is there. For his works
Are known to him from everlasting.

Too long, too long already
Has the glory of the Blessed been viewless.
For almost must they guide
Our fingers for us, and basely
A mighty force teareth our heart from us.
For each of the Blessed demand sacrifice.
Yet if one were passed over
Ne'er did it bring about good.
We have served the earth our mother
And of late we have served
The light of the sun
Unwittingly, but the Father who rules over all
Loves best that the constant Letter be fostered,
And enduring existence
Interpreted well. With this is accordant
The song of my people.

TRANSLATED BY R. F. C. HULL

William Wordsworth

One of the most prolific of the English Romantic poets, he was born in 1770 in Cumberland and educated at Cambridge. In 1792 he spent time in France where he sympathized with the Revolution. In 1793 he began *Guilt and Sorrow*, showing the influence of Godwin; in a period of pessimism (1795-1796) he wrote *The Borderers*. He moved with his sister Dorothy to Somerset to be near Coleridge, with whom he wrote *Lyrical Ballads* vindicating the life of the senses. He lived for a time in Germany; then settled at Grasmere and married Mary Hutchinson. He now became an opponent of liberalism and succeeded Southey as Poet Laureate. He died in 1850.

From LINES COMPOSED A FEW MILES
ABOVE TINTERN ABBEY

These beauteous forms
Through a long absence, have not been to me
As is a landscape to a blind man's eye:
But oft, in lonely rooms, and 'mid the din
Of towns and cities, I have owed to them
In hours of weariness, sensations sweet,
Felt in the blood, and felt along the heart;
And passing even into my purer mind,
With tranquil restoration: — feelings too
Of unremembered pleasure: such, perhaps,
As have no slight or trivial influence
On that best portion of a good man's life.
His little, nameless, unremembered acts
Of kindness and of love. Nor less, I trust,

To them I may have owed another gift,
Of aspect more sublime; that blessed mood,
In which the burthen of the mystery,
In which the heavy and the weary weight
Of all this unintelligible world,
Is lightened: — that serene and blessed mood,
In which the affections gently lead us on, —
Until, the breath of this corporeal frame
And even the motion of our human blood
Almost suspended, we are laid asleep
In body, and become a living soul:
While with an eye made quiet by the power
Of harmony, and the deep power of joy,
We see into the life of things.
                              If this
Be but a vain belief, yet, oh! how oft
In darkness and amid the many shapes
Of joyless daylight; when the fretful stir
Unprofitable, and the fever of the world,
Have hung upon the beatings of my heart —
How oft, in spirit, have I turned to thee,
O sylvan Wye! thou wanderer thro' the woods,
How often has my spirit turned to thee!

      And now, with gleams of half-extinguished thought,
With many recognitions dim and faint,
And somewhat of a sad perplexity,
The picture of the mind revives again:
While here I stand, not only with the sense
Of present pleasure, but with pleasing thoughts
That in this moment there is life and food
For future years. And so I dare to hope,
Though changed, no doubt, from what I was when first
I came among these hills; when like a roe
I bounded o'er the mountains, by the sides

Of the deep rivers, and the lonely streams,
Wherever nature led: more like a man
Flying from something that he dreads, than one
Who sought the thing he loved. For nature then
(The coarser pleasures of my boyish days,
And their glad animal movements all gone by)
To me was all in all. — I cannot paint
What then I was. The sounding cataract
Haunted me like a passion: the tall rock.
The mountain, and the deep and gloomy wood,
Their colours and their forms, were then to me
An appetite; a feeling and a love,
That had no need of a remoter charm,
By thought supplied, nor any interest
Unborrowed from the eye. — That time is past,
And all its aching joys are now no more,
And all its dizzy raptures. Not for this
Faint I, nor mourn nor murmur; other gifts
Have followed; for such loss, I would believe,
Abundant recompense. For I have learned
To look on nature, not as in the hour
Of thoughtless youth; but hearing oftentimes
The still, sad music of humanity,
Nor harsh nor grating, though of ample power
To chasten and subdue. And I have felt
A presence that disturbs me with the joy
Of elevated thoughts; a sense sublime
Of something far more deeply interfused,
Whose dwelling is the light of setting suns,
And the round ocean and the living air,
And the blue sky, and in the mind of man;
A motion and a spirit, that impels
All thinking things, all objects of all thought,
And rolls through all things. Therefore am I still
A lover of the meadows and the woods,

And mountains; and of all that we behold
From this green earth; of all the mighty world
Of eye, and ear, — both what they half create,
And what perceive; well pleased to recognise
In nature and the language of the sense,
The anchor of my purest thoughts, the nurse,
The guide, the guardian of my heart, and soul
Of all my moral being.

From ODE: INTIMATIONS OF IMMORTALITY
FROM RECOLLECTIONS OF
EARLY CHILDHOOD

The Child is father of the Man;
And I could wish my days to be
Bound each to each by natural piety.

There was a time when meadow, grove, and stream,
The earth, and every common sight,
            To me did seem
        Apparelled in celestial light,
The glory and the freshness of a dream.
It is not now as it hath been of yore; —
        Turn wheresoe'er I may,
            By night or day,
The things which I have seen I now can see no more.

        The Rainbow comes and goes,
        And lovely is the Rose,
        The Moon doth with delight
    Look round her when the heavens are bare,
        Waters on a starry night
        Are beautiful and fair;
    The sunshine is a glorious birth;
        But yet I know, where'er I go,
That there hath passed away a glory from the earth.

Now, while the birds thus sing a joyous song,
   And while the young lambs bound
      As to the tabor's sound,
To me alone there came a thought of grief:
A timely utterance gave that thought relief,
      And I again am strong:
The cataracts blow their trumpets from the steep;
No more shall grief of mine the season wrong;
I hear the Echoes through the mountains throng,
The Winds come to me from the fields of sleep,
      And all the earth is gay;
         Land and sea
      Give themselves up to jollity,
         And with the heart of May
      Doth every beast keep holiday —
         Thou child of Joy,
Shout round me, let me hear thy shouts, thou
         happy Shepherd-boy!

Ye blessèd Creatures, I have heard the call
   Ye to each other make; I see
The heavens laugh with you in your jubilee;
      My heart is at your festival,
      My head hath its coronal,
The fullness of your bliss, I feel — I feel it all.
         Oh evil day! if I were sullen
         While earth itself is adorning,
            This sweet May-morning,
         And the children are culling
            On every side,
         In a thousand valleys far and wide,
         Fresh flowers; while the sun shines warm,
And the babe leaps up in his mother's arm —
         I hear, I hear, with joy I hear!
         — But there's a tree, of many, one,

A single field which I have looked upon,
Both of them speak of something that is gone:
    The pansy at my feet
    Doth the same tale repeat:
Whither is fled the visionary gleam?
Where is it now, the glory and the dream?

Our birth is but a sleep and a forgetting:
The Soul that rises with us, our life's Star,
    Hath had elsewhere its setting,
      And cometh from afar:
    Not in entire forgetfulness,
    And not in utter nakedness,
But trailing clouds of glory do we come
    From God, who is our home:
Heaven lies about us in our infancy!
Shades of the prison-house begin to close
    Upon the growing Boy,
But He beholds the light, and whence it flows,
    He sees it in his joy;
The Youth, who daily farther from the east
    Must travel, still is Nature's Priest,
    And by the vision splendid
    Is on his way attended;
At length the Man perceives it die away,
And fade into the light of common day.

Earth fills her lap with pleasures of her own;
Yearnings she hath in her own natural kind,
And, even with something of a Mother's mind,
    And no unworthy aim,
To make her Foster-child, her Inmate Man,
    Forget the glories he hath known,
And that imperial palace whence he came.

Behold the Child among his new-born blisses,
A six years' Darling of a pygmy size!
Fretted by sallies of his mother's kisses,
With light upon him from his father's eyes!
See, at his feet, some little plan or chart,
Some fragment from his dream of human life,
Shaped by himself with newly-learnéd art;
　　A wedding or a festival,
　　A mourning or a funeral;
　　　And this hath now his heart,
　　And unto this he frames his song:
　　　Then will he fit his tongue
To dialogues of business, love, or strife;
　　　But it will not be long
　　　Ere this be thrown aside,
　　　And with new joy and pride
The little Actor cons another part;
Filling from time to time his "humorous stage"
With all the Persons, down to palsied Age,
That Life brings with her in her equipage;
　　　As if his whole vocation
　　　Were endless imitation.

Thou, whose exterior semblance doth belie
　　　Thy Soul's immensity;
Thou best Philosopher, who yet dost keep
Thy heritage, thou Eye among the blind,
That, deaf and silent, read'st the eternal deep,
Haunted for ever by the eternal mind —
　　　Mighty Prophet! Seer blest!
　　　On whom those truths do rest,
Which we are toiling all our lives to find,
In darkness lost, the darkness of the grave;
Thou, over whom thy Immortality
Broods like the Day, a Master o'er a Slave,

A Presence which is not to be put by;
   To whom the grave
Is but a lonely bed without the sense or sight
   Of day or the warm light,
A place of thought where we in waiting lie;
Thou little Child, yet glorious in the might
Of heaven-born freedom on thy being's height,
Why with such earnest pains dost thou provoke
The years to bring the inevitable yoke,
Thus blindly with thy blessedness at strife?
Full soon thy Soul shall have her earthly freight,
And custom lie upon thee with a weight,
Heavy as frost, and deep almost as life!

     O joy! that in our embers
     Is something that doth live,
     That nature yet remembers
     What was so fugitive!
The thought of our past years in me doth breed
Perpetual benediction: not indeed
For that which is most worthy to be blest;
Delight and liberty, the simple creed
Of Childhood, whether busy or at rest,
With new-fledged hope still fluttering in his breast —
     Not for these I raise
     The song of thanks and praise;
    But for those obstinate questionings
    Of sense and outward things,
    Fallings from us, vanishings;
    Blank misgivings of a Creature
Moving about in worlds not realised,
High instincts before which our mortal Nature
Did tremble like a guilty Thing surprised:
    But for those first affections,
    Those shadowy recollections,

Which, be they what they may,
Are yet the fountain-light of all our day,
Are yet a master-light of all our seeing;
   Uphold us, cherish, and have power to make
Our noisy years seem moments in the being
Of the eternal Silence: truths that wake,
      To perish never:
Which neither listlessness, nor mad endeavour,
      Nor Man nor Boy,
Nor all that is at enmity with joy,
Can utterly abolish or destroy!
   Hence in a season of calm weather
      Though inland far we be,
Our Souls have sight of that immortal sea
      Which brought us hither,
   Can in a moment travel thither,
And see the Children sport upon the shore,
And hear the mighty waters rolling evermore.

Then sing, ye Birds, sing, sing a joyous song!
      And let the young Lambs bound
      As to the tabor's sound!
We in thought will join your throng,
      Ye that pipe and ye that play,
      Ye that through your hearts to-day
      Feel the gladness of the May!
What though the radiance which was once so bright
Be now for ever taken from my sight,
   Though nothing can bring back the hour
Of splendour in the grass, of glory in the flower;
      We will grieve not, rather find
      Strength in what remains behind;
      In the primal sympathy
      Which having been must ever be;
      In the soothing thoughts that spring

Out of human suffering;
In the faith that looks through death,
In years that bring the philosophic mind.

And O, ye Fountains, Meadows, Hills, and Groves,
Forebode not any severing of our loves!
Yet in my heart of hearts I feel your might;
I only have relinquished one delight
To live beneath your more habitual sway.
I love the Brooks which down their channels fret,
Even more than when I tripped lightly as they;
The innocent brightness of a new-born Day
            Is lovely yet;
The Clouds that gather round the setting sun
Do take a sober colouring from an eye
That hath kept watch o'er man's mortality;
Another race hath been, and other palms are won.
Thanks to the human heart by which we live,
Thanks to its tenderness, its joys, and fears,
To me the meanest flower that blows can give
Thoughts that do often lie too deep for tears.

From THE PRELUDE

OR, GROWTH OF A POET'S MIND

An Autobiographical Poem
(1850 version)

INTRODUCTION — CHILDHOOD AND SCHOOL-TIME

Dust as we are, the immortal spirit grows
Like harmony in music; there is a dark
Inscrutable workmanship that reconciles
Discordant elements, makes them cling together
In one society. How strange that all
The terrors, pains, and early miseries,

Regrets, vexations, lassitudes interfused
Within my mind, should e'er have borne a part,
And that a needful part, in making up
The calm existence that is mine when I
Am worthy of myself! Praise to the end!
Thanks to the means which Nature deigned to employ;
Whether her fearless visitings, or those
That came with soft alarm, like hurtless light
Opening the peaceful clouds; or she may use
Severer interventions, ministry
More palpable, as best might suit her aim.

One summer evening (led by her) I found
A little boat tied to a willow tree
Within a rocky cove, its usual home.
Straight I unloosed her chain, and stepping in
Pushed from the shore. It was an act of stealth
And troubled pleasure, nor without the voice
Of mountain echoes did my boat move on;
Leaving behind her still, on either side,
Small circles glittering idly in the moon,
Until they melted all into one track
Of sparkling light. But now, like one who rows,
Proud of his skill, to reach a chosen point
With an unswerving line, I fixed my view
Upon the summit of a craggy ridge,
The horizon's utmost boundary; far above
Was nothing but the stars and the gray sky.
She was an elfin pinnace; lustily
I dipped my oars into the silent lake,
And, as I rose upon the stroke, my boat
Went heaving through the water like a swan;
When, from behind that craggy steep till then
The horizon's bound, a huge peak, black and huge,
As if with voluntary power instinct

Upreared its head. I struck and struck again,
And growing still in stature the grim shape
Towered up between me and the stars, and still,
For so it seemed, with purpose of its own
And measured motion like a living thing,
Strode after me. With trembling oars I turned,
And through the silent water stole my way
Back to the covert of the willow tree;
There in her mooring-place I left my bark, —
And through the meadows homeward went, in grave
And serious mood; but after I had seen
That spectacle, for many days, my brain
Worked with a dim and undetermined sense
Of unknown modes of being; o'er my thoughts
There hung a darkness, call it solitude
Or blank desertion. No familiar shapes
Remained, no pleasant images of trees,
Of sea or sky, no colors of green fields;
But huge and mighty forms, that do not live
Like living men, moved slowly through the mind
By day, and were a trouble to my dreams.

Wisdom and Spirit of the universe!
Thou Soul that art the eternity of thought,
That givest to forms and images a breath
And everlasting motion, not in vain
By day or starlight thus from my first dawn
Of childhood didst thou intertwine for me
The passions that build up our human soul;
Not with the mean and vulgar works of man,
But with high objects, with enduring things —
With life and nature — purifying thus
The elements of feeling and of thought,
And sanctifying, by such discipline,
Both pain and fear, until we recognize

A grandeur in the beatings of the heart.
Nor was this fellowship vouchsafed to me
With stinted kindness. In November days,
When vapors rolling down the valley made
A lonely scene more lonesome, among woods,
At noon and 'mid the calm of summer nights,
When, by the margin of the trembling lake,
Beneath the gloomy hills homeward I went
In solitude, such intercourse was mine;
Mine was it in the fields both day and night,
And by the waters, all the summer long.

CAMBRIDGE AND THE ALPS

The melancholy slackening that ensued
Upon those tidings by the peasant given
Was soon dislodged. Downwards we hurried fast,
And, with the half-shaped road which we had missed,
Entered a narrow chasm. The brook and road
Were fellow-travellers in this gloomy strait,
And with them did we journey several hours
At a slow pace. The immeasurable height
Of woods decaying, never to be decayed,
The stationary blasts of waterfalls,
And in the narrow rent at every turn
Winds thwarting winds, bewildered and forlorn,
The torrent shooting from the clear blue sky,
The rocks that muttered close upon our ears,
Black drizzling crags that spake by the way-side
As if a voice were in them, the sick sight
And giddy prospect of the raving stream,
The unfettered clouds and region of the Heavens,
Tumult and peace, the darkness and the light —
Were all like workings of one mind, the features
Of the same face, blossoms upon one tree;
Characters of the great Apocalypse,

The types and symbols of Eternity,
Of first, and last, and midst, and without end.

RESIDENCE IN LONDON

As the black storm upon the mountain-top
Sets off the sunbeam in the valley, so
That huge fermenting mass of human-kind
Serves as a solemn background, or relief,
To single forms and objects, whence they draw,
For feeling and contemplative regard,
More than inherent liveliness and power.
How oft, amid those overflowing streets,
Have I gone forward with the crowd, and said
Unto myself, "The face of every one
That passes by me is a mystery!"
Thus have I looked, nor ceased to look, oppressed
By thoughts of what and whither, when and how,
Until the shapes before my eyes became
A second-sight procession, such as glides
Over still mountains, or appears in dreams;
And once, far-travelled in such mood, beyond
The reach of common indication, lost
Amid the moving pageant, I was smitten
Abruptly, with the view (a sight not rare)
Of a blind Beggar, who, with upright face,
Stood, propped against a wall, upon his chest
Wearing a written paper, to explain
His story, whence he came, and who he was.
Caught by the spectacle my mind turned round
As with the might of waters; an apt type
This label seemed of the utmost we can know,
Both of ourselves and of the universe;
And, on the shape of that unmoving man,
His steadfast face and sightless eyes, I gazed,
As if admonished from another world.

Novalis

Novalis was the pseudonym of Friedrich von Hardenberg, a pioneer of the German romantic movement in poetry and philosophy, born in 1772. A lawyer by profession, he later became a mining engineer. His *Hymns to the Night* express his grief at the death in 1797 of Sophie von Kuhn, to whom he was betrothed. His unfinished allegorical novels *The Disciples at Sais* and *Heinrich von Ofterdingen* also reflect the subtle mysticism and philosophic harmony of his temperament. He died in 1801.

From THOUGHTS ON RELIGION

What is Mysticism? What must be mystically treated? Religion, Love, Nature, the State. — All that is select is related to mysticism. If all men were a pair of lovers, the distinction between mysticism and not-mysticism would fall away.

Mystical faith in what has actual existence, as in the old and known, and mystical hope of all that is to come, or of the new and unknown, are two important characteristics of the humanity of the past.

Why is it that "Virtuosity" cannot find a place in religion? Because it rests upon love. Schleiermacher has proclaimed a kind of love as religion — an art-religion — almost a religion like that of the artist who worships beauty and the ideal. Love is free; it chooses by preference what is poorest and most in need of help. God therefore accepts most readily the poor and sinners. Are there loveless natures? Then there are also irreligious natures.

One must necessarily be terrified when casting a glance into the depths of the spirit. The sense of depth and the will, have no limits. It is with them as it is with the heavens. The imagination stands still, exhausted; and its mere momentary constitution is thereby indicated. Here we come upon the possibility of spiritual diseases, — in short, upon the doctrine of the spiritual life and constitution; and the moral law appears here as the only true and great law of the gradual elevation of the universe, as the fundamental law of harmonious development. Man advances in successive steps, and with every real step he advances more easily; with all acquired velocity space increases. It is only the look that is turned backward which carries forward, as the look that is turned forward leads backward.

From HYMNS TO THE NIGHT

There came from the azure depths, from the heights of my old blessedness, a thrill of twilight, and at once the band of birth, the fetter of light was severed. Away fled the earthly glory, and with it my sorrow. All sadness was gathered into a new unfathomable world; and thou, night's inspiration, heavenly Slumber, camest over me. The scene rose gently aloft, and over the sea hovered my unbound new-born spirit. That mound of earth became a dust-cloud, and through the cloud I beheld the transfigured features of my beloved. In her eyes, eternity reposed; I clasped her hands and my tears became glittering links of an indissoluble chain. Thousands of years moved away into the distance like thunder clouds. On her neck I wept tears that gave the new life rapture. It was my first and only dream;

and ever since do I feel eternal and unchangeable faith in the heaven of Night, and its light, my Beloved.

I now know when the last morning will come: when light shall no more scare away the night and love, when slumber shall be eternal, and but one inexhaustible dream. I feel a heavenly weariness within me. The pilgrimage to the holy sepulchre seemed far and exhausting, and the cross was becoming oppressive. The crystal rill which, unperceived by the common sense, drips in the dark bosom of the hill, breaks forth at its foot in the earthly stream; and whoever has tasted it and hath stood on high on the ridge that bounds the world and looked over into the new land, into the abode of Night: he surely returns no more to the bustle and toil of the world, or to the land where light dwells in eternal unrest.

High up he builds himself his tabernacles — tabernacles of peace — and longs and loves and looks away till the most perfect of all hours draws him to the fountain of the stream. The earthly swims up again borne back by the storm; but what had become sacred from the contact of love, dissolves, and flows through secret channels to the region beyond, where like subtle odors, it mingles with the loved ones in their sleep. Once more dost thou, cheerful Light, awaken the weary to toil, and breathe in me glad life again; yet thou wilt not allure me away from memory and its mossy gravestone. Gladly will I touch the diligent hands, and look around wherever thou needest me; I will laud the full magnificence of thy splendour; unwearied I will pursue the beautiful connections of thy artful work. Gladly will I contemplate the mystic march of thy powerful gleaming recorder of time, and I will explore the equilibrium of the universal forces, and the rules of the wondrous play of numberless spaces and their times. Yet my secret heart remains faithful to Night, and to her daughter creative Love. Canst thou show me a heart that is for ever true?

My heart is swelling,
  And every pain
Feels now indwelling
  Joy's pulse again;
A short time flying,
  Then free I'll rest,
In rapture lying
  On Love's own breast;
An infinite living
  Wakes mighty in me,
I'm looking and giving
  Myself down to thee.
On yon earth upheavèd
  Thy splendours fade,
The garland they weavèd
  Gives cooling shade.
O come, my Belovèd,
  And clasp me with might,
That I with love soothèd
  May slumber the night.
I feel in hot-fever
  Death's youth-giving flood
To balsam and ether
  Transformed is my blood.

From SACRED SONGS

I

Though All Are Faithless Growing . . .

Though all are faithless growing,
Yet will I faithful be,
That one on earth is showing
His thankfulness to Thee.

For me Thou cam'st to suffer
For me Thou had'st to smart,
And now with joy I offer
To Thee my thankful heart.

With tears I oft am grieving
That Thou did'st need to die,
While friends, Thy trust deceiving,
Forgot and passed Thee by.
With naught but love unsparing
Thou cam'st for them and me.
They let Thee die, uncaring,
And thought no more of Thee.

Thou standest still sustaining
Each one with love anew;
With not a friend remaining,
Thou still art ever true.
Yet true love ever winneth,
At last the world will see,
When weeping each one clingeth,
A child before Thy knee.

When now at last I find Thee,
O leave me not alone!
But ever closer bind me
And let me be Thine own!
My brothers too, beholding,
Will soon in Heav'n find rest,
And then Thy love enfolding
Will sink upon Thy breast.

TRANSLATED BY EILEEN HUTCHINS

II
There Come Such Troubled Hours

There come such troubled hours,
So heavy grows our cheer,
When all from far o'erpowers
Our hearts with ghostly fear.

There come wild terrors creeping
With stealthy silent tread,
And night's dark mantle sweeping
O'erweighs the soul with dread.

Our pillars strong are shaking,
No hold remaineth sure,
Our thoughts in whirlpools breaking
Obey our will no more.

Then madness comes and claims us
And none withstands his will,
A senses' dullness maims us,
The pulse of life stands still.

Who raised the Cross, bestowing
A refuge for each heart?
Who lives in heaven all-knowing
And healeth pain and smart?

Go thou where stands that Wonder
And to thy heart give ear.
His flames shall force asunder
And quell thy nightmare fear.

An angel bendeth o'er thee
And bears thee to the strand,

And, filled with joy, before thee
Thou seest the Promised Land.

TRANSLATED BY EILEEN HUTCHINS

III
When in Sad and Weary Hour . . .

When in sad and weary hour
Dark despair hath cast its gloom;
When o'erwhelmed by sickness' power
Fears our inmost soul consume;
When we think of our beloved
Bowed with sorrow and with grief;
All our heav'ns with clouds are covered
Not one hope can bring relief.

God then bendeth to receive us,
With his love he draweth near;
When we long for life to leave us
Then his angel doth appear;
Brings the cup of life, restoring
Strength and comfort from above;
Not in vain our prayers imploring
Peaceful rest for those we love.

TRANSLATED BY EILEEN HUTCHINS

From SELECTED THOUGHTS

The spirit world is in fact revealed to us; it is always open. Could we suddenly become as sensitive as is necessary, we should perceive ourselves to be in its midst. What are the methods for the healing of our present deficient condition? Formerly they were fasts and moral purification; now maybe by invigoration.

From THE DISCIPLES AT SAIS

The Voice must certainly have spoken of our Master, for he knows how to collect the indications that are scattered on all sides. A singular light kindles in his glance when the sublime Rune is unrolled before us, and he looks discerningly into our eyes to find out whether for us too the Star has arisen that shall render the Figure visible and comprehensible. If he see us sad, that our night is not breaking, he comforts us and promises future joy to the faithful and assiduous seer. Often he has told us how, as a child, the impulse to exercise the faculties, to occupy and satisfy them, left him no peace. He looked up to the stars and imitated in the sands their positions and their courses. He gazed into the aerial sea without pause and was never weary of contemplating its transparency, its agitations, its clouds, its lights. He collected stones, flowers and every sort of insect, and set them out in many-fashioned lines. He watched men and animals; he sat by the seashore gathering shells. He listened heedfully to his own heart and to his thoughts. He knew not whither his longing was driving him. When he was older he wandered, beholding other countries, other seas, new skies, strange stars, unknown plants, animals and men; he descended into caves and marked how in courses and coloured strata the Edifice of the Earth had been built up. He manipulated clay into wonderful rock forms. At this time he found everywhere objects already known to him but marvellously mingled and mated, and strange vicissitudes often arose within him. Soon he became aware of the inter-relation of all things, of conjunctions, of coincidences. Ere long he saw nothing singly. The perceptions of his senses thronged together in great variegated Pictures; he heard, saw, felt and thought simultaneously. He took pleasure in bringing strangers together.

Sometimes the stars became men to him, men as stars; stones were as animals, clouds as plants; he sported with forces and phenomena; he knew where and how he could find and bring to light this or that, and thus himself plucked at the strings in his search for tones and sequences. What came to him after this he does not make known to us. He tells us that we ourselves, led on by him and by our own desire, may discover what happened to him. Many of us forsook him. They returned to their parents and learnt to follow a trade. Some have been sent forth by him we know not whither; he chose them out. Of these some had been there but a short time, others longer. One was still a child. Scarcely was he there but the Master wished to resign the teaching into his hands. This child had great dark eyes with blue depths; his skin shone like lilies, and his locks like lustrous cloudlets at eventide. His voice thrilled through our hearts; we would have gladly given him our flowers, stones, feathers, all that we had. He smiled with an infinite gravity; we felt strangely happy to be beside him. One day he will return, said the Master, and live among us. Then the lessons will cease. He sent another pupil with him who often made us impatient. He seemed ever sorrowful. Long years he was here; nothing prospered with him. When we searched for crystals or flowers he did not find them easily. With difficulty, too, he saw from a distance; he knew not how to arrange the motley lines in order. He broke everything so easily. Yet no other had such craving and ardour to see and hear. Some time back — before the Child was come into our circle — he suddenly became both ready and gay. One day he went out sorrowful. He did not return. Night advanced. We were very anxious on his account. Suddenly, when the glimmer of morning came, we heard his voice in a coppice near. He sang a noble, joyous song. We all marvelled. The Master gazed with rapture towards the dawn as I shall never see him gaze again. After a while the singer

came among us, bringing with an expression of ineffable
bliss upon his countenance, a dull little Stone of curious
shape. The Master took it in his hand and kissed his disciple
long; then he looked at us with moist eyes and laid the
Stone in an empty place among the other pebbles, just at
the point where many lines converged. Never shall I forget
that moment. It was as though we had transitorily caught
into our souls a clear vision of this wondrous world.

Jacob Bower

An itinerant Baptist minister of the American frontier, he was born in 1786 of German Baptist (Dunker) parentage in Pennsylvania. He went to Kentucky as a youth, and though always religious by inclination, he seems to have undergone his first movement of profound conversion during a violent earth tremor in 1811. In 1814, he began to preach, and in 1832 accepted a call as a missionary. Bower moved in 1826 to Illinois because he disliked raising his family in a slave state. From 1832 until 1848, Bower organized churches and ordained ministers; in that time he covered over forty thousand miles and preached almost three thousand sermons. He wrote an *Autobiography* of his spiritual, mystic and worldly experience. He died about 1857.

From AUTOBIOGRAPHY OF
JACOB BOWER

I slept but little all night.

Early the next morning before it was quite light, we were on the road. But not without the good mans benediction. Soon we met large companies of Negroes, we passed several companies, at length we met an old man walking by himself, I stoped him, and enquired of him, where they were all going so early this morning. The old negro said, "we are all going to Beards Town to see a fellow servent hung to day for killing his fellow servent." I started on with this thought, how does that man feal, knowing that he must die to day. Suddenly, as if some one had asked me. And how do you feal? You don't know but that you may die before he does.

All of a sudden, (ah I shall never forget it) as if a book had been opened to me, the inside of which I had never seen: I got a sight of the wretchedness of my heart — a cage of every unclean and hateful thing. (ah thought I, here lies the root of bitterness, the fountain from whence all my sinful actions have flowed. My mind & heart have always been enmity against God, who is so holy that he cannot allow of no sin, however small it may appear in the sight of men. How can I ever be admited into Heaven with such a heart? it is utterly imposible. Lost, lost forever lost. Right here, and at this time my crumbly foundation of Universalism gave way. I discovered a just God, who, I thought, could not save me and remain just. I could see no way of escaping eternal punishment.

This day passed away as did the day before, almost in entier silence — four days brought us to my own house, at the sight of which I felt a momentary gladness. My sister who had kept house for us during our absence, met us at the gate and said, "why, Jacob, you look verry pale, have you been sick since you left home? I tryed to pass it by, and made some evasive reply, as though there was not much the matter with me.

It was the morning of the 14th day of October 1811, when the arrow of the Allmighty was made fast in my heart, somtimes I was almost in dispair, at other times I became careless and not so deeply concerned. But the ever memerable morning of the 17th day of December 1811. About 2 o'clock A.M. when most people were in their beds sound asleep. There was an Earthquake, verry violent indeed. I and my wife both awoke about the same time, she spoke first, and said, Lord have mercy upon us, what is it shaking the house so? From a discription given of an Earthquake in Germany by a Tunkard preacher in a sermon when I was about ten years old, I immediately recognized it, and replied, it is an Earthquake. The Lord have mercy

upon us, we shall all be sunk & lost, and I am not prepared.
O God have mercy upon us all. I expected immediate dis-
truction, had no hope of seeing the dawn of another day.
Eternity, oh Eternity was just at hand, and all of us unprepared; just about the time the sun arose, as I supposed,
for it was a thick, dark and foggy morning, there was another verry hard shock — lasted several minutes terible indeed. To see everything touching the earth, shakeing —
quivering, trembling; and mens hearts quaking for fear of
the approaching judgment. Many families ran together and
grasped each other in their arms. One instance near to
where I lived, the woman & five children, all gathered
around her husband, crying O my husband pray for me,
The children crying, Father, pray for me, O, pray for me, for
the day of Judgment is come, and we are unprepared! The
people relinquished all kinds of labour for a time, except
feeding stock, and eat only enough to support nature a few
days. Visiting from house to house, going to meeting Singing — praying, exoting, and once in a while ketch a sermon
from a travelling Minister. Men, Women and children,
everywhere were heard enquiering what they must do to be
saved. This shaking continued more or less for near two
years, sometimes just percievable. Deiists & Universalist in
those days were scarce. But in relation to my own views and
feelings. I thought that the time had been when I viewed
many others much worse, and greater sinners than I was,
and if they were saved, my chance for salvation was as good
as theirs, and I was pretty sure of being saved. But now it
appeared to me, that surely no one was as great a sinner as
I, none had such a wicked heart, and such vile thoughts.
God sees and knows them all, and they are an abomination
in his sight. The time has been when God would have
saved me, but I have passed by the day of his mercy, and I
mite as well give over all hopes of being saved, and return
to my former pleasures again. But my heart would respond,

no, for it is sin I know that has undone me, and I cannot consent to go back into the practice of it again. I became resolved to press forward, I would pray & serve God though he send me to hell, yet I will lye at his feet and beg for mercy as long as I am out of hell. Sin now appeared exceeding sinful to me, I strove to shun it all. Holiness appeared of all things the most desierable but I could not attain to it. I often tryed to pray in the woods, but I felt no better, I could find no relief for my troubled conscience.

For several days past, I had been thinking about giving up to God, and resign myself into his hands, for I can do nothing to save myself, and all I do is so sinful in his sight that he disregards my cries & prayers. But a follish thought suggested itself to my mind, that I must not give up to God to do with me as he pleased, for I thought that the moment I did that, he would kill me and send me instantly to hell, and although I had long ago confessed that he would be just in so doing, Yet I was not willing that Justice should be executed, and I thought that as long as I was not willing, he would not do it. My toung never can till, nor my pen discribe, the struglings & anxities I passed through about this time.

All nature appeared to be dressed in mourning, and the god of nature frowning, oh what a time of melencholy.

Well, on the afternoon of the 8th day of February 1812, I saw one of my neighbors & his wife, passing by my house — going to his wifes fathers. I said to my wife, Robert & Anna are gon to her Fathers this eavning, suppose we go to your Fathers and spend the night with them, (it was about three miles) she readily consented and we went; when we arrived there, almost the first news we heard was. "Your cousin Billy has professed to get religion and is as happy a man as I have ever seen." Joy filled my heart for only a moment, and dispair seized upon my mind. Ah, thought I; God has mercy in story for everybody, and everybody can be saved but me, for me there is no mercy, Gods mercy toards me is clean gon forever — I thought that I had seen the sun set, but alas for me I shall never see it rise again. Before the sun rises again I shall be dead and in hell. I ran away behind the barn and tryed to pray to God for mercy — returned but felt no better reconciled. The more I tryed to pray, the less hope I had of being saved. Just about midnight, I was sittin a chair, absorbed in deep thought about my condition — I well recollect thinking, Oh how much I do suffer in this world, it appeared to me as though the flames of hell kindled on me, where my greatest burdin was, right on my heart, I thought that my sufferings in this world were nothing to what they will be if I fall into the pit of ruin. Suddenly my thoughts turned to the sufferings of Christ, and what he endured on the cross. That he suffered in soul & body, his soul was exceeding sorrowful even unto death, sweting as it had been great drops of blood falling to the ground; and all his painful sufferings for the space of three hours on the cross, and that not for himself; it was for sinners that he thus suffered that they mite be saved. The next thought that passed through my mind was. If it was done for sinners, it was done for me. I believed it. The storm calmed off, my troubled My troubled soul was easy. I felt as light as a fether, and all was quiet — pieceful — tranquil and serene. This transpired about midnight, and I had not slept for several nights previous, for fear that if I went to sleep, I would awake in hell. I thought of lying down. I first walked out of doors, and everything I could see, appeared intierly new. The trees (I thought) lifted their hands up toards Heaven as if they were praising God. I cast my eyes upward, and beheld the bright twinkling stars shining to their makers praise. They appeared as so many holes through which I could look & see the glory of Heaven. Glory to God. Thank God. Bless the Lord O my soul, was busily runing throug my mind — What is the matter with me. I never felt so strange before, strange wonderful — wonderful indeed. A little while ago I felt as if I were hanging by a slender thread over the pit of ruin. God would not have mercy on me — Hell was my portion. God was just in sending me there —This was the last call — the last time, and the last moment with me on Earth. Before morning I shall lift up my eyes in hell. My burdin—my distress of soul was too heavy to be bourn any longer. And now all of a sudden I feal so light — so easy — so happy, so full of glory, and so full of love to everything I see. And so full of love to God. What is it, what can all this mean? It did not then enter my mind that this was religion; or that this was salvation. But in this calm and piecful state of fealing, I laid myself down to sleep, when I awoke, the sun was just then rising, and a bright streak of light shone against the wall, which was the first thing I saw, and the first thought I had was, O the glory of heaven. I arose — walked out, and I never saw the gees — ducks — hogs and every living creature praising God so before. The birds were singing God's praise, and invited me to unite with them in singing the praise of God, for he is good and his mercy endureth forever.

This was the Lords day morning, and the 8th day of February, 1812 I recollected an appointment for a prayer-meeting about six miles off, and I had to pass my house to get there. I made arrangments for my wife to come on after the day got some warmer.

I started verry early and got to the meeting just as the people were singing. I thought that I had never heard such heavenly music; all their singing — praying — exhortation, shakeing of hands accompanied with singing, was certainly the sweetest exercise I had ever witnessed. I wept all the time, the people seamed more like Angels than human beings, O how I loved them and their religious exercises. I had a faint hope that perhaps I would soon get religion. But a great desire to be a christian.

Late in the eavning one of my neighbours and his wife, who had both of them been at the same meeting, came to spend the night with us, she had been a member of the baptist church about four years, and a precious christian. After supper was over, she said to me. "I have come over this eavning on purpose to here you tell your experiance." O, Mrs. Dudley, said I. If that is the errend you have come on, you will be disappointed, for I have no experiance to tell. I think you have, said she, for I noticed you to day all the time of meeting, and I think that you have something to tell. Just tell me how your mind has been exercised of late. I began and related to her the exercise of my mind & feelings from the time my Father spake his last words to me at the edge of the water under the bank of Beech creek in Shelby county the 14th day of October last, till last night about midnight, and how I felt to day at the prayer meeting, but this, said I, is no experiance. I have no religion, but I hope that the Lord will have mercy on me, for I am a poor sinner. She replied, "You speak the language of a Christian, and I think if ever you will be a christian you are one now." Hearing this from one in whose christianity I had the utmost confidence, I began to think & say, why can it be posible that this is religion. O. Mrs. D. the news is too good to be true. Here my eyes poured forth a flood of tears. I exclaimed, Can it be possible, that God is so holy, so just, so righteous, can have mercy on, and save so great a sinner as I am? I have deserved the deepest hell, and I wonder that I am out of it to night. But, said she, "God is love else we all would have been in hell long ago."

John Keats

John Keats, the celebrated English romantic poet, was born in London in 1795, the son of an ostler. He first studied medicine, but abandoned it at twenty-one. As early as 1815, Keats wrote the famous *On First Looking into Chapman's Homer*, and in 1817, the collection of youthful *Poems*. As a member of the literary circle around Leigh Hunt, he met Shelley, Wordsworth and Lamb, and in 1818 published the first of his major poems. *Endymion*. Affected by hereditary consumption, he tried vainly to arrest it by sailing for Italy in 1820. He died in Rome on 23 February 1821, and is buried in the Protestant cemetery there.

Almost all of Keats's great poems appeared in the last two years of his life. His *Letters* reveal an ardent and exquisite nature.

To JOHN HAMILTON REYNOLDS

[Hampstead, February 19, 1818]

My dear Reynolds — I had an idea that a Man might pass a very pleasant life in this manner — Let him on a certain day read a certain page of full Poesy or distilled Prose, and let him wander with it, and muse upon it, and reflect from it, and bring home to it, and prophesy upon it, and dream upon it: until it becomes stale — But when will it do so? Never — When Man has arrived at a certain ripeness in intellect any one grand and spiritual passage serves him as a starting-post towards all "the two-and-thirty Palaces." How happy is such a voyage of conception, what delicious diligent indolence! A doze upon a sofa does not hinder it, and a nap upon Clover engenders ethereal finger-pointings

— the prattle of a child gives it wings, and the converse of middle-age a strength to beat them — a strain of music conducts to "an odd angle of the Isle," and when the leaves whisper it puts a girdle round the earth. — Nor will this sparing touch of noble Books be any irreverence to their Writers — for perhaps the honors paid by Man to Man are trifles in comparison to the benefit done by great works to the "spirit and pulse of good" by their mere passive existence. Memory should not be called Knowledge — Many have original minds who do not think it — they are led away by Custom. Now it appears to me that almost any Man may like the spider spin from his own inwards his own airy Citadel — the points of leaves and twigs on which the spider begins her work are few, and she fills the air with a beautiful circuiting. Man should be content with as few points to tip with the fine Web of his Soul, and weave a tapestry empyrean — full of symbols for his spiritual eye, of softness for his spiritual touch, of space for his wandering, of distinctness for his luxury. But the minds of mortals are so different and bent on such diverse journeys that it may at first appear impossible for any common taste and fellowship to exist between two or three under these suppositions. It is however quite the contrary. Minds would leave each other in contrary directions, traverse each other in numberless points, and at last greet each other at the journey's end. An old man and a child would talk together and the old man be led on his path and the child left thinking. Man should not dispute or assert, but whisper results to his Neighbour, and thus by every germ of spirit sucking the sap from mould ethereal every human might become great, and humanity instead of being a wide heath of furze and briars, with here and there a remote Oak or Pine, would become a grand democracy of forest trees. It has been an old comparison for our urging on — the beehive — however it seems to me that we should rather be the flower than the

Bee — for it is a false notion that more is gained by receiving than giving — no, the receiver and the giver are equal in their benefits. The flower, I doubt not, receives a fair guerdon from the Bee — its leaves blush deeper in the next spring — and who shall say between Man and Woman which is the most delighted? Now it is more noble to sit like Jove than to fly like Mercury: — let us not therefore go hurrying about and collecting honey, bee-like, buzzing here and there impatiently from a knowledge of what is to be arrived at. But let us open our leaves like a flower, and be passive and receptive; budding patiently under the eye of Apollo and taking hints from every noble insect that favours us with a visit — Sap will be given us for meat, and dew for drink. I was led into these thoughts, my dear Reynolds, by the beauty of the morning operating on a sense of Idleness. I have not read any Books — the Morning said I was right — I had no idea but of the Morning, and the Thrush said I was right — seeming to say,

> O thou whose face hath felt the Winter's wind,
> Whose eye has seen the snow-clouds hung in Mist,
> And the black Elmtops 'mong the freezing stars:
> To thee the Spring will be a harvest-time —
> O thou, whose only book has been the light
> Of supreme darkness which thou feddest on
> Night after night, when Phœbus was away,
> To thee the Spring shall be a triple morn —
> O fret not after knowledge — I have none,
> And yet my song comes native with the warmth.
> O fret not after knowledge — I have none,
> And yet the Evening listens. He who saddens
> At thought of idleness cannot be idle,
> And he's awake who thinks himself asleep.

Ralph Waldo Emerson

American poet, essayist and Transcendentalist, he was born in Boston in 1803. Seven of his immediate ancestors were ministers of New England churches. His father was a Unitarian divine. In 1817 Emerson entered Harvard. After graduation he taught school. In 1825 he entered Harvard Divinity School and in 1826 was approved to preach. In 1829 he arrived at the conviction that the Lord's Supper was not a permanent sacrament, and resigned his pastoral office and lectured in Boston. He was influenced by Swedenborg, Wordsworth and Carlyle, and was a great personal friend of the latter. He died in 1882.

From THE JOURNAL

It is the largest part of a man that is not inventoried. He has many enumerable parts: he is social, professional, political, sectarian, literary, and is this or that set and corporation. But after the most exhausting census has been made, there remains as much more which no tongue can tell. And this remainder is that which interests. This is that which the strong genius works upon; the region of destiny, of aspiration, of the unknown. Ah, they have a secret persuasion that as little as they pass for in the world, they are immensely rich in expectancy and power. Nobody has ever yet dispossessed this adhesive self to arrive at any glimpse or guess of the awful life that lurks under it.

Far the best part, I repeat, of every mind is not that which he knows, but that which hovers in gleams, suggestions, tantalizing, unpossessed, before him. His firm recorded knowledge soon loses all interest for him. But this dancing chorus of thoughts and hopes is the quarry of his future, is his possibility, and teaches him that his man's life is of a ridiculous brevity and meanness, but that it is his first age and trial only of his young wings, but that vast revolutions, migrations, and gyres on gyres in the celestial societies invite him. [J, VII, 137-138]

A man is furnished with this superb case of instruments, the senses, and perceptive and executive faculties, and they betray him every day. He transfers his allegiance from Instinct and God to this adroit little committee. A man is an exaggerator. In every conversation see how the main end is still lost sight of by all but the best, and with slight apology or none, a digression made to a creaking door or a buzzing fly. What heavenly eloquence could hold the ear of an audience if a child cried! A man with a truth to express is caught by the beauty of his own words and ends with being a rhymester or critic. And Genius is sacrificed to talent every day. [J, VI, 121]

I can well hear a stranger converse on mysteries of love and romance of character; can easily become interested in his private love and fortunes; but as soon as I learn that he eats cucumbers, or hates parsnip, values his luncheon, and eats his dinner over again in his talk, I can never thenceforward hear that man talk of sentiment.

[J, VI, 527-528]

I finish this morning transcribing my old essay on Love, but I see well its inadequateness. I, cold because I am hot — cold at the surface only as a sort of guard and compensation for the fluid tenderness of the core — have much more experience than I have written there, more than I will, more than I can write. In silence we must wrap much of our life, because it is too fine for speech, because also we cannot explain it to others, and because somewhat we cannot yet understand. We do not live as angels, eager to introduce each other to new perfections in our brothers and sisters, and frankly avowing our delight in each new trait of character, in the magic of each new eyebeam, but that which passes for love in the world gets official, and instead of embracing, hates all the divine traits that dare to appear in other persons. A better and holier society will mend this selfish cowardice, and we shall have brave ties of affection, not petrified by law, not dated or ordained by law to last for one year, for five years, or for life; but drawing their date, like all friendship, from itself only. [J, V, 411-412]

Alfred, Lord Tennyson

English poet, and Poet Laureate after Wordsworth for over forty years, he was born in 1809. His early work (*Poems*, 1851) was chiefly lyrical. The death in 1833 of his dearest friend, Arthur Hallam, occasioned the writing during the next seventeen years of one hundred and eighty-one poems to his memory, published in 1850 as *In Memoriam*. He wrote the narrative poem *Enoch Arden*, historical dramas, and *The Idylls of the King*, first published in 1859 and appearing in several revised editions before its completion in 1885. Tennyson died in 1892.

From IN MEMORIAM
CIII

On that last night before we went
    From out the doors where I was bred,
    I dream'd a vision of the dead,
Which left my after-morn content.

Methought I dwelt within a hall,
    And maidens with me: distant hills
    From hidden summits fed with rills
A river sliding by the wall.

The hall with harp and carol rang.
    They sang of what is wise and good
    And graceful. In the centre stood
A statue veil'd, to which they sang;

And which, tho' veil'd, was known to me,
The shape of him I loved, and love
For ever: then flew in a dove
And brought a summons from the sea:

And when they learnt that I must go
They wept and wail'd, but led the way
To where a little shallop lay
At anchor in the flood below;

And on by many a level mead,
And shadowing bluff that made the banks,
We glided winding under ranks
Of iris, and the golden reed;

And still as vaster grew the shore
And roll'd the floods in grander space,
The maidens gather'd strength and grace
And presence, lordlier than before;

And I myself, who sat apart
And watch'd them, wax'd in every limb;
I felt the thews of Anakim,
The pulses of a Titan's heart;

As one would sing the death of war,
And one would chant the history
Of that great race, which is to be,
And one the shaping of a star;

Until the forward-creeping tides
Began to foam, and we to draw
From deep to deep, to where we saw
A great ship lift her shining sides.

The man we loved was there on deck,
    But thrice as large as man he bent
    To greet us. Up the side I went,
And fell in silence on his neck:

Whereat those maidens with one mind
    Bewail'd their lot; I did them wrong:
    "We served thee here," they said, "so long,
And wilt thou leave us now behind?"

So rapt I was, they could not win
    An answer from my lips, but he
    Replying, "Enter likewise ye
And go with us": they enter'd in.

And while the wind began to sweep
    A music out of sheet and shroud,
    We steer'd her toward a crimson cloud
That landlike slept along the deep.

CXXIV

That which we dare invoke to bless;
    Our dearest faith; our ghastliest doubt;
    He, They, One, All; within, without;
The Power in darkness whom we guess;

I found Him not in world or sun,
    Or eagle's wing, or insect's eye;
    Nor thro' the questions men may try,
The petty cobwebs we have spun:

If e'er when faith had fall'n asleep,
    I heard a voice "believe no more"
    And heard an ever-breaking shore
That tumbled in the Godless deep;

A warmth within the breast would melt
　　The freezing reason's colder part,
　　And like a man in wrath the heart
Stood up and answer'd "I have felt."

No, like a child in doubt and fear:
　　But that blind clamour made me wise;
　　Then was I as a child that cries,
But, crying, knows his father near;

And what I am beheld again
　　What is, and no man understands;
　　And out of darkness came the hands
That reach thro' nature, moulding men.

Sören Aabye Kierkegaard

The great Danish philosopher was born in Copenhagen in 1813 and in 1840 graduated from the University in his native town. He traveled in Germany, and began his literary career by publishing various philosophical works under a pseudonym. He became engaged, but later broke off the engagement. He denounced organized religion on the ground that faith was a personal affair between the individual soul and God. Among his best known and most influential works are *Either-Or* (1943), *Fear and Trembling* (1843) and *The Sickness unto Death* (1845). He died in 1855.

Epilogue

My God, my God, though I be clean forgot,
Let me not love Thee, if I love Thee not.

GEORGE HERBERT

PRAYER

Father in heaven! Hold not our sins up against us but hold us up against our sins, so that the thought of thee when it wakens in our soul, and each time it wakens, should not remind us of what we have committed but of what Thou didst forgive, not of how we went astray but of how Thou didst save us!

NEBUCHADNEZZAR

1. Recollections of my life, when I was a beast of the field and did eat grass; I, Nebuchadnezzar, unto all people, nations and languages.

2. Was not this Babylon, the great city, the greatest among the cities of all nations; and I, Nebuchadnezzar, had built it.

3. No city was like Babylon in renown, and no king like unto me in Babylon, the honour of my majesty.

4. My kingly house was renowned to the ends of the world, and my wisdom was like a mysterious language, which none among the wise could explain.

5. And none could tell me what it was that I had dreamed.

6. And the word came to me that I should be transformed and become as a beast which eats the grass of the fields, while seven times passed over me.

7. Then I called together all my princes and their hosts, and sent forth word that I must be prepared while seven times went over me.

8. But none dared approach Babylon the Great, and I said, Is not this great Babylon which I, Nebuchadnezzar have built.

9. Suddenly a cry was heard and I was changed, quickly, as a woman changes colour.

10. Grass became my food, the dew of heaven fell upon me, and no one knew who I was.

11. But I knew Babylon, and cried out, Is this not Babylon, and none heard my words, and none could understand aught but a cry like that of a beast.

12. My thoughts terrified me, the thoughts in my mind, for my mouth was closed, and none could hear aught but a cry like that of a beast.

13. And I thought, Who is this powerful one, the Lord, the Lord, who is like the darkness of the night and like the depths of the sea, unfathomable.

14. Yes, like a dream, which he alone can unravel, the interpretation of which he has not given into the power of any man, when it suddenly comes upon one and holds one with its powerful arms.

15. No one knows where this powerful one liveth, so that one could point and say: behold, there is his throne;

so that one could journey through the land until it was said: behold, here are the boundaries of his lordship.

16. For he does not dwell on the boundary of my kingdom, as my neighbour, neither does he surround me on all sides like the sea and the mountains.

17. And neither does he live in his temple, for I, Nebuchadnezzar have taken his golden and silver vessels, and laid waste his temple.

18. And no one knows anything of him, who was his father and how he received power, or who taught him the secret of his power.

19. And he has no counsellor, that one might buy his secret for gold, none to whom one can say, What shall I do? and none who say to him, What art thou doing?

20. He has no spies to watch for the opportunity, so that one might catch him, for he does not say, To-morrow; but says, To-day.

21. For he makes no preparations, like a man, and his preparations give the enemy no respite, for he says, Let this happen — and it happens.

22. He sits still and considers with himself; one does not know whether he is present before it has happened.

23. This has he done against me. He does not aim like the archer, so that one can fly from his arrow; he speaks with himself and it happens.

24. In his hands the King's brain is like wax in the melting furnace, and its weight like a feather's weight when he weighs it.

25. And yet he does not live upon the earth like the great and powerful, so that he could take Babylon from me and let me retain a little, or so that he could take everything from me and be the powerful one in Babylon.

26. Then did I think to myself in this loneliness of my mind where none knew me, and the thoughts in my mind terrified me, that there was the Lord.

27. But when the seven ages were run out I became Nebuchadnezzar once more.

28. And I called all the wise men together, that they might explain to me the mystery of that power, and how I had become like a beast of the fields.

29. But one and all, they fell down, upon their faces and said, Great is Nebuchadnezzar! It is imagination, a bad dream, who should be able to do such things against thee.

30. But my anger was upon the wise men in the whole land, and I let them be cut down in their folly.

31. For the Lord, the Lord alone has power, as no man hath it, and I will not envy him his might, but praise it and be near him; for I have taken his gold and silver vessels.

32. Babylon is no more great Babylon, I Nebuchadnezzar, no more Nebuchadnezzar, and my hosts no longer protect me; for none can see the Lord, and none can recognize him.

33. If he should come; and the watchmen would call in vain because I was already become like a bird in the trees, or a fish in the water, known only to other fish.

34. Therefore I will not be renowned in Babylon; but every seventh year there shall be a feast in the land.

35. A great feast for all the people, and it shall be called the Feast of the Transformation.

36. And an astronomer shall be led through the streets, and he shall be dressed as an animal, and he shall carry his calculations with him, torn to shreds like a bundle of hay.

37. And the people shall call out: The Lord, the Lord, the Lord is powerful, and his action is as swift as the leap of a great fish in the sea.

38. For soon my days are numbered, and my lordship past like a night watch, and I know not whither I go;

39. Whether I come to the invisible one in the distance, where the powerful one dwells, so that I must find grace in his eyes;

40. Whether it is he who takes the spirit of life from me, so that I become like a cast-off garment, like my predecessors; so that he should be pleased with me.

41. This have I, Nebuchadnezzar, made known to all people, nations and tongues; and great Babylon shall do my will.

PRAYER

O Thou who art unchangeable, Whom nothing changes! Thou art unchanged in love, precisely for our welfare not subject to any change: may we too will our welfare, submitting ourselves to the direction of Thy unchangeableness, so that we may, in unconditional obedience find our rest and remain at rest in Thy unchangeableness. Thou art not like a man; if he is to preserve only some degree of constancy he must not permit himself too much to be moved nor by too many things. Thou, on the contrary art moved and moved in infinite love, by all things, even that which we human beings call an insignificant trifle and pass by unmoved, the need of the sparrow, even this moves Thee; and what we so often scarcely notice, a human sigh, this moves Thee, o infinite Love! But nothing changes Thee, o Thou who are unchanging. O Thou who in infinite love dost submit to be moved, may this our prayer also move Thee to add Thy blessing, in order that there may be wrought such a change in him who prays as to bring him into conformity with Thy unchanging will, Thou who art unchangeable.

Henry David Thoreau

— • • —

Born in 1817, he became a noted American poet, essayist and naturalist, and scandalized Bostonian sentiment by his choice of a recluse's life near Walden Pond. *Civil Disobedience* appeared in 1849, and *Walden* in 1854. His massive *Journal* was published posthumously in fourteen volumes. A critic has spoken of Thoreau's "indulgence in fine renouncements," and in 1853 he described himself: "I was obliged to speak to their condition and to describe to them that poor part of me which alone they can understand. The fact is, I am a mystic, a transcendentalist and a natural philosopher to boot." He died of consumption in 1862.

From JOURNALS

My path hitherto has been like a road through a diversified country, now climbing high mountains, then descending into the lowest vales. From the summits I saw the heavens; from the vales I looked up to the heights again. In prosperity I remember God, or memory is one with consciousness; in adversity I remember my own elevations, and only hope to see God again.

It is vain to talk. What do you want? To bandy words, or deliver some grains of truth which stir within you? Will you make a pleasant rumbling sound after feasting, for digestion's sake, or such music as the birds in springtime?

The death of friends should inspire us as much as their lives. If they are great and rich enough, they will leave consolation to the mourners before the expenses of their funerals. It will not be hard to part with any worth, because it is worthy. How can any good depart? It does not go and come, but we. Shall we wait for it? Is it slower than we?

Feb. 21. I must confess there is nothing so strange to me as my own body. I love any other piece of nature, almost, better.

I was always conscious of sounds in nature which my ears could never hear, — that I caught but the prelude to a strain. She always retreats as I advance. Away behind and behind is she and her meaning. Will not this faith and expectation make to itself ears at length? I never saw to the end, nor heard to the end; but the best part was unseen and unheard.

I am like a feather floating in the atmosphere; on every side is depth unfathomable.

I feel as if years had been crowded into the last month, and yet the regularity of what we call time has been so far preserved as that I . . . will be welcome in the present. I have lived ill for the most part because too near myself. I have tripped myself up, so that there was no progress for my own narrowness. I cannot walk conveniently and pleasantly but when I hold myself far off in the horizon. And the soul dilutes the body and makes it passable. My soul and body have tottered along together of late, tripping and hindering one another like unpracticed Siamese twins. They two should walk as one, that no obstacle may be nearer than the firmament.

July 16. *Wednesday.* Methinks my present experience is nothing; my past experience is all in all. I think that no experience which I have to-day comes up to, or is comparable with, the experiences of my boyhood. And not only this is true, but as far back as I can remember I have unconsciously referred to the experiences of a previous state of existence. "For life is a forgetting," etc. Formerly, methought, nature developed as I developed, and grew up with me. My life was ecstasy. In youth, before I lost any of my senses, I can remember that I was all alive, and inhabited my body with inexpressible satisfaction; both its weariness and its refreshment were sweet to me. This earth was the most glorious musical instrument, and I was audience to its strains. To have such sweet impressions made on us, such ecstasies begotten of the breezes! I can remember how I was astonished. I said to myself, — I said to others, — "There comes into my mind such an indescribable, infinite, all-absorbing, divine, heavenly pleasure, a sense of elevation and expansion, and [I] have had nought to do with it. I perceive that I am dealt with by superior powers. This is a pleasure, a joy, an existence which I have not procured myself. I speak as a witness on the stand, and tell what I have perceived." The morning and the evening were sweet to me, and I led a life aloof from society of men. I wondered if a mortal had ever known what I knew. I looked in books for some recognition of a kindred experience, but, strange to say, I found none. Indeed, I was slow to discover that other men had had this experience, for it had been possible to read books and to associate with men on other grounds. The maker of me was improving me. When I detected this interference I was profoundly moved. For years I marched as to a music in comparison with which the military music of the streets is noise and discord. I was daily intoxicated, and yet no man could call me intemperate. With all your science can you tell how it is, and whence it is, that light comes into the soul? . . .

The water which so calmly reflects the fleeting clouds and the primeval trees I have never seen before. It may have washed some distant shore, or framed a glacier or iceberg at the north, when I last stood here. Seen through a mild atmosphere, the works of the husbandman, his plowing and reaping, have a beauty to the beholder which the laborer never sees.

I seem to see somewhat more of my own kith and kin in the lichens on the rocks than in any books. It does seem as if mine were a peculiarly wild nature, which so yearns toward all wildness. I know of no redeeming qualities in me but a sincere love for some things, and when I am reproved I have to fall back on to this ground. This is my argument in reserve for all cases. My love is invulnerable. Meet me on that ground, and you will find me strong. When I am condemned, and condemn myself utterly, I think straightway, "But I rely on my love for some things." Therein I am whole and entire. Therein I am God-propped.

What more glorious condition of being can we imagine than from impure to be becoming pure? It is almost desirable to be impure that we may be the subject of this improvement. That I am innocent to myself! That I love and reverence my life! That I am better fitted for a lofty society to-day than I was yesterday! To make my life a sacrament! What is nature without this lofty tumbling? May I treat myself with more and more respect and tenderness. May I not forget that I am impure and vicious. May I not cease to love purity. May I go to my slumbers as expecting to arise to a new and more perfect day. May I so live and refine my life as fitting myself for a society ever higher than I actually enjoy. May I treat myself tenderly as I would treat the most innocent child whom I love; may I treat children and my friends as my newly discovered self. Let me forever go in search of myself; never for a moment think that I have found myself; be as a stranger to myself, never a familiar, seeking acquaintance still. May I be to myself as one is to me whom I love, a dear and cherished object. What temple, what fane, what sacred place can there be but the innermost part of my own being? The possibility of my own improvement, that is to be cherished. As I regard myself, so I am. O my dear friends, I have not forgotten you. I will know you to-morrow. I associate you with my ideal self.

I had ceased to have faith in myself. I thought I was grown up and become what I was intended to be, but it is earliest spring with me. In relation to virtue and innocence the oldest man is in the beginning spring and vernal season of life. It is the love of virtue makes us young ever. That is the fountain of youth, the very aspiration after the perfect. I love and worship myself with a love which absorbs my love for the world.

Our ecstatic states, which appear to yield so little fruit, have this value at least: though in the seasons when our genius reigns we may be powerless for expression, yet, in calmer seasons, when our talent is active, the memory of those rarer moods comes to color our picture and is the permanent paint-pot, as it were, into which we dip our brush. Thus no life or experience goes unreported at last; but if it be not solid gold it is gold-leaf, which gilds the furniture of the mind. It is an experience of infinite beauty on which we unfailingly draw, which enables us to exaggerate ever truly. Our moments of inspiration are not lost though we have no particular poem to show for them; for those experiences have left an indelible impression, and we are ever and anon reminded of them. Their truth subsides, and in cooler moments we can use them as paint to gild and adorn our prose. When I despair to sing them, I will remember that they will furnish me with paint with which to adorn and preserve the works of talent one day. They are like a pot of pure ether. They lend the writer when the moment comes a certain superfluity of wealth, making his expression to overrun and float itself. It is the difference between our river, now parched and dried up, exposing its unsightly and weedy bottom, and the same when, in the spring, it covers all the meads with a chain of placid lakes, reflecting the forests and the skies.

We are receiving our portion of the infinite. The art of life! Was there ever anything memorable written upon it?

By what disciplines to secure the most life, with what care to watch our thoughts. To observe what transpires, not in the street, but in the mind and heart of me! I do not remember any page which will tell me how to spend this afternoon. I do not so much wish to know how to economize time as how to spend it, by what means to grow rich, that the day may not have been in vain.

What if one moon has come and gone with its world of poetry, its weird teachings, its oracular suggestions? So divine a creature, freighted with hints for me, and I not use her! One moon gone by unnoticed! ! Suppose you attend to the hints, to the suggestions, which the moon makes for one month, — commonly in vain, — will they not be very different from anything in literature or religion or philosophy?

The scenery, when it is truly seen, reacts on the life of the seer. How to live. How to get the most life. As if you were to teach the young hunter how to entrap his game. How to extract its honey from the flower of the world. That is my every-day business. I am as busy as a bee about it. I ramble over all fields on that errand, and am never so happy as when I feel myself heavy with honey and wax. I am like a bee searching the livelong day for the sweets of nature. Do I not impregnate and intermix the flowers, produce rare and finer varieties by transferring my eyes from one to another? I do as naturally and as joyfully, with my own humming music, seek honey all the day. With what honeyed thought any experience yields me I take a bee line to my cell. It is with flowers I would deal. Where is the flower, there is the honey, — which is perchance the nectareous portion of the fruit, — there is to be the fruit, and no doubt flowers are thus colored and painted to attract and guide the bee. So by the dawning or radiance of beauty are we advertised where is the honey and the fruit of thought, of discourse, and of action. We are first attracted by the beauty of the flower, before we discover the honey which is a foretaste of the future fruit. Did not the young Achilles (?) spend his youth learning how to hunt? The art of spending a day. If it is possible that we may be addressed, it behooves us to be attentive. If by watching all day and all night I may detect some trace of the Ineffable, then will it not be worth the while to watch? Watch and pray without ceasing, but not necessarily in sadness. Be of good cheer. Those Jews were too sad: to another people a still deeper revelation may suggest only joy. Don't I know what gladness is? Is it but the reflex of sadness, its back side? In the Hebrew gladness, I hear but too distinctly still the sound of sadness retreating. Give me a gladness which has never given place to sadness.

I am convinced that men are not well employed, that this is not the way to spend a day. If by patience, if by watching, I can secure one new ray of light, can feel myself elevated for an instant upon Pisgah, the world which was dead prose to me become living and divine, shall I not watch ever? shall I not be a watchman henceforth? If by watching a whole year on the city's walls I may obtain a communication from heaven, shall I not do well to shut up my shop and turn a watchman? Can a youth, a man, do more wisely than to go where his life is to [be] found? As if I had suffered that to be rumor which may be verified. We are surrounded by a rich and fertile mystery. May we not probe it, pry into it, employ ourselves about it, a little?

Emily Brontë

English novelist and poet, she was born in 1818, the daughter of a clergyman. She was the sister of Charlotte, Anne, and Branwell. She and her two sisters attended boarding school together and later became teachers for a time. All three were writers. Emily wrote poems under the name of Ellis Bell. Her most famous work is *Wuthering Heights*, her only novel, which reflects the unhappiness of her life. "No Coward Soul Is Mine" was her last poem, written shortly before her death in 1848.

THE PRISONER

Still let my tyrants know, I am not doom'd to wear
Year after year in gloom and desolate despair;
A messenger of Hope comes every night to me,
And offers for short life, eternal liberty.

He comes with Western winds, with evening's wandering
    airs,
With that clear dusk of heaven that brings the thickest stars:
Winds take a pensive tone, and stars a tender fire,
And visions rise, and change, that kill me with desire.

Desire for nothing known in my maturer years,
When Joy grew mad with awe, at counting future tears:
When, if my spirit's sky was full of flashes warm,
I knew not whence they came, from sun or thunder-storm.

But first, a hush of peace — a soundless calm descends;
The struggle of distress and fierce impatience ends.

Mute music soothes my breast — unutter'd harmony
That I could never dream, till Earth was lost to me.

Then dawns the Invisible; the Unseen its truth reveals;
My outward sense is gone, my inward essence feels;
Its wings are almost free — its home, its harbour found,
Measuring the gulf, it stoops, and dares the final bound.

O dreadful is the check — intense the agony —
When the ear begins to hear, and the eye begins to see;
When the pulse begins to throb — the brain to think again —
The soul to feel the flesh, and the flesh to feel the chain.

Yet I would lose no sting, would wish no torture less;
The more that anguish racks, the earlier it will bless;
And robed in fires of hell, or bright with heavenly shine,
If it but herald Death, the vision is divine.

NO COWARD SOUL IS MINE

No coward soul is mine
No trembler in the world's storm-troubled sphere:
I see Heaven's glories shine,
And Faith shines equal arming me from Fear.

O God within my breast,
Almighty ever-present Deity!
Life, that in me hast rest,
As I Undying Life, have power in Thee!

Vain are the thousand creeds
That move men's hearts, unutterably vain,
Worthless as withered weeds,
Or idlest froth amid the boundless main,

To waken doubt in one
Holding so fast by thy infinity,
So surely anchored on
The steadfast rock of Immortality.

With wide-embracing love
Thy spirit animates eternal years,
Pervades and broods above,
Changes, sustains, dissolves, creates and rears.

Though Earth and moon were gone,
And suns and universes ceased to be,
And thou wert left alone,
Every Existence would exist in thee.

There is not room for Death
Nor atom that his might could render void:
Since thou art Being and Breath,
And what thou art may never be destroyed.

Walt Whitman

Born in 1819, he worked at a variety of jobs, finally becoming editor of the Brooklyn *Eagle* from 1846 to 1848. He held other journalistic positions and served in several government posts. *Leaves of Grass*, his most famous book of verse, was published in 1855. *Specimen Days* (1882) is his spontaneous prose celebrations and recollections. He died in 1892.

From SPECIMEN DAYS

Hours for the Soul

July 22d, 1878 — Living down in the country again. A wonderful conjunction of all that goes to make those sometime miracle hours after sunset — so near and yet so far. Perfect, or nearly perfect days, I notice, are not so very uncommon; but the combinations that make perfect nights are few, even in a lifetime. We have one of those perfections tonight. Sunset left things pretty clear; the larger stars were visible soon as the shades allowed. A while after 8, three or four great black clouds suddenly rose, seemingly from different points, and sweeping with broad swirls of wind but no thunder, underspread the orbs from view everywhere, and indicated a violent heat storm. But without storm, clouds, blackness, and all, sped and vanished as suddenly as they had risen; and from a little after 9 till 11 the atmosphere and the whole show above were in that state of exceptional clearness and glory just alluded to. In the northwest turned the Great Dipper with its pointers round the Cynosure. A little south of east the constellation of the scorpion was fully up, with red Antares glowing in its neck; while dominating, majestic Jupiter swam, an hour and a half risen, in the east (no moon till after 11). A large part of the sky seemed just laid in great splashes of phosphorus. You could look deeper in, farther through, than usual; the orbs thick as heads of wheat in a field. Not that there was any special brilliancy either — nothing near as sharp as I have seen of keen winter nights, but a curious general luminousness throughout to sight, sense, and soul. The latter had much to do with it. (I am convinced there are hours of Nature, especially of the atmosphere, mornings and evenings, addressed to the soul. Night transcends, for that purpose, what the proudest day can do.) Now, indeed, if never before, the heavens declared the glory of God. It was to the full the sky of the Bible, of Arabia, of the prophets, and of the oldest poems. There, in abstraction and stillness (I had gone off by myself to absorb the scene, to have the spell unbroken), the copiousness, the removedness, vitality, loose-clear-crowdedness, of that stellar concave spreading overhead, softly absorbed into me, rising so free, interminably high, stretching east, west, north, south — and I, though but a point in the center below, embodying all.

As if for the first time, indeed, creation noiselessly sank into and through me its placid and untellable lesson, beyond — O, so infinitely beyond! — anything from art, books, sermons, or from science, old or new. The spirit's hour — religion's hour — the visible suggestion of God in space and time — now once definitely indicated, if never told again. The untold pointed at — the heavens all paved with it. The Milky Way, as if some superhuman symphony, some ode of universal vagueness, disdaining syllable and sound — a flashing glance of Diety, addressed to the soul. All silently — the indescribable night and stars — far off and silently.

THE DAWN — *July 23* — This morning, between one and two hours before sunrise, a spectacle wrought on the same background, yet of quite different beauty and meaning. The moon well up in the heavens, and past her half, is shining brightly — the air and sky of that cynical-clear, Minerva-like quality, virgin cool — not the weight of sentiment or mystery, or passion's ecstasy indefinable — not the religious sense, the varied All, distilled and sublimated into one, of the night just described. Every star now clear-cut, showing for just what it is, there in the colorless ether.

From SONG OF MYSELF

I believe a leaf of grass is no less than the journey-work of
    the stars,
And the pismire is equally perfect, and a grain of sand, and
    the egg of the wren.
And the tree-toad is a chef-d'œuvre for the highest,
And the running blackberry would adorn the parlours of
    heaven,
And the narrowest hinge in my hands puts to scorn all
    machinery,
And the cow crunching with depress'd head surpasses any
    statue,
And a mouse is miracle enough to stagger sextillions of
    infidels.

I think I could turn and live with animals, they are so placid
    and self-contain'd.
I stand and look at them long and long.
They do not sweat and whine about their condition,
They do not lie awake in the dark and weep for their sins,
They do not make me sick discussing their duty to God,

Not one is dissatisfied, not one is demented with the mania
   of owning things,
Not one kneels to another, nor to his kind that lived
   thousands of years ago,
Not one is respectable or unhappy over the whole earth.

My faith is the greatest of faiths and the least of faiths,
Enclosing worship ancient and modern and all between
   ancient and modern.
Believing I shall come again upon the earth after five
   thousand years,
Waiting responses from oracles, honouring the gods, saluting
   the sun,
Making a fetish of the first rock or stump, powowing with
   sticks in the circle of obis,
Helping the Lama or Brahmin as he trims the lamps of the
   idols . . .
Accepting the Gospels, accepting him that was crucified,
   knowing assuredly that he is divine,
To the mass kneeling or the puritan's prayer rising, or sitting
   patiently in a pew,
I know every one of you, I know the sea of torment, doubt,
   despair and unbelief.

Henri Frederic Amiel

He was a Swiss philosopher and critic, born in Geneva in 1821. He became Professor of Aesthetics at the Academy of Geneva in 1849 and in 1854 become Professor of Moral Philosophy there. These appointments were conferred by the democratic party, which deprived him of the support of the aristocratic party which comprised nearly all the culture of the city. This isolation inspired the one book by which Amiel lives, the *Intimate Journal*. It attracted many readers, partly because it interpreted many lonely souls to themselves. He died in Geneva 11 May 1881.

From INTIMATE JOURNAL

Afternoon — Shall I ever enjoy again those marvelous reveries of past days, as, for instance, once, when I was still quite a youth, in the early dawn, sitting among the ruins of the castle of Faucigny; another time in the mountains above Lavey, under the midday sun, lying under a tree and visited by three butterflies; and again another night on the sandy shore of the North Sea, stretched full length upon the beach, my eyes wandering over the Milky Way? Will they ever return to me, those grandiose, immortal, cosmogonic dreams, in which one seems to carry the world in one's breast, to touch the stars, to possess the infinite? Divine moments, hours of ecstasy, when thought flies from world to world, penetrates the great enigma, breathes with a respiration large, tranquil, and profound, like that of the ocean, and hovers serene and boundless like the blue heaven! Visits from the muse, Urania, who traces around the foreheads of those she loves the phosphorescent nimbus of contemplative power, and who pours into their hearts the tranquil intoxication, if not the authority of genius, moments of irresistible intuition in which a man feels himself great like the universe and calm like a god! From the celestial spheres down to the shell or the moss, the whole of creation is then submitted to our gaze, lives in our breast, and accomplishes in us its eternal work with the regularity of destiny and the passionate ardor of love. What hours, what memories! The traces which remain to us of them are enough to fill us with respect and enthusiasm, as though they had been visits of the Holy Spirit. And then, to fall back again from these heights with their boundless horizons into the muddy ruts of triviality! what a fall! Poor Moses! Thou too sawest undulating in the distance the ravishing hills of the promised land, and it was thy fate nevertheless to lay thy weary bones in a grave dug in the desert! Which of us has not his promised land, his day of ecstasy and his death in exile? What a pale counterfeit is real life of the life we see in glimpses, and how these flaming lightnings of our prophetic youth make the twilight of our dull monotonous manhood more dark and dreary!

October 27, 1853. — I thank Thee, my God, for the hour that I have just passed in Thy presence. Thy will was clear to me; I measured my faults, counted my griefs, and felt Thy goodness toward me. I realized my own nothingness, Thou gavest me Thy peace. In bitterness there is sweetness; in affliction, joy; in submission, strength; in the God who punishes, the God who loves. To lose one's life that one may gain it, to offer it that one may receive it, to possess nothing that one may conquer all, to renounce self that God may give Himself to us, how impossible a problem, and how sublime a reality! No one truly knows happiness who has not suffered, and the redeemed are happier than the elect.

(Same day.) — The divine miracle *par excellence* consists surely in the apotheosis of grief, the transfiguration of
evil by good. The work of creation finds its consummation,
and the eternal will of the infinite mercy finds its fulfillment only in the restoration of the free creature to God
and of an evil world to goodness, through love. Every soul
in which conversion has taken place is a symbol of the
history of the world. To be happy, to possess eternal life,
to be in God, to be saved, all these are the same. All alike
mean the solution of the problem, the aim of existence.
And happiness is cumulative, as misery may be. An eternal
growth is an unchangeable peace, an ever profounder depth
of apprehension, a possession constantly more intense and
more spiritual of the joy of heaven — this is happiness.
Happiness has no limits, because God has neither bottom
nor bounds, and because happiness is nothing but the conquest of God through love.

The center of life is neither in thought nor in feeling, nor
in will, nor even in consciousness, so far as it thinks, feels,
or wishes. For moral truth may have been penetrated and
possessed in all these ways, and escape us still. Deeper even
than consciousness there is our being itself, our very substance, our nature. Only those truths which have entered
into this last region, which have become ourselves, become
spontaneous and involuntary, instinctive and unconscious,
are really our life — that is to say something more than our
property. So long as we are able to distinguish any space
whatever between the truth and us we remain outside it.
The thought, the feeling, the desire, the consciousness of
life, are not yet quite life. But peace and repose can nowhere be found except in life, and in eternal life and the
eternal life is the divine life, is God. To become divine is
then the aim of life: then only can truth be said to be ours
beyond the possibility of loss, because it is no longer outside us, nor even in us, but we are it, and it is we; we our-

selves are a truth, a will, a work of God. Liberty has become nature; the creature is one with its creator — one through love. It is what it ought to be; its education is finished, and its final happiness begins. The sun of time declines and the light of eternal blessedness arises.

Our fleshly hearts may call this mysticism. It is the mysticism of Jesus: "I am one with my Father; ye shall be one with me. We will be one with you."

April 21, 1865. (*Mornex*). — A morning of intoxicating beauty, fresh as the feelings of sixteen, and crowned with flowers like a bride. The poetry of youth, of innocence, and of love, overflowed my soul. Even to the light mist hovering over the bosom of the plain — image of that tender modesty which veils the features and shrouds in mystery the inmost thoughts of the maiden — everything that I saw delighted my eyes and spoke to my imagination. It was a sacred, a nuptial day! and the matin bells ringing in some distant village harmonized marvelously with the hymn of nature. "Pray," they said, "and love! Adore a fatherly and beneficent God." They recalled to me the accent of Haydn; there was in them and in the landscape a childlike joyousness, a naïve gratitude, a radiant heavenly joy innocent of pain and sin, like the sacred, simplehearted ravishment of Eve on the first day of her awakening in the new world. How good a thing is feeling, admiration! It is the bread of angels, the eternal food of cherubim and seraphim.

George Macdonald

He was born in 1824 at Huntley, in Aberdeenshire, and ordained a minister in the Congregational Church but resigned to devote himself to literature. He was a prolific author, writing both in prose and verse, for children and adults. Among his friends were Matthew Arnold, Carlyle, Emerson, Ruskin, and Tennyson. His most famous book is *At the Back of the North Wind*. He died in 1905.

From LILITH

43: *The Dreams that Came*

I grew aware of existence, aware also of the profound, the infinite cold. I was intensely blessed — more blessed, I know, than my heart, imagining, can now recall. I could not think of warmth with the least suggestion of pleasure. I knew that I had enjoyed it, but could not remember how. The cold had soothed every care, dissolved every pain, comforted every sorrow. *Comforted?* Nay; sorrow was swallowed up in the life drawing nigh to restore every good and lovely thing a hundredfold. I lay at peace, full of the quietest expectation, breathing the damp odors of Earth's bountiful bosom, aware of the souls of primroses, daisies and snowdrops, patiently waiting in it for the Spring.

How convey the delight of that frozen, yet conscious sleep! I had no more to stand up, had only to lie stretched out and still. How cold I was, words cannot tell; yet I grew colder and colder — and welcomed the cold yet more and more. I grew continuously less conscious of myself, continuously more conscious of bliss, unimaginable yet felt. I had neither made it nor prayed for it: it was mine in virtue of existence and existence was mine in virtue of a Will that dwelt in mine.

Then the dreams began to arrive — and came crowding. — I lay naked on a snowy peak. The white mist heaved below me like a billowy sea. The cold moon was in the air with me, and above the moon and me the colder sky, in which the moon and I dwelt. I was Adam, waiting for God to breathe into my nostrils the breath of life. — I was not Adam, but a child in the bosom of a mother white with a radiant whiteness. I was a youth on a white horse, leaping from cloud to cloud of a blue heaven, hasting calmly to some blessed goal. For centuries I dreamed — or was it chiliads? or only one long night? — But why ask? for time had nothing to do with me; I was in the land of thought — farther in, higher up than the seven dimensions, the ten senses: I think I was where I am — in the heart of God. — I dreamed away dim cycles in the center of a melting glacier, the spectral moon drawing nearer and nearer, the wind and the welter of a torrent growing in my ears. I lay and heard them: the wind and the water and the moon sang a peaceful waiting for a redemption drawing nigh. I dreamed cycles, I say, but, for aught I knew or can tell, they were the solemn, aeonian march of a second, pregnant with eternity.

Then, of a sudden, but not once troubling my conscious bliss, all the wrongs I had ever done, from far beyond my earthly memory down to the present moment, were with me. Fully in every wrong lived the conscious I, confessing, abjuring, lamenting the deed, making atonement with each person I had injured, hurt, or offended. Every human soul to which I had caused a troubled thought, was now grown unspeakably dear to me, and I humbled myself before it, agonizing to cast from between us the clinging offense. I wept at the feet of the mother whose commands I had slighted; with bitter shame I confessed to my father that I had told him two lies, and long forgotten them: now for long had remembered them, and kept them in memory to crush at last at his feet. I was the eager slave of all whom I had thus or anyhow wronged. Countless services I devised to render them: for this one I would build such a house as had never grown from the ground, for that one I would train such horses as had never yet been seen in any world, for a third I would make such a garden as had never bloomed, haunted with still pools, and alive with running waters. I would write songs to make their hearts swell, and tales to make them glow; I would turn the forces of the world into such channels of invention as to make them laugh with the joy of wonder. Love possessed me: love was my life: love was to me, as to Him that made me, all in all.

45: The Journey Home

It had ceased to be dark; we walked in a dim twilight, breathing through the dimness the breath of the spring. A wondrous change had passed upon the world — or was it not rather that a change more marvelous had taken place in us? Without light enough in the sky or the air to reveal anything, every heather-bush, every small shrub, every blade of grass was perfectly visible, either by light that went out from it, as fire from the bush Moses saw in the desert, or by light that went out of our eyes. Nothing cast a shadow; all things interchanged a little light. Every growing thing showed me, by its shape and color, its indwelling idea — the informing thought, that is, which was its being, and sent it out. My bare feet seemed to love every plant they trod upon. The world and my being, its life and mine, were one. The microcosm and macrocosm were at length atoned, at length in harmony. I lived in everything; everything entered and lived in me. To be aware of a thing, was to know its life at once and mine, to know whence we came, and where we were at home — was to know that we are all what we are, because Another is what he is. Sense after sense, hitherto asleep, awoke in me — sense after sense indescribable, because no correspondent words, no likenesses or imaginations exist, wherewithal to describe them. Full indeed — yet ever expanding, ever making room to receive — was the conscious being where things kept entering by so many open doors. When a little breeze brushing a bush of heather set its purple bells a-ringing, I was myself in the joy of the bells, myself in the joy of the breeze to which responded their sweet *tin-tinning*,* myself in the joy of the sense, and of the soul that received all the joys together. To everything glad I lent the hall of my being wherein to revel. I was a peaceful ocean upon which the ground swell of a living joy was continually lifting new waves; yet was the joy ever the same joy, the eternal joy, with tens of thousands of changing forms. Life was a cosmic holiday.

Now I knew that life and truth were one; that life mere and pure is in itself bliss; that where being is not bliss, it is not life, but life-in-death. Every inspiration of the dark wind that blew where it listed, went out a sigh of thanksgiving. At last I was. I lived, and nothing could touch my life. My darling walked beside me, and we were on our way home to the Father.

So much was ours ere ever the first sun rose upon our freedom: what must not the eternal day bring with it.

We came to the fearful hollow where once had wallowed the monsters of the earth: it was indeed, as I had beheld it in my dream, a lovely lake. I gazed into its pellucid depths. A whirlpool had swept out the soil in which the abortions burrowed, and at the bottom lay visible the whole horrid

---

* Tin tin sonando con sì dolce nota
Che 'l ben disposto spirito d' amor turge.
Del Paradiso, x., 142.

brood: a dim greenish light pervaded the crystalline water, and revealed every hideous form beneath it. Coiled in spires, folded in layers, knotted on themselves, or "extended long and large," they weltered in motionless heaps — shapes more fantastic in ghoulish, blasting dismay, than ever wine-sodden brain of exhausted poet fevered into misbeing. He who dived in the swirling Maelstrom saw none to compare with them in horror: tentacular convolutions, tumid bulges, glaring orbs of sepia deformity, would have looked to him innocence beside such incarnations of hatefulness — every head the wicked flower that, bursting from an abominable stalk, perfected its evil significance.

Not one of them moved as we passed. But they were not dead. So long as exist men and women of unwholesome mind, that lake will still be peopled with loathsomenesses.

But hark the herald of the sun, the auroral wind, softly trumpeting his approach. The master-minister of the human tabernacle is at hand, heaping before his prow a huge ripple-fretted wave of crimson and gold, he rushes aloft, as if new launched from the urging hand of his maker into the upper sea — pauses, and looks down on the world. White-raving storm of molten metals, he is but a coal from the altar of the Father's never-ending sacrifice to his children. See every little flower straighten its stalk, lift up its neck, and with outstretched head stand expectant: something more than the sun, greater than the light, is coming, is coming — none the less surely coming that it is long upon the road! What matters to-day, or to-morrow, or ten thousand years to Life himself, to Love himself! He is coming, is coming, and the necks of all humanity are stretched out to see him come! Every morning will they thus outstretch themselves, every evening will they droop and wait — until he comes. — Is this but an air-drawn vision? When he comes, will he indeed find them watching thus?

It was a glorious resurrection-morning. The night had been spent in preparing it.

The children went gamboling before, and the beasts came after us. Fluttering butterflies, darting dragon-flies hovered or shot hither and thither about our heads, a cloud of colors and flashes, now descending upon us like a snow-storm of rainbow flakes, now rising into the humid air like a rolling vapor of embodied odors. It was a summer-day more like itself, that is, more ideal, than ever man that had not died found summer-day in any world. I walked on the new earth, under the new heaven, and found them the same as the old, save that now they opened their minds to me, and I saw into them. Now, the soul of everything I met came out to greet me and make friends with me, telling me we came from the same, and meant the same. I was going to him, they said, with whom they always were, and whom they always meant; they were, they said, lightnings that took shape as they flashed from him to his. The dark rocks drank like sponges the rays that showered upon them; the great world soaked up the light, and sent out the living. Earth breathed heavenward her sweet-savored smoke; we breathed homeward our longing desires. For thanksgiving, our very consciousness was that.

Emily Dickinson

This American poet was born in 1830 and lived as a recluse and spinster in Amherst, Massachusetts, completely dominated by her strict Congressman father. She began writing in 1861, but only two poems were published during her lifetime. Six volumes of poetry have appeared since her death in 1886, bringing her recognition as one of America's most original poets.

From POEMS

Going to heaven!
I don't know when,
Pray do not ask me how, —
Indeed, I'm too astonished
To think of answering you!
Going to heaven! —
How dim it sounds!
And yet it will be done
As sure as flocks go home at night
Unto the shepherd's arm!

Perhaps you're going too!
Who knows?
If you should get there first,
Save just a little place for me
Close to the two I lost!
The smallest "robe" will fit me,
And just a bit of "crown";

For you know we do not mind our dress
When we are going home.

I'm glad I don't believe it,
For it would stop my breath,
And I'd like to look a little more
At such a curious earth!
I am glad they did believe it
Whom I have never found
Since the mighty autumn afternoon
I left them in the ground.

Water is taught by thirst;
Land, by the oceans passed;
 Transport, by throe;
Peace, by its battles told;
Love, by memorial mould;
 Birds, by the snow.

Though I get home how late, how late!
So I get home, 'twill compensate.
Better will be the ecstasy
That they have done expecting me,
When, night descending, dumb and dark,
They hear my unexpected knock.
Transporting must the moment be,
Brewed from decades of agony!

To think just how the fire will burn,
Just how long-cheated eyes will turn

To wonder what myself will say,
And what itself will say to me,
Beguiles the centuries of way!

I shall know why, when time is over,
And I have ceased to wonder why;
Christ will explain each separate anguish
In the fair schoolroom of the sky.

He will tell me what Peter promised,
And I, for wonder at his woe,
I shall forget the drop of anguish
That scalds me now, that scalds me now.

I felt a funeral in my brain,
   And mourners, to and fro,
Kept treading, treading, till it seemed
   That sense was breaking through.

And when they all were seated,
   A service like a drum
Kept beating, beating, till I thought
   My mind was going numb.

And then I heard them lift a box,
   And creak across my soul
With those same boots of lead, again.
   Then space began to toll

As all the heavens were a bell,
    And Being but an ear,
And I and silence some strange race,
    Wrecked, solitary, here.

From LETTERS OF EMILY DICKINSON

To Miss Maria Whitney

1879

DEAR FRIEND, — Your touching suggestion . . . is a
tender permission. . . .

We cannot believe for each other — thought is too sacred a despot, but I hope that God, in whatever form, is
true to our friend. . . . Consciousness is the only home of
which we *now* know. That sunny adverb had been enough,
were it not foreclosed.

When not inconvenient to your heart, please remember
us, and let us help you carry it, if you grow tired. Though
we are each unknown to ourself and each other, 'tis not
what well conferred it, the dying soldier asks, it is only the
water.

> We knew not that we were to live,
> Nor when we are to die
> Our ignorance our cuirass is;
> We wear mortality
> As lightly as an option gown
> Till asked to take it off.
> By His intrusion God is known —
> It is the same with life.

EMILY

To Mrs. Helen Hunt Jackson

March, 1885

DEAR FRIEND, — To reproach my own foot in behalf of
yours is involuntary, and finding meager solace in "whom

He loveth He chasteneth," your valor astounds me. It was only a small wasp, said the French physician repairing the sting, but the strength to perish is sometimes withheld — though who but you can tell a foot.

> Take all away from me
> But leave me ecstasy,
> And I am richer then
> Than all my fellow-men.
> Is it becoming me
> To dwell so wealthily,
> When at my very door
> Are those possessing more,
> In abject poverty?

That you glance at Japan as you breakfast, not in the least surprises me, thronged only with music, like the decks of birds.

Thank you for hoping I am well. Who could be ill in March, that month of proclamation? Sleighbells and jays contend in my matinée, and the north surrenders instead of the south, a reverse of bugles.

Pity me, however, I have finished *Ramona*. Would that like Shakespeare it were just published!

Knew I how to pray, to intercede for your foot were intuitive, but I am but a pagan.

Oh God we ask one favor, that we may be forgiven. For what, He is presumed to know. The crime, from us, is hidden.

> Immured the whole of life
> Within a magic prison,
> We reprimand the happiness
> That too competes with Heaven.

May I once more know, and that you are saved?

Yours,

E. DICKINSON

Hannah Whitall Smith

She was born on February 7, 1832, the first child of John Mickle Whitall and Mary Tatum. Hannah, her brother James and her three sisters were all brought up strict Quakers. She married Robert Pearsall Smith in June 1851. He joined her in her preaching, and they went to England, where they conducted religious services. She wrote *The Christian's Secret of a Happy Life* and *The Unselfishness of God and How I Discovered It*. She died in 1911.

From THE CHRISTIAN'S SECRET OF
A HAPPY LIFE

I feel sure that to each one of you have come some divine intimations or forshadowings of the life I here describe. Have you not begun to feel dimly conscious of the voice of God speaking to you, in the depths of your soul, about these things? Has it not been a pain and a distress to you of late to discover how full your lives are of self? Has not your soul been plunged into inward trouble and doubt about certain dispositions or pursuits in which you have been formerly accustomed to indulge? Have you not begun to feel uneasy with some of your habits of life, and to wish that you could do differently in certain respects? Have not paths of devotedness and of service begun to open out before you, with the longing thought, "Oh that I could walk in them!" All these questions and doubts and this inward yearning are the voice of the Good Shepherd in your heart, seeking to call you out of that which is contrary to His will. Let me entreat of you not to turn away from His gentle pleadings! You little know the sweet paths into which He means to lead you by these very steps, nor the wonderful stores of blessedness that lie at their end, or you would spring forward with an eager joy to yield to every one of His requirements. The heights of Christian perfection can only be reached by each moment faithfully following the Guide who is to lead you there; and He reveals the way to us one step at a time, in the little things of our daily lives, asking only on our part that we yield ourselves up to His guidance. Be perfectly pliable then in His dear hands, to go where He entices you, and to turn away from all from which He makes you shrink. Obey Him perfectly the moment you are sure of His will; and you will soon find that He is leading you out swiftly and easily into such a wonderful life of conformity to Himself that it will be a testimony to all around you, beyond what you yourself will ever know.

I knew a soul thus given up to follow the Lord whithersoever He might lead her, who in a very little while traveled from the depths of darkness and despair, into the realization and actual experience of a most blessed union with the Lord Jesus Christ. Out of the midst of her darkness she consecrated herself to the Lord, surrendering her will up altogether to Him, that He might work in her to will and to do of His own good pleasure. Immediately He began to speak to her by His Spirit in her heart, suggesting to her some little acts of service for Him, and troubling her about certain things in her habits and her life, showing her where she was selfish and un-Christlike, and how she could be transformed. She recognized His voice, and yielded to Him each thing He asked for the moment she was sure of His will. Her swift obedience was rewarded by a rapid progress, and day by day she was conformed more and more to the image of Christ, until very soon her life became such a testimony to those around her that some even who had begun by opposing and disbelieving were forced to acknowledge that it was of God, and were won to a similar surrender. And, finally, in a little while it came to pass, so swiftly had she gone, that her Lord was able to reveal to her wondering soul some of the deepest secrets of His love, and to fulfil to her the marvelous promise of Acts 1: 5 by giving her to realize the baptism of the Holy Ghost. Think you she has ever regretted her whole-hearted following of Him? Or that aught but thankfulness and joy can ever fill her soul when she reviews the steps by which her feet have been led to this place of wondrous blessedness, even though some of them may have seemed at the time hard to take? Ah, dear soul, if thou wouldst know a like blessing abandon thyself, like her, to the guidance of thy divine Master, and shrink from no surrender for which He may call.

W. H. Hudson

Novelist and naturalist, was born in 1841 in Argentina of American parentage, but became a British subject. He wrote numerous
essays for the London Society for the Protection of Birds. His books
include *Green Mansions* (1904), *Adventures Among Birds* (1913),
the autobiographical *Far Away and Long Ago* (1918). He died in
1922.

From FAR AWAY AND LONG AGO

About noon that day old Caesar, dead and stiff, was
taken by one of the workmen to a green open spot among
the old peach trees, where his grave had already been dug.
We followed our schoolmaster and watched while the body
was lowered and the red earth shovelled in. The grave was
deep, and Mr. Trigg assisted in filling it, puffing very much
over the task and stopping at intervals to mop his face
with his coloured cotton handkerchief.

Then, when all was done, while we were still standing
silently around, it came into Mr. Trigg's mind to improve
the occasion. Assuming his schoolroom expression he
looked round at us and said solemnly: "That's the end.
Every dog has his day and so has every man; and the end
is the same for both. We die like old Caesar, and are put
into the ground and have the earth shovelled over us."

Now these simple, common words affected me more
than any other words I have heard in my life. They pierced
me to the heart. I had heard something terrible — too
terrible to think of, incredible — and yet — and yet if it
was not so, why had he said it? Was it because he hated us,

just because we were children and he had to teach us our lessons, and wanted to torture us? Alas! no, I could not believe that! Was this, then, the horrible fate that awaited us all? I had heard of death — I knew there was such a thing; I knew that all animals had to die, also that some men died. For how could any one, even a child in its sixth year, overlook such a fact, especially in the country of my birth — a land of battle, murder, and sudden death? I had not forgotten the young man tied to the post in the barn who had killed some one, and would perhaps, I had been told, be killed himself as a punishment. I knew, in fact, that there was good and evil in the world, good and bad men, and the bad men — murderers, thieves, and liars — would all have to die, just like animals; but that there was any life after death I did not know. All the others, myself and my own people included, were good and would never taste death. How it came about that I had got no further in my system or philosophy of life I cannot say; I can only suppose that my mother had not yet begun to give me instruction in such matters on account of my tender years, or else that she had done so and that I had understood it in my own way. Yet, as I discovered later, she was a religious woman, and from infancy I had been taught to kneel and say a little prayer each evening: "Now I lay me down to sleep, I pray the Lord my soul to keep"; but who the Lord was or what my soul was I had no idea. It was just a pretty little way of saying in rhyme that I was going to bed. My world was a purely material one, and a most wonderful world it was, but how I came to be in it I didn't know; I only knew (or imagined) that I would be in it always, seeing new and strange things every day, and never, never get tired of it. In literature it is only in Vaughan, Traherne, and other mystics, that I find any adequate expression of that perpetual rapturous delight in nature and my own existence which I experienced at that period.

And now these never-to-be-forgotten words spoken over
the grave of our old dog had come to awaken me from that
beautiful dream of perpetual joy!

When I recall this event I am less astonished at my ignorance than at the intensity of the feeling I experienced,
the terrible darkness it brought on so young a mind. The
child's mind we think, and in fact know, is like that of the
lower animals; or if higher than the animal mind, it is not
so high as that of the simplest savage. He cannot concen-
trate his thought — he cannot think at all; his consciousness is in its dawn; he revels in colours, in odours, is thrilled
by touch and taste and sound, and is like a well-nourished
pup or kitten at play on a green turf in the sunshine. This
being so, one would have thought that the pain of the revelation I had received would have quickly vanished — that
the vivid impressions of external things would have blotted
it out and restored the harmony. But it was not so; the
pain continued and increased until it was no longer to be
borne; then I sought my mother, first watching until she
was alone in her room. Yet when with her I feared to speak
lest with a word she should confirm the dreadful tidings.
Looking down, she all at once became alarmed at the sight
of my face, and began to question me. Then, struggling
against my tears, I told her of the words which had been
spoken at the old dog's burial, and asked her if it was true,
if I — if she — if all of us had to die and be buried in the
ground? She replied that it was not wholly true; it was only
true in a way, since our bodies had to die and be buried in
the earth, but we had an immortal part which could not
die. It was true that old Caesar had been a good, faithful
dog, and felt and understood things almost like a human
being, and most persons believed that when a dog died he
died wholly and had no after-life. We could not know that;
some very great, good men had thought differently; they
believed that the animals, like us, would live again. That

was also her belief — her strong hope; but we could not know for certain, because it had been hidden from us. For ourselves, we knew that we could not really die, because God Himself, who made us and all things, had told us so, and His promise of eternal life had been handed down to us in His Book — in the Bible.

To all this and much more I listened trembling, with a fearful interest, and when I had once grasped the idea that death when it came to me, as it must, would leave me alive after all — that, as she explained, the part of me that really mattered, the myself, the I am I, which knew and considered things, would never perish, I experienced a sudden immense relief. When I went out from her side again I wanted to run and jump for joy.

William James

American psychologist and philosopher, he was the brother of the
novelist Henry James. Born in 1842, he died in 1910.

From THE WILL TO BELIEVE

I confess that I do not see why the very existence of an
invisible world may not in part depend on the personal
response which any one of us may make to the religious appeal. God himself, in short, may draw vital strength and increase of very being from our fidelity. For my own part, I do
not know what the sweat and blood and tragedy of this life
mean, if they mean anything short of this. If this life be not
a real fight, in which something is eternally gained for the
universe by success, it is no better than a game of private
theatricals from which one may withdraw at will. But it
feels like a real fight — as if there were something really
wild in the universe which we, with all our idealities and
faithfulnesses, are needed to redeem; and first of all to redeem our own hearts from atheisms and fears. For such a
half-wild half-saved universe our nature is adapted. The
deepest thing in our nature is this dumb region of the heart
in which we dwell alone with our willingnesses and our
unwillingnesses, our faiths and our fears. As through the
cracks and crannies of caverns, those waters exude from
the earth's bosom which then form the fountain-heads of
springs, so in these crepuscular depths of personality the
sources of all our outer deeds and decisions take their rise.

Here is our deepest organ of communication with the nature of things; and compared with these concrete movements of our soul all abstract statements and scientific arguments — the veto, for example, which the strict positivist pronounces upon our faith — sound to us like mere chatterings of the teeth . . .

These then are my last words to you: Be not afraid of life. Believe that life *is* worth living, and your belief will help create the fact. The 'scientific' proof that you are right may not be clear before the day of judgment (or some stage of being which that expression may serve to symbolise) is reached. But the faithful fighters of this hour, or the beings that then and there will represent them, may turn to the faint-hearted, who here decline to go on, with words like those with which Henry IV greeted the tardy Crillon after a great battle had been gained: "Hang yourself, brave Crillon! We fought at Arques, and you were not there!"

Richard Jefferies

<hr>

A writer noted for his descriptions of nature, he was born in 1848 at Coate Farm, near Swindon, England, and married Jessie Baden. They had two sons who predeceased him, and a daughter who survived. He worked as a reporter on the *North Wilts Herald*. His first novel, *The Scarlet Shawl*, was published in 1877. Other works include *The Story of My Heart*, *Red-Deer*, and *Amaryllis at the Fair*. He died in 1887.

From THE STORY OF MY HEART

With disbelief, belief increased. The aspiration and hope, the prayer, was the same as that which I felt years before on the hills, only it now broadened.

Experience of life, instead of curtailing and checking my prayer, led me to reject experience altogether. As well might the horse believe that the road the bridle forces it to traverse every day encircles the earth as I believe in experience. All the experience of the greatest city in the world could not withhold me. I rejected it wholly. I stood bareheaded before the sun, in the presence of the earth and air, in the presence of the immense forces of the universe. I demand that which will make me more perfect now, this hour. London convinced me of my own thought. That thought has always been with me, and always grows wider.

One midsummer I went out of the road into the fields, and sat down on the grass between the yellowing wheat and the green hawthorn bushes. The sun burned in the sky, the wheat was full of a luxuriant sense of growth, the grass high, the earth giving its vigour to tree and leaf, the heaven blue. The vigour and growth, the warmth and light, the beauty and richness of it entered into me; an ecstasy of soul accompanied the delicate excitement of the senses: the soul rose with the body. Rapt in the fullness of the moment, I prayed there with all that expansion of mind and frame; no words, no definition, inexpressible desire of physical life, of soul-life, equal to and beyond the highest imagining of my heart.

These memories cannot be placed in exact chronological order. There was a time when a weary restlessness came upon me, perhaps from too-long-continued labour. It was like a drought — a moral drought — as if I had been absent for many years from the sources of life and hope. The inner nature was faint, all was dry and tasteless; I was weary for the pure, fresh springs of thought. Some instinctive feeling uncontrollable drove me to the sea; I was so under its influence that I could not arrange the journey so as to get the longest day. I merely started, and of course had to wait and endure much inconvenience. To get to the sea at some quiet spot was my one thought; to do so I had to travel farther, and from want of prearrangement it was between two and three in the afternoon before I reached the end of my journey. Even then, being too much preoccupied to inquire the way, I missed the road and had to walk a long distance before coming to the shore. But I found the sea at last; I walked beside it in a trance away from the houses out into the wheat. The ripe corn stood up to the beach, the waves on one side of the shingle, and the yellow wheat on the other.

There, alone, I went down to the sea. I stood where the foam came to my feet, and looked out over the sunlit waters. The great earth bearing the richness of the harvest, and its hills golden with corn, was at my back; its strength and firmness under me. The great sun shone above, the wide sea was before me, the wind came sweet and strong from the waves. The life of the earth and the sea, the glow of the sun filled me; I touched the surge with my hand, I lifted my face to the sun, I opened my lips to the wind. I prayed aloud in the roar of the waves — my soul was strong as the sea and prayed with the sea's might. Give me fullness of life like to the sea and the sun, to the earth and the air; give me fullness of physical life, mind equal and beyond their fullness; give me a greatness and perfection of soul higher than all things; give me my inexpressible desire which swells in me like a tide — give it to me with all the force of the sea.

Then I rested, sitting by the wheat; the bank of beach was between me and the sea, but the waves beat against it; the sea was there, the sea was present and at hand. By the dry wheat I rested, I did not think, I was inhaling the richness of the sea, all the strength and depth of meaning of the sea and earth came to me again. I rubbed out some of the wheat in my hands, I took up a piece of clod and crumbled it in my fingers — it was a joy to touch it — I held my hand so that I could see the sunlight gleam on the slightly moist surface of the skin. The earth and sun were to me like my flesh and blood, and the air of the sea life.

With all the greater existence I drew from them I prayed for a bodily life equal to it, for a soul-life beyond my thought, for my inexpressible desire of more than I could shape even into idea. There was something higher than idea, invisible to thought as air to the eye; give me bodily life equal in fullness to the strength of earth, and sun, and sea; give me the soul-life of my desire. Once more I went down to the sea, touched it, and said farewell. So deep was the inhalation of this life that day, that it seemed to remain in me for years. This was a real pilgrimage.

Vincent van Gogh

Dutch painter, lithographer, and etcher of the post-impressionist movement, he was born in 1853 in Brabant, where his father was a Calvinist pastor. At the age of sixteen he began to work for his uncle, a picture dealer in The Hague. In 1876 he became a language teacher in a school at Ramsgate, but returned to Holland the next year to study theology. In 1880 he went to Brussels to paint and in 1885 joined his brother Theo in Paris. In 1888 he settled at Arles, where the painter Gauguin joined him. Among his canvases are *The Potato Eaters, The Restaurant on Montmartre, The Sunflowers*, and *Berceuse*. He died in 1890.

Now for more than five years — I do not know exactly how long — I have been more or less without employment, wandering here and there. You say, Since a certain time you have gone down, you have deteriorated, you have not done anything. Is this quite true?

It is true that occasionally I have earned my crust of bread, occasionally a friend has given it to me in charity. I have lived as I could, as luck would have it, haphazardly. It is true that I have lost the confidence of many; it is true that my financial affairs are in a sad state; it is true that the future is only too gloomy; it is true that I might have done better; it is true that I've lost time in terms of earning my bread; it is true that even my studies are in a rather sad and hopeless condition, and that my needs are greater — infinitely greater — than my possessions. But is this what you call "going down," is this what you call "doing nothing"?

You will perhaps say, But why didn't you continue as they wanted you to — they wanted you to go through the university?

My only answer is, the expenses were too heavy, and besides, that future was not much better than the one on the road now before me.

But I must continue on the path I have taken now. If I don't do anything, if I don't study, if I don't go on seeking any longer, I am lost. Then woe is me. That is how I look at it : to continue, to continue, that is what is necessary.

But you will ask, What is your definite aim?

That aim becomes more definite, will stand out slowly and surely, as the rough draft becomes a sketch, and the sketch becomes a picture — little by little, by working seriously on it, by pondering over the idea, vague at first, over the thought that was fleeting and passing, till it gets fixed.

I must tell you that with evangelists it is the same as with artists. There is an old academic school, often detestable, tyrannical, the accumulation of horrors, men who wear a cuirass, a steel armor, of prejudices and conventions; when these people are in charge of affairs, they dispose of positions, and by a system of red tape they try to keep their protégés in their places and to exclude the other man. Their God is like the God of Shakespeare's drunken Falstaff, *le dedans d'une église* [the inside of a church]; indeed, by a curious chance some of these evangelical (???) gentlemen find themselves with the same point of view on spiritual things as that drunken character (perhaps they would be somewhat surprised to discover this if they were capable of human emotions). But there is little fear of their blindness ever changing to clear-sightedness in such matters.

This state of affairs has its bad side for him who does not agree, but protests against it with all his soul and all his heart and all the indignation of which he is capable. For my part I respect academicians who are not like these, but the respectable ones are rarer than one would first believe. One of the reasons why I am unemployed now, why I have been unemployed for years, is simply that I have different ideas than the gentlemen who give the places to men who think as they do. It is not merely the question of dress which they have hypocritically reproached me with; it is a much more serious question, I assure you.

Why do I tell you all this? — not to complain, not to excuse myself for things in which I may or may not have been wrong, but simply to answer you. During your visit last summer, when we walked together near the abandoned pit which they call *La Sorcière*, you reminded me that there had been another time when we two had walked together — near the old canal and mill of Rijswijk. "And then," you said, "we agreed in many things." But you added, "Since then you have changed so much, you are not the same any longer."

Well, that is not quite true. What has changed is that my life then was less difficult and my future seemed less dark; but the inner state, my way of looking at things and my way of thinking, has not changed. If there has been any change at all, it is that I think and believe and love more seriously now what I already thought and believed and loved then.

So you must not think that I disavow things — I am rather faithful in my unfaithfulness and, though changed, I am the same; my only anxiety is, How can I be of use in the world? Can't I serve some purpose and be of any good? How can I learn more and study certain subjects profoundly? You see, that is what preoccupies me constantly; and then I feel imprisoned by poverty, excluded from participating in certain work, and certain necessities are beyond my reach. That is one reason for being somewhat melancholy. And then one feels an emptiness where there might be friendship and strong and serious affections, and one feels a terrible discouragement gnawing at one's very moral energy, and fate seems to put a barrier to the instincts of affection, and a choking flood of disgust envelops one. And one exclaims, "How long, my God!"

Well, what shall I say? Do our inner thoughts ever show outwardly? There may be a great fire in our soul, yet no one ever comes to warm himself at it, and the passers-by see only a wisp of smoke coming through the chimney, and go along their way. Look here, now, what must be done? Must one tend that inner fire, have salt in oneself, wait patiently yet with how much impatience for the hour when somebody will come and sit down near it — maybe to stay? Let him who believes in God wait for the hour that will come sooner or later.

For the moment it seems that things are going very badly with me, and it has already been so for a considerable time and may continue awhile in the future; but after everything has seemed to go wrong, perhaps a time will come when things will go right. I don't count on it, perhaps it will never happen; but if there is a change for the better, I should consider it so much gain, I should be contented, I should say, At last! you see *there was something after all!*

But you will say, Yet you are an intolerable being because you have impossible ideas about religion and childish scruples of conscience.

If my ideas are impossible or childish, I hope to get rid of them — I ask no better. But this is approximately what I think on the subject. In *Un Philosophe sous les toits*, by Souvestre, you will find how a man of the people, a simple miserable laborer, imagines his own country. "Perhaps you have never thought what your own country really is," he said, putting his hand on my shoulder. "It is everything around you, everything that has brought you up and nourished you, everything you have loved; those fields that you see, those houses, those trees, those young girls laughing as they pass — that is your country! The laws that protect you, the bread which rewards your labor, the words you speak, the joy and the sorrow that come to you from the people and the things among which you live — that is your country! The little room where you used to see your mother, the memories which she has left you, the earth in which she reposes — that is your country! You see it, you breathe it, everywhere! Figure to yourself the rights and the duties, the affections and the needs, the memories and the gratitude; gather it all under one name, and that name will be your country."

In the same way I think that everything which is really good and beautiful — of inner moral, spiritual and sublime beauty in men and their works — comes from God, and that all which is bad and wrong in men and in their works is not of God, and God does not approve of it.

But I always think that the best way to know God is to love many things. Love a friend, a wife, something — whatever you like — you will be on the way to knowing more about Him; that is what I say to myself. But one must love with a lofty and serious intimate sympathy, with strength, with intelligence; and one must always try to know deeper, better and more. That leads to God, that leads to unwavering faith.

To give you an example: someone loves Rembrandt, but seriously — that man will know there is a God, he will surely believe it. Someone studies the history of the French Revolution — he will not be unbelieving, he will see that in great things also there is a sovereign power manifesting itself. Maybe for a short time somebody takes a free course at the great university of misery, and pays attention to the things he sees with his eyes and hears with his ears, and thinks them over; he, too, will end in believing, and he will perhaps have learned more than he can tell. To try to understand the real significance of what the great artists, the serious masters, tell us in their masterpieces, *that* leads to God; one man wrote or told it in a book; another, in a picture. Then simply read the Gospel and the Bible: it makes you think, and think much, and think all the time. Well, think much and think all the time, it raises your thoughts above the ordinary level without your knowing it. We know how to read — well then, let us read!

It is true that there may be moments when one becomes somewhat absentminded, somewhat visionary; some become too absent-minded, too visionary. This is perhaps the case with me, but it is my own fault; maybe there is some excuse after all — I was absorbed, preoccupied, troubled, for some reason — but one overcomes this. The dreamer sometimes falls into a well, but is said to get out of it afterward. And the absent-minded man also has his lucid intervals in compensation. He is sometimes a person who has his reasons for being as he is, but they are not always understood at first, or are unconsciously forgotten most of the time, from lack of interest. A man who has been tossed back and forth for a long time, as if on a stormy sea, at last reaches his destination; a man who has seemed good-for-nothing and incapable of any employment, any function, ends in finding one and becoming active and capable of action — he shows himself quite different from what he seemed at first.

A caged bird in spring knows quite well that he might serve some end; he is well aware that there is something for him to do, but he cannot do it. What is it? He does not quite remember. Then some vague ideas occur to him, and he says to himself, "The others build their nests and lay their eggs and bring up their little ones"; and he knocks his head against the bars of the cage. But the cage remains, and the bird is maddened by anguish.

"Look at that lazy animal," says another bird in passing, "he seems to be living at ease."

Yes, the prisoner lives, he does not die; there are no outward signs of what passes within him — his health is good, he is more or less gay when the sun shines. But then the season of migration comes, and attacks of melancholia — "But he has everything he wants," say the children that tend him in his cage. He looks through the bars at the overcast sky where a thunderstorm is gathering, and inwardly he rebels against his fate. "I am caged, I am caged, and you tell me I do not want anything, fools! You think I have everything I need! Oh! I beseech you liberty, that I may be a bird like other birds!"

A certain idle man resembles this idle bird.

And circumstances often prevent men from doing things, prisoners in I do not know what horrible, horrible, most horrible cage. There is also — I know it — the deliverance, the tardy deliverance. A justly or unjustly ruined reputation, poverty, unavoidable circumstances, adversity — that is what makes men prisoners.

One cannot always tell what it is that keeps us shut in, confines us, seems to bury us; nevertheless, one feels certain barriers, certain gates, certain walls. Is all this imagination, fantasy? I don't think so. And one asks, "My God! is it for long, is it forever, is it for all eternity?"

Do you know what frees one from this captivity? It is every deep, serious affection. Being friends, being brothers, love, that is what opens the prison by some supreme power, by some magic force. Without this, one remains in prison. Where sympathy is renewed, life is restored.

George Gissing

He was born in 1857. He reflected, in his autobiographical *The Private Papers of Henry Ryecroft*, what V. S. Pritchett has called "a self . . . chronically at variance with the world." Gissing's novels of working-class realism, notably *New Grub Street* (1891) and *Demos* (1886), are important documents of late Victorian society, showing the profound influences of poverty on character and introducing into the English novel something of French naturalism. He died in 1903.

From THE PRIVATE PAPERS OF HENRY RYECROFT

10

It may well be that what we call the unknowable will be for ever the unknown. In that thought is there not a pathos beyond words? It may be that the human race will live and pass away; all mankind, from him who in the world's dawn first shaped to his fearful mind an image of the Lord of Life, to him who, in the dusking twilight of the last age, shall crouch before a deity of stone or wood; and never one of that long lineage have learned the wherefore of his being. The prophets, the martyrs, their noble anguish vain and meaningless; the wise whose thought strove to eternity and was but an idle dream; the pure in heart whose life was a vision of the living God, the suffering and the mourners whose solace was in a world to come, the victims of injustice who cried to the Judge Supreme — all gone down into silence, and the globe that bare them circling dead and cold through soundless space. The most tragic aspect of such a tragedy is that it is not unthinkable. The soul revolts, but dare not see in this revolt the assurance of its higher destiny. Viewing our life thus, is it not easier to believe that the tragedy is played with no spectator? And of a truth, of a truth, what spectator can there be? The day may come when, to all who live, the Name of Names will be but an empty symbol, rejected by reason and by faith. Yet the tragedy will be played on.

It is not, I say, unthinkable; but that is not the same thing as to declare that life has no meaning beyond the sense it bears to human intelligence. The intelligence itself rejects such a supposition; in my case, with impatience and scorn. No theory of the world which ever came to my knowledge is to me for one moment acceptable: the possibility of an explanation which would set my mind at rest is to me inconceivable; no whit the less am I convinced that there is a reason of the all; one which transcends my understanding, one no glimmer of which will ever touch my apprehension; a reason which must imply a creative power, and therefore, even whilst a necessity of my thought, is by the same criticized into nothing. A like antinomy with that which affects our conception of the infinite in time and space. Whether the rational processes have reached their final development, who shall say? Perhaps what seem to us the impassable limits of thought are but the conditions of a yet early stage in the history of man. Those who make them a proof of a "future state" must necessarily suppose gradations in that futurity; does the savage, scarce risen above the brute, enter upon the same "new life" as the man of highest civilization? Such gropings of the mind certify our ignorance; the strange thing is that they can be held by any one to demonstrate that our ignorance is final knowledge.

14

I have had one of my savage headaches. For a day and a night I was in blind torment. Have at it now with the stoic remedy. Sickness of the body is no evil. With a little resolution and considering it as a natural issue of certain natural processes, pain may well be borne. One's solace is to remember that it cannot affect the soul, which partakes of the eternal nature. This body is but as "the clothing or the cottage of the mind." Let flesh be racked; I, the very I, will stand apart, lord of myself.

Meanwhile, memory, reason, every faculty of my intellectual part is being whelmed in muddy oblivion. Is the soul something other than the mind? If so, I have lost all consciousness of its existence. For me, mind and soul are one, and as I am too feelingly reminded, that element of my being is *here*, where the brain throbs and anguishes. A little more of such suffering, and I were myself no longer; the body representing me would gesticulate and rave, but I should know nothing of its motives, its fantasies. The very I, it is too plain, consists but with a certain balance of my physical elements, which we call health. Even in the light beginnings of my headache, I was already not myself; my thoughts followed no normal course, and I was aware of the abnormality. A few hours later, I was but a walking disease; my mind — if one could use the word — had become a barrel-organ, grinding in endless repetition a bar or two of idle music.

What trust shall I repose in the soul that serves me thus? Just as much, one would say, as in the senses, through which I know all that I can know of the world in which I live, and which, for all I can tell, may deceive me even more grossly in their common use than they do on certain occasions where I have power to test them; just as much, and no more — if I am right in concluding that mind and soul are merely subtle functions of body. If I chance to become deranged in certain parts of my physical mechanism, I shall straightway be deranged in my wits; and behold that something in me which "partakes of the eternal," prompting me to pranks which savour little of the infinite wisdom. Even in its normal condition (if I can determine what that is) my mind is obviously the slave of trivial accidents; I eat something that disagrees with me, and of a sudden the whole aspect of life is changed; this impulse has lost its force, and another, which before I should not for a moment have entertained, is all-powerful over me. In short, I know just as little about myself as I do about the eternal essence, and I have a haunting suspicion that I may be a mere automaton, my every thought and act due to some power which uses and deceives me.

Why am I meditating thus, instead of enjoying the life of the natural man, at peace with himself and the world, as I was a day or two ago? Merely, it is evident, because my health has suffered a temporary disorder. It has passed; I have thought enough about the unthinkable; I feel my quiet returning. Is it any merit of mine that I begin to be in health once more? Could I, by any effort of the will, have shunned this pitfall?

Rufus Jones

Rufus Jones, born in 1863, was a member of the Society of Friends in America. A professor of philosophy at Haverford College, he was interested in mysticism, and was for many years chairman of the American Friends Service Committee for European Relief. Wrote *Practical Christianity*, *The Quakers in the American Colonies*, and *The Church's Debt to Heretics*. He died in 1948.

The plain-looking meeting-house with unpainted seats and undecorated walls stood on a sightly hill from which we could see the Kennebago Mountains of Western Maine, eighty miles away. It formed the center of a small community of houses and farms, surrounded by a fringe of ancient forests in which, at least to my imagination, roamed deer and moose and bears, and where "loupcervies" and catamounts and plain wildcats were waiting to pounce upon anyone who ventured into its depths. We lived three miles away from the Meeting and could reach it only by a drive in wagon or sleigh through the "dangerous" woods. Thither on Thursdays and Sundays we always went. In the winter there was a huge hot soapstone under the buffalo robe, and I used to slip down and sit on it or near it as we creaked through the snow. There were many other boys in the group, as the neighbors from near and far gathered to fill the meeting-house, which in my youth seemed to be of vast dimensions. There was no bell, no organ, no choir, no pulpit, no order of service, no ritual. There was always silence and then more silence. It was strange that these hard-working toilers kept awake through these long hushes, but they did keep awake, for it was "unbecoming behavior" to nod or to doze. For them this "silence of all flesh" was a sacrament of awe and wonder. They were in faith and practice meeting with God, and the occasion called for all their powers of mind and spirit. It might be supposed that a little boy, keyed to action and charged with animal spirits, on a hard bench, with feet unsupported, would have hated this silence and would have longed for a chance to hit the boy in the next seat over the head. But that was not the case. Sooner or later the boy would get hit no doubt when the proper time came for it. But the silence came over us as a kind of spell. It had a life of its own. There was something "numinous" about it, which means, in simpler non-Latin words, a sense of divine presence, which even a boy could feel. It was almost never explained to us. There was very little said about it. No theories were expounded. No arguments were promulgated. We "found" ourselves in the midst of a unique laboratory experiment which *worked*. A boy responds to reality the moment he feels it, almost quicker than an adult does. He has not yet travelled so far inland from "the immortal sea that brought him hither," and he hasn't yet been "debauched" by commonplace words and phrases and the dull mechanics of life. Anyway that experiment with silence in the far-off period of my youth, sitting in the hush with the moveless group, concentrated on the expectation of divine presence, did something to me and for me which has remained an unlost possession.

I had got over the sky-idea very early in life and thought of God as a Presence in the midst with whom I could commune without any ladder. He came to our meeting with us, and we did not need to go somewhere else to find Him. I cannot remember when I first discovered that there was a meeting place within, where Spirit met with spirit and

where the Above and the below belonged together. I knew
it certainly as early as I knew that the water in our lake was
buoyant and held up the young swimmer instead of
drowning him. The two things came together. I learned to
swim and to enjoy silent worship at about the same time.
Almost always the silence was broken in the early part of
the meeting by a vocal prayer.

> Haply some one felt
> On his moved lips the seal of silence melt,

as Whittier has expressed it. The prayer always came out of
the silence and was more or less the expression of the
group-feeling. The prayer was tremulous with emotion and
it voiced for the waiting group the yearning for fellowship
and communion. We all stood with bowed heads as the
spontaneous prayer was being poured out. I was glad to get
my little feet on the floor for a few minutes change of position, though I felt even then, and more emphatically
later, that the act of rising and sitting down again disturbed
the attitude of hush and reverence. But as soon as we
were seated again the silence took on a new depth of penetration. The whole burden of worship was thrown upon
each individual soul. One could be vacant and unconcerned
with empty mind, *or* one could mount up as with wings of
eagles into the heavenlies and find the Fatherland to
which he belonged. Whatever was done in this period of
silence had to be done by the person himself. It was once
more like swimming. Nobody could do it for you. You
either did your swimming or your worshipping *yourself,* or
it wasn't done. There were no substitutes to perform for
you in either of these activities.

William Butler Yeats

An Irish Nobel Prize-winning poet and dramatist, he was born in 1865. One of the leaders of the Irish Revival, one of the founders of the Abbey Theatre, Dublin, Yeats led an active political life as well as leaving a considerable body both of prose and verse. He became an Irish senator. His brother was an excellent painter. Yeats's mystical experiences are described in his *Celtic Twilight*, the autobiographical *Reveries over Childhood*, and *Dramatis Personae*. He died in 1939.

A VOICE

One day I was walking over a bit of marshy ground close to Inchy Wood when I felt, all of a sudden, and only for a second, an emotion which I said to myself was the root of Christian mysticism. There had swept over me a sense of weakness, of dependence on a great personal Being somewhere far off yet near at hand. No thought of mine had prepared me for this emotion, for I had been pre-occupied with Ængus and Edain, and with Mannanan, son of the sea. That night I awoke lying upon my back and hearing a voice speaking above me and saying, "No human soul is like any other human soul, and therefore the love of God for any human soul is infinite, for no other soul can satisfy the same need in God." A few nights after this I awoke to see the loveliest people I have ever seen. A young man and a young girl dressed in olive-green raiment, cut like old Greek raiment, were standing at my bedside. I looked at the girl and noticed that her dress was gathered about her neck into a kind of chain, or perhaps into some kind of stiff embroidery which represented ivy-leaves. But what filled me with wonder was the miraculous mildness of her face. There are no such faces now. It was beautiful, as few faces are beautiful, but it had neither, one would think, the light that is in desire or in hope or in fear or in speculation. It was peaceful like the faces of animals, or like mountain pools at evening, so peaceful that it was a little sad. I thought for a moment that she might be the beloved of Ængus, but how could that hunted, alluring, happy, immortal wretch have a face like this? Doubtless she was from among the children of the Moon, but who among them I shall never know.

1902

Forbes Robinson

He was born in 1867, and became an Anglican chaplain and theological lecturer at Emmanuel and Christ's Colleges, Cambridge. He died in 1904, and his letters were first published privately in 1916.

From LETTERS

I feel more and more the necessity of being alone occasionally for some time — to get time enough to pray. I think my supreme desire is to be a man of prayer. You must help me to accomplish the desire: "Gutta cavat lapidem non vi, sed saepe cadendo."

So it is with prayer. As the stone gets worn away, not by the force of the drop of water but by its constant trickling, so prayer often renewed must at length attain its end. It is a wonderful privilege to be able to state all one's wishes and hopes for others in prayer — to know that there can be there no possibility of misunderstanding — to tell to God the incomprehensible depth of one's love, and to feel that He knows what it means, because He Himself is love. It is glorious to be made in His image, and to be sure that all one's highest yearnings are a reflection — however broken, partial and unsightly — of His own marvellous life. We have indeed cause to be grateful for our "creation." I often look at the poor dumb creatures, and thank God that He has given me such full powers of love, which they cannot understand: for I would rather have the pains of love than any other pleasure.

Æ

This was the pseudonym of George William Russell, Irish poet, essayist and journalist born in 1867 and known for his mystical verse. He organized agricultural societies and edited Irish newspapers. A great friend of the poet Yeats, and one of the leaders in the Irish revival, Æ after the liberation of Ireland became a senator. His most famous books are *The Candle of Vision, Song and Its Fountains* and *The Avatars*. He died in 1935.

From SONG AND ITS FOUNTAINS

I

A child sits on the grass or strays in darkening woods, and its first going inward in dream may make inevitable a destiny. When inner and outer first mingle it is the bridal night of soul and body. A germ is dropped from which inevitably evolves the character and architecture of the psyche. It is seed as truly as if it were dropped into earth or womb. Only what is born from it is a spirit thing, and it grows up and takes its abode in the body with its other inhabitants, earth-born or heaven-born. There may be many other minglings of heaven and earth in childhood which beget a brood which later become desires, thoughts or imaginations, but the earliest are the masters and they lie subtly behind other impulses of soul.

This I found many years ago when I began to practise a meditation the ancient sages spoke of. In this meditation we start from where we are and go backwards through the day; and later, as we become quicker in the retracing of our way, through weeks, through years, what we now are passing into what we did or thought the moment before, and that into its antecedent; and so we recall a linked medley of action, passion, imagination or thought. It is most difficult at first to retrace our way, to remember what we thought or did even an hour before. But if we persist the past surrenders to us and we can race back fleetly over days or months. The sages enjoined this meditation with the intent that we might, where we had been weak, conquer in imagination, kill the dragons which overcame us before and undo what evil we might have done. I found, when I had made this desire for retrospect dominant in meditation, that an impulse had been communicated to everything in my nature to go back to origins. It became of myself as if one of those moving pictures we see in the theatres, where in a few moments a plant bursts into bud, leaf and blossom, had been reversed and I had seen the blossom dwindling into the bud. My moods began to hurry me back to their first fountains. To see our lives over again is to have memories of two lives and intuitions of many others, to discover powers we had not imagined in ourselves who were the real doers of our deeds, to have the sense that a being, the psyche, was seeking incarnation in the body. As a tribe of gay or dusky winged creatures we followed might lead us home to their nest, so a crowd of delicately coloured desires led me back to the moment in childhood when, about four or five years of age, beauty first dawned on me. I had strayed into a park, and I remembered how I lay flat on grass overcome by some enchantment flickering about a clump of daffodils. A little later I read a child's story, and in this what fascinated me was that the hero had a magic sword with a hilt of silver and a blade of blue steel. The word "magic" stirred me, though I knew not what it meant, as if there was some being within me which could foresee the time when the whole universe from wheeling stars to the least motion of life would appear to be wrought by, or depend on, the magic of some mighty mind. It lay in memory, that word, without meaning, until a dozen years later its transcendental significance emerged as a glittering dragon-fly might come out of a dull chrysalis. But the harmony of blue and silver at once bewitched me. I murmured to myself, "blue and silver! blue and silver!" And then, the love of colour awakened, a few days later I saw primroses and laid the cool and gentle glow of these along with the blue and silver in my heart, and then lilac was added to my memory of colours to be treasured. And so, by harmony or contrast, one colour after another entered the imagination. They became mine or were denied, as they could or would not shine in company with those delicate originals of blue and silver. This love of colour seemed instinctive in the outer nature, and it was only in that retrospective meditation I could see that the harmonies which delighted me had been chosen by a deeper being and were symbolic of its nature and not of that unthinking child's.

Johannes Anker-Larsen

A Danish novelist, he was born in 1874 on the island of Langeland. His father was a sailor. Johannes became an actor, later a pro-
ducer of plays in Copenhagen. His first book, *The Philosopher's
Stone*, won the Gyldendal prize of 70,000 kroner in 1923, and he
left the stage, but later returned as literary censor. The quest of a
living faith has been the mainspring of all his novels.

From WITH THE DOOR OPEN

As far back as my memory goes, I can recall a sense of
the Eternal. "Eternity," "heaven," "the Kingdom of God,"
that was a reality which, though I was unable to see it, was
nevertheless so much around me that I could feel it sometimes — in some such way as I could feel the rays of the
sun on my hand on a summer's day. The picture is crude
but striking; only, the rays of the Eternal Sun were more
tenuous; they warmed not the surface but penetrated my
inner self. Religion was not much discussed in my home,
nor was there an active religious life in our part of the country. I was told that God existed, and I thought that I
could "feel" heaven. I also remember the words, "Beware
lest the Lord punish you." I cannot say that they impressed
me very much; they harmonized so poorly with my own
sense of heaven, where God dwelt. On the other hand, I
never doubted that He would help me if I should be in
need. This I probably deemed self-evident, since I regarded heaven as something good. For the rest, I relished
life without restriction. I hardly think that there was any

fruit in the garden which I would not willingly have tasted. However, it happened now and again that the sun of the Eternal Kingdom was so strong, and entered so deeply into me that I forgot to eat. But there were enough beclouded days on which I was up to all the pranks that boys like to go in for. The "heaven" or "Eternity" which surrounded me was so close that it could reach me with its beneficence; not so close, however, that I was in danger of being entirely engulfed by it before I died. I feared to die before I had tasted all the delights (right and wrong) for which I was yearning, and before I had gained enough time in peace and quietness to "sense" heaven so clearly that I was ready to walk straight into it.

Such, at least, is my recollection of that time. The earth was the earth, but it lay in the light of Eternity.

Slowly, unperceived, the light grew dimmer, the shadows grew thick, and became a coarser reality. In the end, Eternity was like a day that had passed away; I had ceased to sense it.

But I missed it, and became religious.

I was young, and the world was beautiful, but I kept looking for a sunrise which was to make everything more alive.

I looked for it in the theological Faculty. To a thirsting soul, this is like a desert. It reminded me of a time during the war, when one day I entered a café where I hoped to get a cup of coffee, and got something which was called coffee and looked like coffee, but wasn't.

One winter's day I was taking a walk in the Geels forest. It was cold; I had walked long and fast to get warm. Now I could feel every fiber of my body warmed by the central-heating system of the red blood. With every breath the fresh air poured into my lungs. I was intoxicated with health; I had my fill of it; I could not hold any more. The whole

wood wafted it into my face, I could *see* health and
strength filling out the spaces between the bare tree trunks,
I exalted in *seeing* — until I was saturated, and turned my
eyes away like a child who has been so long under the spell
of a Christmas display that the inconceivable happens:
it is no longer interested to see hardly even to possess, anything of it. Thus I walked home mechanically, in more than
one sense. I was too elated to rejoice over the possession of
anything. My usual sense of ego had gone to sleep like a little child in its crib. I only just remember how the frozen
dead leaves crunched under my big, heavy boots. Otherwise my consciousness was not very active, but as I looked
up to get my bearings, I became quite confused in regard
to place and time, for I beheld before me a small wood
path, so fresh, pure and fairylike that it must have been a
path in the Garden of Paradise. There could be no doubt
about it, my own joy at the sight of it belonged likewise to
Paradise. That lasted perhaps a second — measured by the
temporal clock. I went on standing there with my gaze
fixed on the footpath — and now it was merely the one
which led to the house in which I lived. It looked commonplace, unalluring and insignificant. But in my memory still
shone the image of the path in the Garden of Paradise, accompanied by the feeling that it was familiar. And now I
remembered it quite distinctly. It is one that lies in a small
wood near a village school on the island of Langeland. But
it is not worth the trouble to journey thither to find it; it
certainly looks commonplace, unalluring and insignificant.
I had been in those parts one winter morning with a few
comrades. I was seven years old. It may be that later on I
was there again once or twice, but that is all. Until now I
had completely forgotten that the path existed. It had
never figured among the home scenes which used to visit
me; it had been stored away far below the "threshold of
consciousness." I scrutinized the path in the Geels forest

closely so as to search out the similarity which had recalled that other from the depth of oblivion. I found it quite impossible to discover any resemblance except that they were both wood paths. I stood still, swayed by two feelings which it would be hard to conceive of as being present simultaneously: by a profound happiness which declared itself as indestructible, and a verdict upon my whole life as being fundamentally misdirected.

These were the first faint traces of the way homeward, as one might say. It took time and attention to get farther.

That brief moment had held such abundance that I soon demanded a repetition. I looked at my wood path in hopes that I might discover the resemblance between it and the "path in the Garden of Paradise": it developed into a puzzle-picture within which the Path of Paradise lay concealed. I had seen it once, but could not find it again. It was as if a streak of lightning had illumined the wood; I could recall the picture as a memory, but I could not produce the lightning again and really see it.

One day the "lightning" was suddenly resumed. It was on a wide crossroad hemmed in on both sides by pine forest. In the instant I could read the puzzle picture. It was a road in a manor wood near my father's house. I was six or seven years old, and was there for the first time. Generally speaking, I believe that the places which appeared in the lightning flash were old familiar places as I had seen them for the first time. I know of no instance where they appeared through the remembrance of later wanderings. As soon as I hunted them out consciously in memory they were always connected with a history. These consciously warmed-up servings failed to satisfy. They were thin gruel.

The lightning flashes came of their own accord when

they came. They sprang out of a direct perception of reality.

One day I was loitering in the garden with no particular object in view. I had been working hard, and had to stop to recover breath. I was tired of my work in my study, and so I strolled idly along the garden paths. I walked and walked, until I found myself standing in front of a dyke by the wood. As I glanced at it, there was a flash of lightning, and the puzzle picture was easy to read. It was a dyke by one of the fields belonging to the estate where I was born. I actually saw it. That is to say, at that moment I did not distinguish between this dyke and the old one, between my present ego and the one of the past. The two phenomena were *simultaneous and one.* Yes, by magic, the place itself seemed to be the same. Suddenly a change occurred. I saw another dyke by another field at home — with the same feeling of present experience. Fortunately, no reflections intervened; I only stood there and looked. The dyke here by the wood revealed itself as a great actor; seven fields belonged to our native estate, all of them surrounded by dykes and growing hedges, and in a trice he impersonated the whole series — then took off the masks, standing there with his own undisputable countenance, and leaving me to my contemplations.

Now it was quite evident that this dyke resembled the others just as much as any other dyke. I had seen it often enough, and not discovered any native fields. No, the similarity did not lie outside of myself, in what I was looking at, but within myself, in the manner of my perception. I had succeeded in seeing this dyke *honestly and straightforwardly* with the eyes which were my birthright. The profound joy of reality filled me; my own inner condition opened out, and became one with all the homogeneous conditions. It was not a question of remembrance, but of a state of being. I did not miss the old dykes, for they were present.

I took courage, however, and learned to tarry in the moment whenever it came to me. I had not the feeling of wasting time or of inactivity, as I felt sure that while it lasted something significant was going on. The feeling of joy which it brought was the deepest, purest, and most precious joy I had experienced. The outcome of abiding in these moments was invariably the same; the feeling of joy became so profound that I felt it quite impossible to disregard the consciousness thereof; then it developed into enjoyment, and the moment had passed.

I venture the suspicion that just here may be lurking the great temptation toward ecstasy. Intensive concentration (perhaps supported by prayer) upon a feeling of joy — or merely the remembrance of a feeling of joy — which must be named bliss can certainly produce a state of self-hypnotism, which passes from intoxication to insensibility, and thus precludes either direct consciousness or a healthy unconsciousness. Thus the ecstatic is for ever swinging between the intoxication of "unification" and the slump of "separation."

The feeling of joy was accompanied by something which I must call clairvoyance, but I shall refer to this later. The most significant thing about these moments was their will-determining power. A definite aim was imparted to my life which can never change. Even though I may now and again run along a sidetrack, I know at least that it is a sidetrack.

The flashes of lightning ceased to be lightning; they began to last. At this time I began to become really conscious of the accompanying clairvoyance. At first it was almost bewildering. The two policemen Time and Space loosened the handcuffs, but I did not trust myself to believe in it altogether. Even now, in my attempt to give an account of it, I feel that to him who knows nothing about it it must sound like the words of a lunatic. But everything is insane babbling that we do not yet understand, so I shall go right on.

As I walked along a certain street in Holte, it might be that a bunch of common chervil in the gutter would bring to my mind the road from Henninge to Rudköbing where I have walked many a time. That was a memory, and I was now quite different from the small lad who wandered in the direction of Rudköbing. It came hard to me to believe that he was really I. Time and Space had me in chains.

But I might also have walked in the same street in Holte and merely contemplated how the chervil was growing there all alone, and suddenly have found myself *on* the road from Henninge to Rudköbing; then I *was* the small lad walking there all by myself. This actually happened *now*, but if, knowing better, I wanted to protest and prove that my papers, years and dates were in good order, policeman Time, as a private person, hands in pockets, would declare with a smile: "Just at present I am not on duty." And I was no better off if I turned to his colleague Space; he was also on leave. If I looked at the Holte road, in order to establish my identity, it *opened* itself out, and I *saw within it* the road to Rudköbing. If anyone is convinced that this clairvoyance is madness, it may cheer him if I add a warning that the worst is yet to come.

A child is out in the dark, alone; it is supporting itself with a stick, because the road is slippery. Nevertheless, it stumbles here and there, and gets hurt. Suddenly it feels a grown-up taking it by the hand. The warmth of the large hand is communicated to the small one immediately.

It is the warmth of the grown-up, but now it is his warmth too. Besides, the hand is a good support and the child does not stumble any more, so long as it holds on firmly. It needs the stick no longer, and the hand leads forward; there is a good will in the hand. All the child knows about this great, great grown-up is that he is warm, strong, and good, and it is confident that he knows the way — though it may perhaps keep its own eyes watchfully open. It knows the grown-up only through the warmth, the support, and the security it receives from him. This warmth, strength, and security flow into us, and in gratitude we say "God," because that is the word which expresses our feelings. As far as I am concerned one might just as well put it: "He learned to know God's guidance," or "he poetized a God into being, because something had become free within himself," or "he calls it God, but we know that it was not *our* God; he might as well have said Allah, or Brahma or the impersonal Tao." That is immaterial to me. We are dealing here with actual, practical life and not with philosophies of life which one spins in one's easy-chair. I am just as ready to solve a cross-word puzzle as to discuss philosophies of life.

God had thus entered my universe, and he brought with him a remembrance of childhood and the fulfillment of a childhood wish — one that I never understood before, as its folly seemed as great as its fervor.

Now I come to that which is the most difficult to explain — the meeting with Eternity.

While I was still on my way, I noticed how Time and Space had loosened my handcuffs. Yearnings and painful longings were diminished, whether it be toward places or people to whom I had become attached. Not that my feelings had grown cold, but I could no longer feel *separation* with the old force. There is a condition in which it ceases to exist.

Every object which we know has been christened by Time and Space. Every name means limitation, every word is an expression for something in distinction to something else. In the everlasting Now there is neither Space nor Time, neither limitation nor distinction. Even the language of the gods would be inadequate to describe it, and the "language of Heaven" cannot be spoken or written; it is *lived*. Tongue and pen can tell lies, the language of Heaven is the life of true reality in man and imparts itself directly from soul to soul, with those who are wholly and really living in truth. Words cannot describe the wordless, and I am no artist in handling words, even within the realm of words.

But now I will try to express myself on the subject as plainly and simply as I can. I select a summer day's meeting between Time and Eternity and describe it in as far as it can be described.

I had been sitting in the garden working and had just finished. That afternoon I was to go to Copenhagen, but it was still an hour and a half before the departure of the train. The weather was beautiful, the air clear and pure. I lighted a cigar and sat down in one of the easy-chairs in front of the house. It was still and peaceful — around me and within me. Too good, in fact, to allow one to think much about anything. I just sat there. Then it began to come, that infinite tenderness, which is purer and deeper than that of lovers, or of a father toward his child. It was in me, but it also came to me, as the air came to my lungs. As usual, the breathing became sober and reverent, became, as it were, incorporeal; I inhaled the tenderness. Needless to say the cigar went out. I did not cast it away like a sin, I simply had no use for it.

This deep tenderness which I felt, first within myself

and then even stronger around and above me, extended further and further — it became all-present. I saw it, and it developed into knowing, into knowing all, at the same time it became power, omnipotence, and drew me into the eternal Now.

That was my first actual meeting with Reality; because such is the real life: a Now which *is* and a Now which *happens*. There is no beginning and no end. I cannot say any more about this Now. I sat in my garden, but there was no place in the world where I was not.

During the whole time my consciousness was clear and sober. I sat in the garden and acknowledged it with a smile. There was something to smile over, for time and space, characteristics of the Now which happens were so to speak "outside." But what is the Now which happens? It is the continuously active creation with all its birth throes. I saw time and space as instruments or functions of this creation. They come into existence with it and in the course of it, and with it they come to an end. The Newly Created stands in the Now and discards these tools. The freedom, the real *Being* begins.

John Masefield

————•·•————

Poet, novelist and dramatist, he was born in 1878. He ran away to sea when he was thirteen. He finally settled near London and has devoted himself to writing since 1897. His works include the autobiographical *So Long to Learn*, *Salt Water Ballads*, *Live and Kicking Ned*, and *Generation Risen*. He became England's Poet Laureate in 1930.

From WANDERINGS

It is difficult for me to describe the ecstatic bliss of my earliest childhood. All that I looked upon was beautiful, and known by me to be beautiful, but also known by me to be, as it were, only the shadow of something much more beautiful, very, very near, and almost to be reached, where there was nothing but beauty itself in ecstasy, undying, inexhaustible.

This feeling is probably present in most children: it was strong in me. I was sure that a greater life was near us: in dreams I sometimes seemed to enter a part of it, and woke with rapture and longing. Then, on one wonderful day, when I was a little more than five years old, as I stood looking north, over a clump of honeysuckle in flower, I entered that greater life; and that life entered into me with a delight that I can never forget. I found suddenly that I could imagine imaginary beings complete in every detail, with every faculty and possession, and that these imaginations did what I wished for my delight, with an incredible perfection, in a brightness not of this world.

Something, I know not what, in the very reality of the
joy, told me that this could not be talked about, it was too
intense for that: and, indeed, even if I had had a confidant
(which I had not) the sympathy might have been strained
by the tallness of the tale. But from that wonderful hour, I
had a life for myself, better than any life of men; and for
some years I lived in that life, and could enter it at will,
or almost at will, unknown to anybody.

Certain sorrows then crushed my power to enter it: and
for a long time I mourned, thinking that I had been
damned, as some of my elders had said I should be. The effect upon myself could not be distinguished from damnation. However, the power to enter that life returned to me
later, not for always, but at intervals.

I believe that life to be the source of all that is of glory or
goodness in this world; and that modern man, not knowing that life, is dwelling in death.

From SO LONG TO LEARN

On a Sunday morning in that blackness of despair I set
out upon a memorable walk in a late April, after a winter
of much ill-health and disappointment. Being alone in the
country for the week-end I went away through some woodland, in parts that I had never before seen, and have never
seen since. It was a sad walk, for my work was not what I
had hoped, and on my way into the country a fact had
come to my knowledge that filled my mind with bitterness.
The prospect before me seemed black.

Seeing a likely ash-plant in a pile of hedge-trimmings, I
took it, and trimmed some five feet of it, with a knife, to be
my walking-staff. The day was sunny and fine, but it had
been a cold and snowy April. On my walk, I came to a hollow on the northern side of a hedge (it was more than a

ditch: it looked like an overgrown shallow quarry). It
was still full of dirty unmelted snow-drift, for no sun
could reach it and rain had not fallen since the snow. I
probed the snow with my staff, and found it to be,
roughly, three feet four inches deep; not a bad record for
late April; not a cheerful sight, but one well according
with my mood.

Presently, on my return journey, being then on the
southern side of that hedge, I found the bank starred with
primroses. They were the first that I had seen for a year,
and in any case would have given me delight; but as I
looked at them a voice within me, that I did not know (a
man's voice), said clearly, "The spring is beginning."

I walked home, feeling that the difficulties that beset
me in what I was then trying to write would now clear
away. I had no doubt of this: a message of hope had been
given to me.

However, the difficulties did not clear away, the work
seemed in a tangle, and not to be cleared by any effort of
mine. I took it with me into another part of the country,
where I stayed alone, working and worrying for a few days,
finding no light upon it, yet sure that the promised light
would come.

In an evening in May, having written myself weary, I
went out for a walk through woodland, then in all the
beauty of young leaf and life. I was in a state of great inner joy from a sight that I had seen that morning. I came
home uphill through a wood, feeling that the incredible
and the impossible were on each side of me. At the wood's
edge there was a sort of fence to shut it from the common
beyond. The fence was something to step over with the
feet, and easily to push through with the body. As I went
over and through this division, I said to myself, "Now I
will make a poem about a blackguard who becomes converted." Instantly, the poem appeared to me in its complete

form, with every detail distinct; the opening lines poured out upon the page as fast as I could write them down. I had written between fourteen and twenty lines before I reached home. I then lit the lamp and sat down to write, till I had done some sixty-odd lines more.

I was alone in the house. It was not a very lonely house: there were two other little houses, one about thirty, the other sixty yards away. However, it was deep country, nearly midnight, and everybody near me must have been abed and asleep.

Suddenly, as I wrote, the door of the room in which I wrote flung itself noisily wide open.

Do not think that I was scared: no, no; I was terrified, almost out of my wits.

Why the door had opened in that way, I do not know. It had never opened like that before, and never did again. The hint was not lost upon me: I packed up my writing and went to bed.

This brings me to the important thing in all the arts, the breaking of the tomb, the resurrection of the dead, known as the coming of inspiration. What is this illumination that adds so much to human happiness?

In conversation with many writers and painters, I have learned that not all experience what I mean by the word. Some say, "The subject comes, or it sticks, one or the other; and that is that." Perhaps, with a good many, after the first enthusiasms of beginning, the work is a trial to be overcome, then put aside, so that something else can be attempted. With others, there is a knowledge, that very near at hand, whatever the subject may be, there is the possibility of illumination.

This illumination is an intense experience, and so wonderful that it cannot be described. While it lasts, the momentary problem is merged into a dazzlingly clear perception of the entire work in all its detail. In a mood of mental ecstasy, the writer (and in some cases at least the painter also) perceives what seems to be an unchangeable way of statement, so full, and so insistent, that he cannot set down one half of what there is to utter. The mood may last for some hours or for some weeks, it goes as strangely and as suddenly as it comes, having, in its passing, revealed something that will be more sure to please and to illumine others than work done in moods less glowing.

Some writers and painters say that, of course, all this is but one of the manifestations or ways of the mysterious thing called Mind, that it is an intensely personal thing, owing to a rare yet perfect functioning of the being. One or two writers whom I have known have called it "the individual's realization of his Higher Being." Two or three others (poets) have felt that it is the perception by a mortal of an undying reality, to which all mortals may have access by effort, and from which all beauty, good, wisdom and rightness forever come to man.

Certainly, to myself, this last is the explanation of the term. I cannot doubt that this universe of glory and of energy exists and that man may in some strange ways enter into it or partake of its nature. This belief, in many forms, has been held by many.

Margaret Prescott Montague

———•••———

A West Virginian, whose brother was a well-known Episcopalian minister, Margaret Prescott Montague was a novelist, short-story writer and poet. She was born in 1878. Menaced from childhood by progressive blindness, and later by almost total deafness, she published *Leaves from a Secret Journal* under the name Jane Steger; her other books and many articles under her own name. Despite a long life of incurable suffering, she was able to share with many her perception that, as she put it "if the world be shut without, I'll sail the hidden seas within." She died in 1955.

From TWENTY MINUTES OF REALITY

As a child I was afraid of world without end, of life everlasting. The thought of it used to clutch me at times with a crushing sense of the inevitable, and make me long to run away. But where could one run? If never-ending life were true, then I was already caught fast in it, and it would never end. Perhaps it had never had a beginning. Life everlasting, eternity, forever and ever: these are tremendous words for even a grown person to face; and for a child — if he grasp their significance at all — they may be hardly short of appalling. The picture that Heaven presented to my mind was of myself, a desperate little atom, dancing in a streak of light around and around and around forever and ever. I do not know what could have suggested such an idea; I only know that I could not think of myself caught there in eternity like a chip in a whirlpool, or say "round again, and round again, and round again" for more than a minute, without hypnotizing myself into a state of sheer terror. Of course, as I grew older I threw off this truly awful conception; yet shorn of its crudeness and looked at with grown-up eyes, there were moments when, much as I believed in, and desired, eternal life, that old feeling of "round again, and round again" would swoop back upon me with all its unutterable weariness, and no state of bliss that I could imagine seemed to me proof forever against boredom. Nevertheless, I still had faith to believe that eternity and enjoyment of life could in some way be squared, though I did not see how it was to be done. I am glad that I had, for I came at last to a time when faith was justified by sight, and it is of that time that I wish to write here.

I do not really know how long the insight lasted. I have said, at a rough guess, twenty minutes. It may have been a little shorter time, it may have been a little longer. But at best it was very transitory.

It happened to me about two years ago, on the day when my bed was first pushed out of doors to the open gallery of the hospital. I was recovering from a surgical operation. I had undergone a certain amount of physical pain, and had suffered for a short time the most acute mental depression which it has ever been my misfortune to encounter. I suppose that this depression was due to physical causes, but at the time it seemed to me that somewhere down there under the anesthetic, in the black abyss of unconsciousness, I had discovered a terrible secret, and the secret was that there was no God; or if there was one, He was indifferent to all human suffering.

Though I had hardly reëstablished my normal state of faith, still the first acuteness of that depression had faded, and only a scar of fear was left when, several days later, my bed was first wheeled out to the porch. There other patients took their airing and received their visitors; busy internes and nurses came and went, and one could get a glimpse of the sky, with bare gray branches against it, and of the ground, with here and there a patch of melting snow.

It was an ordinary cloudy March day. I am glad to think that it was. I am glad to remember that there was nothing extraordinary about the weather, nor any unusualness of setting — no flush of spring or beauty of scenery — to induce what I saw. It was, on the contrary, almost a dingy day. The branches were bare and colorless, and the occasional half-melted piles of snow were a forlorn gray rather than white. Colorless little city sparrows flew and chirped in the trees, while human beings, in no way remarkable, passed along the porch.

There was, however, a wind blowing, and if any outside thing intensified the experience, it was the blowing of that wind. In every other respect it was an ordinary commonplace day. Yet here, in this everyday setting, and entirely unexpectedly (for I had never dreamed of such a thing), my eyes were opened, and for the first time in all my life I caught a glimpse of the ecstatic beauty of reality.

I cannot now recall whether the revelation came suddenly or gradually; I only remember finding myself in the very midst of those wonderful moments, beholding life for the first time in all its young intoxication of loveliness, in its unspeakable joy, beauty, and importance. I cannot say exactly what the mysterious change was. I saw no new thing, but I saw all the usual things in a miraculous new light — in what I believe is their true light. I saw for the first time how wildly beautiful and joyous, beyond any words of mine to describe, is the whole of life. Every human being moving across that porch, every sparrow that flew, every branch tossing in the wind, was caught in and was a part of the whole mad ecstasy of loveliness, of joy, of importance, of intoxication of life.

It was not that for a few keyed-up moments I *imagined* all existence as beautiful, but that my inner vision was cleared to the truth so that I *saw* the actual loveliness which is always there, but which we so rarely perceive; and I knew that every man, woman, bird, and tree, every living thing before me, was extravagantly beautiful, and extravagantly important. And, as I beheld, my heart melted out of me in a rapture of love and delight. A nurse was walking past; the wind caught a strand of her hair and blew it out in a momentary gleam of sunshine, and never in my life before had I seen how beautiful beyond all belief is a woman's hair. Nor had I ever guessed how marvelous it is for a human being to walk. As for the internes in their white suits, I had never realized before the whiteness of white linen; but much more than that, I had never so much as dreamed of the mad beauty of young manhood. A little sparrow chirped and flew to a nearby branch, and I honestly believe that only "the morning stars singing together, and the sons of God shouting for joy" can in the least express the ecstasy of a bird's flight. I cannot express it, but I have seen it.

Once out of all the gray days of my life I have looked into the heart of reality; I have witnessed the truth; I have seen life as it really is — ravishingly, ecstatically, madly beautiful, and filled to overflowing with a wild joy, and a value unspeakable. For those glorified moments I was in love with every living thing before me — the trees in the wind, the little birds flying, the nurses, the internes, the people who came and went. There was nothing that was alive that was not a miracle. Just to be alive was in itself a miracle. My very soul flowed out of me in a great joy.

Stark Young

American dramatic critic for the New York *Times* and the *New Republic*, he was born in 1881. Formerly an English teacher, he was also a novelist, essayist, and playwright. Among his books are *So Red the Rose, Immortal Shadows* and *The Pavilion*. He died in 1963.

From THE PAVILION

I felt the impurity of the heart that arises when we move towards what may become ours only by will and conquest instead of towards what is naturally and simply ours by vision. I began to know from both waking and sleeping that in all dreams there is something hoped for, something passionate and cold and final. But I saw also, or else read somewhere, that while our wills are infinite our intelligences are finite, and that because of this our wildest dreams in reveries and fictions are peopled or furnished with distortions of the usual. I thought a great deal on this matter, but often in despair and defeat at getting no further with it. Meanwhile in the midst of this life in that mountainous country I felt always growing clearer to me the belief that body, idea, and spirit are for us as simply and wholly a part of the surrounding universe as the trees or the stars or the falling of water; and that there can be no miracles, not because they are contrary to possibility and fact, but because what we call a miracle is itself the fact, which we judge to be superhuman and supernatural because we cannot follow it to its source. But still the seasons came, and the moon and the stars, all in their due moments, and I was baffled and comforted and whipped by their rightness. I have always been led by a sense that the natural world is our tutor and redeemer, and that genius, even, is only an intelligence that works like nature.

I was led to the reflection, often repeated, as to whom in the fields of human love and to what enveloping arms, what lovely love, shall we turn? . . .

But I was too young except in some rapturous confusion, which by my instinct and my epoch I mistrusted, to accept all that with any fullness; and I was too sincere, with the intense, personal and callous sincerity of youth, to pretend to do so. Lines from the mystics and poets, which in fact often turned out to be my own lines, gathered in my mind — "Thou are my rest from care, Thou in the black night a light, and a crowd to me in lonely places. For Thou alone art my house, Thou all my hours of happiness." . . .

But speaking, meanwhile, for the classic tradition and for the clear, lovely daylight of the classic thought and its avoidance of the murky, ethereal and turgid, I could put my small mind and timid wonder against the confused shadows of mystical desire.

Virginia Woolf

———— • ————

English novelist and critic, she was born in 1882. She was in large part responsible for the stream-of-consciousness technique of character development. Her novels include *Mrs. Dalloway, To the Lighthouse,* and *Orlando.* She died in 1941, and A *Writer's Diary* was published posthumously in 1953.

From A WRITER'S DIARY

Mrs. Webb's book has made me think a little what I could say of my own life. I read some of 1923 this morning, being headachy again, and taking a delicious draught of silence. But then there were causes in her life: prayer; principle. None in mine. Great excitability and search after something. Great content — almost always enjoying what I'm at, but with constant change of mood. I don't think I'm ever bored. Sometimes a little stale; but I have a power of recovery — which I have tested; and am now testing for the 50th time. I have to husband my head still very carefully: but then, as I said to Leonard today, I enjoy epicurean ways of society; sipping and then shutting my eyes to taste. I enjoy almost everything. Yet I have some restless searcher in me. Why is there not a discovery in life? Something one can lay hands on and say "This is it"? My depression is a harassed feeling. I'm looking: but that's not it — that's not it. What is it? And shall I die before I find it? Then (as I was walking through Russell Square last night) I see the mountains in the sky: the great clouds; and the moon which is risen over Persia; I have a great and astonishing sense of something there, which is "it." It is not exactly beauty that I mean. It is that the thing is in itself enough: satisfactory; achieved. A sense of my own strangeness, walking on the earth is there too: of the infinite oddity of the human position; trotting along Russell Square with the moon up there and those mountain clouds. Who am I, what am I, and so on: these questions are always floating about in me: and then I bump against some exact fact — a letter, a person, and come to them again with a great sense of freshness. And so it goes on. But on this showing, which is true, I think, I do fairly frequently come upon this "it"; and then feel quite at rest.

Description of a Total Eclipse (1927)

Then, for a moment, we saw the sun, sweeping — it seemed to be sailing at a great pace and clear in a gap; we had out our smoked glasses; we saw it crescent, burning red; next moment it had sailed fast into the cloud again; only the red streamers came from it; then only a golden haze, such as one has often seen. The moments were passing. We thought we were cheated; we looked at the sheep; they showed no fear; the setters were racing round; everyone was standing in long lines, rather dignified, looking out. I thought how we were like very old people, in the birth of the world — druids on Stonehenge; (this idea came more vividly in the first pale light though). At the back of us were great blue spaces in the cloud. These were still blue. But now the colour was going out. The clouds were turning pale; a reddish black colour. Down in the valley it was an extraordinary scrumble of red and black; there was the one light burning; all was cloud down there, and very beautiful, so delicately tinted. Nothing could be seen through the cloud. The 24 seconds were passing. Then one looked back again at the blue; and rapidly, very very quickly, all the colours faded; it became darker and darker as at the beginning of a violent storm; the light sank and sank; we kept saying this is the shadow; and we thought now it is over — this is the shadow; when suddenly the light went out. We had fallen. It was extinct. There was no colour. The earth was dead. That was the astonishing moment; and the next when as if a ball had rebounded the cloud took colour on itself again, only a sparky ethereal colour and so the light came back. I had very strongly the feeling as the light went out of some vast obeisance; something kneeling down and suddenly raised up when the colours came. The colour for some moments was of the most lovely kind — fresh, various; here blue and there brown; all new colours, as if washed over and repainted. They came back astonishingly lightly and quickly and beautifully in the valley and over the hills — at first with a miraculous glittering and ethereality, later normally almost, but with a great sense of relief. It was like recovery. We had been much worse than we had expected. We had seen the world dead. This was within the power of nature. Our greatness had been apparent too.

Thursday, September 30th

I wished to add some remarks to this, on the mystical side of this solicitude; how it is not oneself but something in the universe that one's left with. It is this that is frightening and exciting in the midst of my profound gloom, depression, boredom, whatever it is. One sees a fin passing far out. What image can I reach to convey what I mean? Really there is none, I think. The interesting thing is that in all my feeling and thinking I have never come up against this before. Life is, soberly and accurately, the oddest affair; has in it the essence of reality. I used to feel this as a child — couldn't step across a puddle once, I remember, for thinking how strange — what am I? etc. But by writing I don't reach anything. All I mean to make is a note of a curious state of mind. I hazard the guess that it may be the impulse behind another book. At present my mind is totally blank and virgin of books. I want to watch and see how the idea at first occurs. I want to trace my own process.

Saturday, February 7th

Here in the few minutes that remain, I must record, heaven be praised, the end of *The Waves*. I wrote the words O Death fifteen minutes ago, having reeled across the last ten pages with some moments of such intensity and intoxication that I seemed only to stumble after my own voice, or almost, after some sort of speaker (as when I was mad) I was almost afraid, remembering the voices that used to fly ahead. Anyhow, it is done; and I have been sitting these 15 minutes in a state of glory, and calm, and some tears, thinking of Thoby and if I could write Julian Thoby Stephen 1881-1906 on the first page. I suppose not. How physical the sense of triumph and relief is! Whether good or bad, it's done; and, as I certainly felt at the end, not merely finished, but rounded off, completed, the thing stated — how hastily, how fragmentarily I know; but I mean that I have netted that fin in the waste of water which appeared to me over the marshes out of my window at Rodmell when I was coming to an end of *To the Lighthouse*.

What interests me in the last stage was the freedom and boldness with which my imagination picked up, used and tossed aside all the images, symbols which I had prepared. I am sure that this is the right way of using them — not in set pieces, as I had tried at first, coherently, but simply as images, never making them work out; only suggest. Thus I hope to have kept the sound of the sea and the birds, dawn and garden subconsciously present, doing their work under ground.

Frank C. Laubach

American Congregationalist minister, scientist, and mystic, Frank C. Laubach was born at Benton, Pennsylvania, in 1884. Educated at Princeton, he was subsequently ordained. Married in 1912 to Effa Seely, a nurse, he and his wife both left three years later for service as missionaries to Mindanao in the Philippine Islands. There Dr. Laubach began the mass program of teaching reading and writing which has subsequently brought him prestige as the world's foremost expert on literacy. He has done similar work in India and Latin America. His books include *The People of the Philippines* (Doran, 1925) and *Towards World Literacy* (Syracuse University Press, 1960). In 1937, *Letters by a Modern Mystic* was compiled from letters written by Dr. Laubach to his father from Lake Lanao in the Philippines.

From LETTERS BY A MODERN MYSTIC

January 26, 1930

You who will read these letters will know that I am here exploring two lands which for me are new. One of them is within my own soul, the other is in the soul of the Moros.

For the past few days I have been experimenting in a more complete surrender than ever before. I am taking by deliberate act of will, enough time from each hour to give God much thought. Yesterday and today I have made a new adventure, which is not easy to express. I am feeling

God in each movement, by an act of will — willing that
He shall direct these fingers that now strike this typewriter
— willing that He shall pour through my steps as I walk —
willing that He shall direct my words as I speak, and my
very jaws as I eat!

You will object to this intense introspection. Do not try
it, unless you feel dissatisfied with your own relationship
with God, but at least allow me to realize all the leadership
of God I can. I am disgusted with the pettiness and futility
of my unled self. If the way out is not more perfect slavery
to God then what is the way out? Paul speaks of our liberty
in Christ. I am trying to be utterly free from everybody,
free from my own self, but completely enslaved to the will
of God every moment of this day.

We used to sing a song in the church in Benton which I
liked, but which I never really practiced until now. It runs:

> "Moment by moment I'm kept in His love;
> Moment by moment, I've life from above;
> Looking to Jesus till glory doth shine;
> Moment by moment, O Lord, I am Thine."

It is exactly that "moment by moment," every waking
moment, surrender, responsiveness, obedience, sensitive-
ness, pliability, "lost in His love," that I now have the
mind-bent to explore with all my might. It means two
burning passions: First, to be like Jesus. Second, to respond
to God as a violin responds to the bow of the master.

In defense of my opening my soul and laying it bare to
the public gaze in this fashion, I may say that it seems to
me that we really seldom do anybody much good excepting
as we share the deepest experiences of our souls in this way.
It is not the fashion to tell your inmost thoughts, but there
are many wrong fashions, and concealment of the best in
us is wrong. I disapprove of the usual practice of talking

"small talk" whenever we meet, and holding a veil over our souls. If we are so impoverished that we have nothing to reveal but small talk, then we need to struggle for more richness of soul. As for me I am convinced that this spiritual pilgrimage which I am making is infinitely worth while, the most important thing I know of to talk about. And talk I shall while there is anybody to listen. And I hunger — O how I hunger! for others to tell me their soul adventures.

Edwin Muir

British critic, novelist, and poet, he was born in 1887. He wrote *The Marionette, First Poems,* and *The Structure of the Novel.* He and his wife collaborated on translations of Franz Kafka and Hermann Broch. He died in 1959.

From FROM DARKNESS TO LIGHT

The Adoration of the Beasts

I dreamed that I was lying asleep, when a light in my room wakened me. A man was standing by my bedside. He was wearing a long robe, which fell about him in motionless folds, while he stood like a column. The light that filled the room came from his hair, which rose straight up from his head, burning, like a motionless brazier. He raised his hand, and without touching me, merely by making that sign, lifted me to my feet in one movement so that I stood before him. He turned and went out through the door, and I followed him. We were in the gallery of a cloister; the moon was shining, and the shadows of the arches made black ribs on the flagstones. We went through a street, at the end of which there was a field, and while we walked on the moonlight changed to the white light of early morning. As we passed the last houses I saw a dark, shabby man with a dagger in his hand; he was wearing rags bound round his feet, so that he walked quite soundlessly; there was a stain as of blood on one of his sleeves; I took him to be a robber or a murderer and was afraid. But as he came nearer I saw that his eyes, which were fixed immovably on the figure beside me, were filled with a profound, violent adoration such as I had never seen in human eyes before. Then, behind him, I caught sight of a confused crowd of other men and women in curious or ragged clothes, and all had their eyes fixed with the same look on the man walking beside me. I saw their faces only for a moment. Presently we came to the field, which as we drew near changed into a great plain dotted with little conical hills a little higher than a man's head. All over the plain animals were standing or sitting on their haunches on these little hills; lions, tigers, bulls, deer, elephants, were there; serpents too wreathed their lengths on the knolls; and each was separate and alone, and each slowly lifted its head upward as if in prayer. This upward-lifting motion had a strange solemnity and deliberation; I watched head after head upraised as if proclaiming some truth just realized, and yet as if moved by an irresistible power beyond them. The elephant wreathed its trunk upward, and there was something pathetic and absurd in that indirect act of adoration. But the other animals raised their heads with the inevitability of the sun's rising, as if they knew, like the sun, that a new day was about to begin, and were giving the signal for its coming. Then I saw a little dog busily running about with his nose tied to the ground, as if he did not know that the animals had been redeemed. He was a friendly little dog, officiously going about his business, and it seemed to me that he too had a place in this day, and that his oblivious concern with the earth was also a sort of worship. How the dream ended I do not remember: I have now only a memory of the great animals with all their heads raised to heaven.

From AN AUTOBIOGRAPHY

My dissatisfaction with myself made me turn against other people as well . . . I was sometimes haunted by animal traits in human beings, as I had been many years before, sitting in a Glascow tramcar looking at a man like a pig. . . . After that there came a turn for the better.

I can see men and women as really human only when I see them as immortal souls. Otherwise they are unnatural, self-evidently not what they are by their nature; they do not exist in their *own* world.

This dialogue with myself went on. Meanwhile the world was darkening, and our work was growing precarious. Then my wife fell ill and had to go into a nursing home. After she began to recover, I was returning from the nursing home one day — it was the last day of February 1939, when I saw some schoolboys playing at marbles on the pavement; the old game had "come round" again at its own time, known only to children, and it seemed a simple little rehearsal for a resurrection, promising a timeless renewal of life. I wrote in my diary next day:

Last night, going to bed alone, I suddenly found myself (I was taking off my waistcoat) reciting the Lord's Prayer in a loud, emphatic voice — a thing I had not done for many years — with deep urgency and profound disturbed emotion. While I went on I grew more composed; as if it had been empty and craving and were being replenished, my soul grew still; every word had a strange fullness of meaning which astonished and delighted me. It was late; I had sat up reading; I was sleepy; but as I stood in the middle of the floor half-undressed, saying the prayer over and over, meaning after meaning sprang from it, overcoming me again with joyful surprise; and I realized that this simple petition was always universal and always inexhaustible, and day by day sanctified human life.

I had believed for many years in God and the immortality of the soul; I had clung to the belief even when, in horrifying glimpses, I saw animals peeping through human eyes. My belief receded then, it is true, to an unimaginable distance, but it still stood there, not in any territory of mine, it seemed, but in a place of its own. Now I realized that, quite without knowing it, I was a Christian, no matter how bad a one . . .

THE TRANSFIGURATION

So from the ground we felt that virtue branch
Through all our veins till we were whole, our wrists
As fresh and pure as water from a well,
Our hands made new to handle holy things,
The source of all our seeing rinsed and cleansed
Till earth and light and water entering there
Gave back to us the clear unfallen world.
We would have thrown our clothes away for lightness
But that even they, though sour and travel stained,
Seemed, like our flesh, made of immortal substance,
And the soiled flax and wool lay light upon us
Like friendly wonders, flower and flock entwined
As in a morning field. Was it a vision?
Or did we see that day the unseeable
One glory of the everlasting world
Perpetually at work, though never seen
Since Eden locked the gate that's everywhere
And nowhere? Was the change in us alone,
And the enormous earth still left forlorn
An exile or a prisoner? Yet the world
We saw that day made this unreal, for all
Was in its place. The painted animals
Assembled there in gentle congregations
Or sought apart their leafy oratories
Or walked in peace, the wild and tame together

As if, also for them, the day had come.
The shepherds' hovels shone, for underneath
The soot we saw the stone clean as the heart
As on the starting-day. The refuse heaps
Were grained with that fine dust that made the world;
For he had said "to the pure all things are pure."
And when we went into the town, he with us,
The lurkers under doorways, murderers,
With rags tied round their feet for silence, came
Out of themselves to us and were with us,
And those who hide within the labyrinth
Of their own loneliness and greatness came,
And those entangled in their own devices
The silent and the garrulous liars, all
Stepped out of their own dungeons and were free.
Reality or vision, this we have seen.
If it had lasted but another moment
It might have held for ever! But the world
Rolled back into its place, and we are here,
And all that radiant kingdom lies forlorn
As if it had never stirred; no human voice
Is heard among its meadows, but it speaks
To itself alone, alone it flowers and shines
And blossoms for itself while time runs on.

T. S. Eliot

Anglo-American poet and critic, he was born in 1888. His early works, including *Prufrock and Other Observations*, reflected pessimism, but his later ones make use of Anglican liturgy to convey an attitude of faith and hope. *Four Quartets* and *Ash Wednesday* are typical of this latter group. Eliot has also written the poetic dramas *Murder in the Cathedral*, *The Cocktail Party*, and *Family Reunion*.

From FOUR QUARTETS

IV

The wounded surgeon plies the steel
That questions the distempered part;
Beneath the bleeding hands we feel
The sharp compassion of the healer's art
Resolving the enigma of the fever chart.

Our only health is the disease
If we obey the dying nurse
Whose constant care is not to please
But to remind of our, and Adam's curse,
And that, to be restored, our sickness must grow worse.

The whole earth is our hospital
Endowed by the ruined millionaire,
Wherein, if we do well, we shall
Die of the absolute paternal care
That will not leave us, but prevents us everywhere.

The chill ascends from feet to knees,
The fever sings in mental wires.
If to be warmed, then I must freeze
And quake in frigid purgatorial fires
Of which the flame is roses, and the smoke is briars.

The dripping blood our only drink,
The bloody flesh our only food:
In spite of which we like to think
That we are sound, substantial flesh and blood —
Again, in spite of that, we call this Friday good.

Thomas Raymond Kelly

Born on 4 June 1893 near Chillicothe, in southwest Ohio, of Quaker parents, he was educated at Wilmington College. He worked at Harvard and then taught at Earlham. In 1934, he went to Pendle Hill. In 1935 he went to the University of Hawaii, to Haverford in 1937 and to Germany in 1938. He died in 1941.

From A TESTAMENT OF DEVOTION

There is a way of ordering our mental life on more than one level at once. On one level we may be thinking, discussing, seeing, calculating, meeting all the demands of external affairs. But deep within, behind the scenes, at a profounder level, we may also be in prayer and adoration, song and worship and a gentle receptiveness to divine breathings.

The secular world of today values and cultivates only the first level, assured that *there* is where the real business of mankind is done, and scorns, or smiles in tolerant amusement, at the cultivation of the second level — a luxury enterprise, a vestige of superstition, an occupation for special temperaments. But in a deeply religious culture men know that the deep level of prayer and of divine attendance is the most important thing in the world. It is at this deep level that the real business of life is determined. The secular mind is an abbreviated, fragmentary mind, building only upon a part of man's nature and neglecting a part — the most glorious part — of man's nature, powers and resources. The religious mind involves the whole of man, embraces his relations with time within their true ground and setting in the Eternal Lover. It ever keeps close to the fountains of divine creativity. In lowliness it knows joys and stabilities, peace and assurances, that are utterly incomprehensible to the secular mind. It lives in resources and powers that make individuals radiant and triumphant, groups tolerant and bonded together in mutual concern, and is bestirred to an outward life of unremitting labor.

Between the two levels is fruitful interplay, but ever the accent must be upon the deeper level, where the soul ever dwells in the presence of the Holy One. For the religious man is forever bringing all affairs of the first level down into the Light, holding them there in the Presence, reseeing them and the whole of the world of men and things in a new and overturning way, and responding to them in spontaneous, incisive and simple ways of love and faith. Facts remain facts, when brought into the Presence in the deeper level, but their value, their significance, is wholly realigned. Much apparent wheat becomes utter chaff, and some chaff becomes wheat. Imposing powers? They are out of the Life, and must crumble. Lost causes? If God be for them, who can be against them? Rationally plausible futures? They are weakened or certified in the dynamic Life and Light. Tragic suffering? Already He is there, and we actively move, in His tenderness, toward the sufferers. Hopeless debauchees? These are children of God, His concern and ours. Inexorable laws of nature? The dependable framework for divine reconstruction. The fall of a sparrow? The Father's love. For faith and hope and love for all things are engendered in the soul, as we practice their submission and our own to the Light Within, as we humbly see all things, even darkly and as through a glass, yet through the eye of God.

But the upper level of our mind plays upon the deeper

level of divine immediacy of internal communion and of prayer. It furnishes us with the objects of divine concern, "the sensualized material of our duty," as Fichte called it. It furnishes us with those culture-patterns of our group which are at one and the same time the medium and the material for their regeneration, our language, our symbols, our traditions, and our history. It provides for the mystic the suggestions for his metaphors, even the metaphor of the Light, the Seed, the Sanctuary, whereby he would suggest and communicate the wonder of God's immediacy and power. It supplies the present-day tools of reflection whereby the experience of Eternity is knit into the fabric of time and thought. But theologies and symbols and creeds, though inevitable, are transient and become obsolescent, while the Life of God sweeps on through the souls of men in continued revelation and creative newness. To that divine Life we must cling. In that Current we must bathe. In that abiding yet energizing Center we are all made one, behind and despite the surface differences of our forms and cultures. For the heart of the religious life is in commitment and worship, not in reflection and theory.

How, then, shall we lay hold of that Life and Power, and live the life of prayer without ceasing? By quiet, persistent practice in turning of all our being, day and night, in prayer and inward worship and surrender, toward Him who calls in the deeps of our souls. Mental habits of inward orientation must be established. An inner, secret turning to God can be made fairly steady, after weeks and months and years of practice and lapses and failures and returns. It is as simple an art as Brother Lawrence found it, but it may be long before we achieve any steadiness in the process. Begin now, as you read these words, as you sit in your chair, to offer your whole selves, utterly and in joyful abandon, in quiet, glad surrender to Him who is within. In secret ejaculations of praise, turn in humble wonder to the Light, faint though it may be. Keep contact with the outer world of sense and meanings. Here is no discipline in absent-mindedness. Walk and talk and work and laugh with your friends. But behind the scenes, keep up the life of simple prayer and inward worship. Keep it up throughout the day. Let inward prayer be your last act before you fall asleep and the first act when you awake. And in time you will find as did Brother Lawrence, that "those who have the gale of the Holy Spirit go forward even in sleep."

The first days and weeks and months are awkward and painful, but enormously rewarding. Awkward, because it takes constant vigilance and effort and reassertions of the will, at the first level. Painful, because our lapses are so frequent, the intervals when we forget Him so long. Rewarding, because we have begun to live. But these weeks and months and perhaps even years must be passed through before He gives us greater and easier stayedness upon Himself.

Lapses and forgettings are so frequent. Our surroundings grow so exciting. Our occupations are so exacting. But when you catch yourself again, lose no time in self-recriminations, but breathe a silent prayer for forgiveness and begin again, just where you are. Offer *this* broken worship up to Him and say: "This is what I am except Thou aid me." Admit no discouragement, but ever return quietly to Him and wait in His Presence.

At first the practice of inward prayer is a process of alternation of attention between outer things and the Inner Light. Preoccupation with either brings the loss of the other. Yet what is sought is not alternation, but simultaneity, worship undergirding every moment, living prayer, the continuous current and background of all moments of life. Long practice indeed is needed before alternation yields to concurrent immersion in both levels at once. The "plateaus in the learning curve" are so long, and many falter and give up, assenting to alternation as the best that they can do. And no doubt in His graciousness God gives us His gifts, even in intermittent communion, and touches us into flame, far beyond our achievements and deserts. But the hunger of the committed one is for unbroken communion and adoration, and we may be sure He longs for us to find it and supplements our weakness. For our quest is of His initiation, and is carried forward in His tender power and completed by His grace.

The first signs of simultaneity are given when at the moment of recovery from a period of forgetting there is a certain sense that we have not completely forgotten Him. It is as though we are only coming back into a state of vividness which had endured in dim and tenuous form throughout. What takes place now is not reinstatement of a broken prayer but return to liveliness of that which had endured, but mildly. The currents of His love have been flowing, but whereas we had been drifting in Him, now we swim. It is like the background of a picture which extends all the way across behind a tree in the foreground. It is not that we merely know intellectually that the background of the picture has unbroken extension; we experience aesthetically that it *does* extend across. Again, it is like waking from sleep yet knowing, not by inference but by immediate awareness, that we have lived even while we were asleep. For sole preoccupation with the world is sleep, but immersion in Him is life.

But to some at least He gives an amazing stayedness in Him, a well-nigh unbroken life of humble quiet adoration in His Presence, in the depths of our being. Day and night, winter and summer, sunshine and shadow, He is here, the great Champion. And we are with Him, held in His Tenderness, quickened into quietness and peace, children in Paradise before the Fall, walking with Him in the garden in the heat as well as the cool of the day. Here is not ecstasy but serenity, unshakableness, firmness of life-orientation. We are become what Fox calls "established men."

But longer discipline in this inward prayer will establish more enduring upreachings of praise and submission and relaxed listening in the depths, unworded but habitual orientation of all one's self about Him who is the Focus. The process is much simpler now. Little glances, quiet breathings of submission and invitation suffice. Voluntary or stated times of prayer merely join into and enhance the steady undercurrent of quiet worship that underlies the hours. Behind the foreground of the words continues the background of heavenly orientation, as all the currents of our being set toward Him. Through the shimmering light of divine Presence we look out upon the world, and in its turmoil and its fitfulness, we may be given to respond, in some increased measure, in ways dimly suggestive of the Son of Man.

We may suppose these depths of prayer are our achievement, the precipitate of our own habits at the surface level settled into subconscious regions. But this humanistic account misses the autonomy of the life of prayer. It misses the fact that this inner level has a life of its own, invigorated not by us but by a divine Source. There come times when prayer pours forth in volumes and originality such as we cannot create. It rolls through us like a mighty tide. Our prayers are mingled with a vaster Word, a Word that at one time was made flesh. We pray, and yet it is not we who pray, but a Greater who prays in us. Something of our punctiform selfhood is weakened, but never lost. All we can say is, Prayer is taking place, and I am given to be in the orbit. In holy hush we bow in Eternity, and know the Divine Concern tenderly enwrapping us and all things within His persuading love. Here all human initiative has passed into acquiescence, and He works and prays and seeks His own through us, in exquisite, energizing life. Here the autonomy of the inner life becomes complete and we are joyfully *prayed through*, by a Seeking Life that flows through us into the world of men. Sometimes this prayer is particularized, and we are impelled to pray for particular persons or particular situations with a quiet or turbulent energy that, subjectively considered, seems utterly irresistible. Sometimes the prayer and this Life that flows through us reaches out to all souls with kindred vision and upholds them in His tender care. Sometimes it flows out to the world of blinded struggle, and we become cosmic Saviors, seeking all those who are lost.

This "infused prayer" is not frequently given, in full intensity. But something of its autonomous character remains, not merely as a memory of a time when the fountains of creation were once revealed and we were swept along in their rising waters. It remains as an increasing awareness of a more-than-ourselves, working persuadingly and powerfully at the roots of our own soul, and in the depths of all men. It is an experimental assurance of Divine Labor and persuasion pervading the world, impelling men to their cross. In holy awe we are drawn anew to "keep close to the fresh up-springings of the Life," amazed at that which is revealed as at work, at the base of all being, all men and ourselves. And we have our first-hand assurance that He who began that good work in us, as in Timothy, can establish us in Him, can transform intermittency and alternation into simultaneity and continuity.

Guidance of life by the Light within is not exhausted as is too frequently supposed, in special leadings toward particular tasks. It begins first of all in a mass revision of our total reaction to the world. Worshipping in the light we become new creatures, making wholly new and astonishing responses to the entire outer setting of life. These responses are not reasoned out. They are, in large measure, spontaneous reactions of felt incompatibility between "the world's" judgments of value and the Supreme Value we adore deep in the Center. There is a total Instruction as well as specific instructions from the Light within. The dynamic illumination from the deeper level is shed upon the judgments of the surface level, and lo, the "former things are passed away, behold, they are become new."

Paradoxically, this total Instruction proceeds in two opposing directions at once. We are torn loose from earthly attachments and ambitions — *contemptus mundi*. And we are quickened to a divine but painful concern for the world — *amor mundi*. He plucks the world out of our hearts, loosening the chains of attachment. And He hurls the world into our hearts, where we and He together carry it in infinitely tender love.

Edward Estlin Cummings

An American poet and painter, born in 1894. His *The Enormous Room* is an account of the misunderstanding that led to his imprisonment by the French as a spy during World War I. *EIMI* is an account of a trip to the USSR. He also published a collection of drawings and paintings, and *Tom* (1935), a satirical ballet based on *Uncle Tom's Cabin*. Other works include *Christmas Tree*, 1/20, and *50 Poems*. He died in 1962.

From I: SIX NON-LECTURES

Only a butterfly's glide from my home began a mythical domain of semiwilderness; separating cerebral Cambridge and orchidaceous Somerville. Deep in this magical realm of Between stood a palace, containing Harvard University's far-famed Charles Eliot Norton: and lowly folk, who were neither professors nor professors' children, had nicknamed the district Norton's Woods. Here, as a very little child, I first encountered that mystery who is Nature; here my enormous smallness entered Her illimitable being; and here someone actually infinite or impossibly alive — someone who might almost (but not quite) have been myself — wonderingly wandered the mortally immortal complexities of Her beyond imagining imagination

O sweet spontaneous
earth how often have
the
doting

      fingers of
prurient philosophers pinched

and
poked

thee
, has the naughty thumb
of science prodded
thy

    beauty   .how
often have religions taken
thee upon their scraggy knees
squeezing and

buffeting thee that thou mightest conceive
gods
      (but
true

to the incomparable
couch of death thy
rhythmic
lover

      thou answerest

them only with

        spring)

— later, this beyond imagining imagination revealed a not
believably mountaining ocean, at Lynn; and, in New Hamp-
shire, oceaning miraculously mountains. But the wonder of my
first meeting with Herself is with me now; and also with me is
the coming (obedient to Her each resurrection) of a roguish
and resistless More Than Someone: Whom my deepest selves
unfailingly recognized, though His disguise protected him from
all the world

i thank You God for most this amazing
day:for the leaping greenly spirits of trees
and a blue true dream of sky;and for everything
which is natural which is infinite which is yes

(i who have died am alive again today,
and this is the sun's birthday;this is the birth
day of life and of love and wings;and of the gay
great happening illimitably earth)

how should tasting touching hearing seeing
breathing any — lifted from the no
of all nothing — human merely being
doubt unimaginable You?

(now the ears of my ears awake and
now the eyes of my eyes are opened)

C. S. Lewis

Born in 1898, he was an English writer and Cambridge don, who called his spiritual autobiography, *Surprised by Joy* (1956), "the shape of my early life." *The Screwtape Letters* (1943), an imaginary correspondence of demons, is among the most notable and unorthodox works of contemporary Christian apologetics. His other works include *Pilgrim's Regress* and *Out of the Silent Planet*. He died in 1963.

From SURPRISED BY JOY

As I stood beside a flowering currant bush on a summer day there suddenly arose in me without warning, and as if from a depth not of years but of centuries, the memory of that earlier morning at the Old House when my brother had brought his toy garden into the nursery. It is difficult to find words strong enough for the sensation which came over me; Milton's "enormous bliss" of Eden (giving the full, ancient meaning to "enormous") comes somewhere near it. It was a sensation, of course, of desire; but desire for what? not, certainly, for a biscuit tin filled with moss, nor even (though that came into it) for my own past. Ἰούλιαν ποθῶ * — and before I knew what I desired, the desire itself was gone, the whole glimpse withdrawn, the world turned commonplace again, or only stirred by a longing for the longing that had just ceased. It had taken only a moment of time; and in a certain sense everything else

* Oh, I desire too much.

that had ever happened to me was insignificant in comparison.

The odd thing was that before God closed in on me, I was in fact offered what now appears a moment of wholly free choice. In a sense. I was going up Headington Hill on the top of a bus. Without words and (I think) almost without images, a fact about myself was somehow presented to me. I became aware that I was holding something at bay, or shutting something out. Or, if you like, that I was wearing some stiff clothing, like corsets, or even a suit of armor, as if I were a lobster. I felt myself being, there and then, given a free choice. I could open the door or keep it shut; I could unbuckle the armor or keep it on. Neither choice was presented as a duty; no threat or promise was attached to either, though I knew that to open the door or to take off the corslet meant the incalculable. The choice appeared to be momentous but it was also strangely unemotional. I was moved by no desires or fears. In a sense I was not moved by anything. I chose to open, to unbuckle, to loosen the rein. I say, "I chose," yet it did not really seem possible to do the opposite. On the other hand, I was aware of no motives. You could argue that I was not a free agent, but I am more inclined to think that this came nearer to being a perfectly free act than most that I have ever done. Necessity may not be the opposite of freedom, and perhaps a man is most free when, instead of producing motives, he could only say, "I am what I do." Then came the repercussion on the imaginative level. I felt as if I were a man of snow at long last beginning to melt. The melting was starting in my back — drip-drip and presently trickle-trickle. I rather disliked the feeling.

From THE SCREWTAPE LETTERS

XXXI

My dear, my very dear, Wormwood, my poppet, my pigsnie,

How mistakenly now that all is lost you come whimpering to ask me whether the terms of affection in which I address you meant nothing from the beginning. Far from it! Rest assured, my love for you and your love for me are as like as two peas. I have always desired you, as you (pitiful fool) desired me. The difference is that I am the stronger. I think they will give you to me now; or a bit of you. Love you? Why, yes. As dainty a morsel as ever I grew fat on.

You have let a soul slip through your fingers. The howl of sharpened famine for that loss re-echoes at this moment through all the levels of the Kingdom of Noise down to the very Throne itself. It makes me mad to think of it. How well I know what happened at the instant when they snatched him from you! There was a sudden clearing of his eyes (was there not?) as he saw you for the first time, and recognised the part you had had in him and knew that you had it no longer. Just think (and let it be the beginning of your agony) what he felt at that moment; as if a scab had fallen from an old sore, as if he were emerging from a hideous, shell-like tetter, as if he shuffled off for good and all a defiled, wet, clinging garment. By Hell, it is misery enough to see them in their mortal days taking off dirtied and uncomfortable clothes and splashing in hot water and giving little grunts of pleasure — stretching their eased limbs. What, then, of this final stripping, this complete cleansing?

The more one thinks about it, the worse it becomes. He

got through so easily! No gradual misgivings, no doctor's
sentence, no nursing home, no operating theatre, no false
hopes of life; sheer, instantaneous liberation. One moment it seemed to be all our world; the scream of bombs,
the fall of houses, the stink and taste of high explosive on
the lips and in the lungs, the feet burning with weariness,
the heart cold with horrors, the brain reeling, the legs aching; next moment all this was gone, gone like a bad dream,
never again to be of any account. Defeated, out-manoeuvred
fool! Did you mark how naturally — as if he'd been born
for it — the earth-born vermin entered the new life? How
all his doubts became, in the twinkling of an eye, ridiculous?
I know what the creature was saying to itself! "Yes. Of
course. It always was like this. All horrors have followed
the same course, getting worse and worse and forcing you
into a kind of bottle-neck till, at the very moment when
you thought you must be crushed, behold! you were out of
the narrows and all was suddenly well. The extraction hurt
more and more and then the tooth was out. The dream
became a nightmare and then you woke. You die and die
and then you are beyond death. How could I ever have
doubted it?"

As he saw you, he also saw Them. I know how it was.
You reeled back dizzy and blinded, more hurt by them
than he had ever been by bombs. The degradation of it!
— that this thing of earth and slime could stand upright
and converse with spirits before whom you, a spirit, could
only cower. Perhaps you had hoped that the awe and
strangeness of it would dash his joy. But that is the cursed
thing; the gods are strange to mortal eyes, and yet they are
not strange. He had no faintest conception till that very
hour of how they would look, and even doubted their
existence. But when he saw them he knew that he had
always known them and realised what part each one of
them had played at many an hour in his life when he had

supposed himself alone, so that now he could say to them, one by one, not "Who *are* you?" but "So it was *you* all the time." All that they were and said at this meeting woke memories. The dim consciousness of friends about him which had haunted his solitudes from infancy was now at last explained; that central music in every pure experience which had always just evaded memory was now at last recovered. Recognition made him free of their company almost before the limbs of his corpse became quiet. Only you were left outside.

He saw not only Them; he saw Him. This animal, this thing begotten in a bed, could look on Him. What is blinding, suffocating fire to you, is now cool light to him, is clarity itself, and wears the form of a Man. You would like, if you could, to interpret the patient's prostration in the Presence, his self-abhorrence and utter knowledge of his sins (yes, Wormwood, a clearer knowledge even than yours) on the analogy of your own choking and paralysing sensations when you encounter the deadly air that breathes from the heart of Heaven. But it's all nonsense. Pains he may still have to encounter, but they *embrace* those pains. They would not barter them for any earthly pleasure. All the delights of sense, or heart, or intellect, with which you could once have tempted him, even the delights of virtue itself, now seem to him in comparison but as the half nauseous attractions of a raddled harlot would seem to a man who hears that his true beloved whom he has loved all his life and whom he had believed to be dead is alive and even now at his door. He is caught up into that world where pain and pleasure take on transfinite values and all our arithmetic is dismayed. Once more, the inexplicable meets us. Next to the curse of useless tempters like yourself the greatest curse upon us is the failure of our Intelligence Department. If only we could find out what He is really up to! Alas, alas, that knowledge, in itself so hateful and mawkish a thing, should yet be necessary for Power! Sometimes I am almost in despair. All that sustains me is the conviction that our Realism, our rejection (in the face of all temptations) of all silly nonsense and claptrap, *must* win in the end. Meanwhile, I have you to settle with. Most truly do I sign myself

Your increasingly and ravenously
affectionate uncle
SCREWTAPE

John Betjeman

———•—•———

A member of the Church of England, John Betjeman was born in 1906 and educated at Oxford, and began writing satirical verse at an early age. His books include *Old Lights for New Chancels* and the autobiographical *Summoned by Bells*, from which the following extract is taken.

From SUMMONED BY BELLS

There wasn't much to see, there wasn't much
The *Little Guide* could say about the church.
Holy and small and heavily restored,
It held me for the length of Evensong,
Said rapidly among discoloured walls,
Impatient of my diffident response.
"Better come in and have a cup of tea."
The Rectory was large, uncarpeted;
Books and oil-lamps and papers were about;
The study's pale green walls were mapped with damp;
The pitch-pine doors and window-frames were cracked;
Loose noisy tiles along the passages
Let to a waste of barely furnished rooms:
Clearly the Rector lived here all alone.
    He talked of poetry and Cornish saints;
He kept an apiary and a cow;
He asked me which church service I liked best —
I told him Evensong . . . "And I suppose
You think religion's mostly singing hymns
And feeling warm and comfortable inside?"

And he was right: most certainly I did.
"Borrow this book and come to tea again."
With Arthur Machen's *Secret Glory* stuffed
Into my blazer pocket, up the hill
On to St. Merryn, down to Padstow Quay
In time for the last ferry back to Rock,
I bicycled — and found Trebetherick
A worldly contrast with my afternoon.

    I would not care to read that book again.
It so exactly mingled with the mood
Of those impressionable years, that now
I might be disillusioned. There were laughs
At public schools, at chapel services,
At masters who were still "big boys at heart" —
While all the time the author's hero knew
A Secret Glory in the hills of Wales:
Caverns of light revealed the Holy Grail
Exhaling gold upon the mountain-tops;
At "Holy! Holy! Holy!" in the Mass
King Brychan's sainted children crowded round,
And past and present were enwrapped in one.

    In quest of mystical experience
I knelt in darkness at St. Enodoc;
I visited our local Holy Well,
Whereto the native Cornish still resort
For cures for whooping cough, and drop bent pins
Into its peaty water . . . Not a sign:
No mystical experience was vouchsafed:
The maidenhair just trembled in the wind
And everything looked as it always looked . . .
But somewhere, somewhere underneath the dunes,
Somewhere among the cairns or in the caves
The Celtic saints would come to me, the ledge
Of time we walk on, like a thin cliff-path
High in the mist, would show the precipice.

Dietrich Bonhoeffer

He was born in 1906 and became a philosopher among the pastors
of the German evangelical Confessional Church. He died in a Nazi
concentration camp in April 1945.

CHRISTIANS AND UNBELIEVERS

Men go to God when they are sore bestead,
Pray to him for succour, for his peace, for bread,
For mercy for them sick, sinning or dead:
All men do so, Christian and unbelieving.

Men go to God when he is sore bestead,
Find him poor and scorned, without shelter or bread,
Whelmed under weight of the wicked, the weak, the dead:
Christians stand by God in his hour of grieving.

God goeth to every man when he is sore bestead,
Feedeth body and spirit with his bread,
For Christians, heathens alike he hangeth dead:
And both alike forgiving.

Helmuth James, Count von Moltke

German jurist and statesman, was born in 1907. He wrote these last letters to his wife shortly before his execution by the Nazis in January 1945.

From DYING WE LIVE

Tegel, January 10, 1945

DEAR HEART: First I must tell you that quite evidently the last twenty-four hours of one's life are no different from any others. I had always imagined that it would come as a shock to say to oneself: "Now the sun is setting for the last time for you, now the hour hand will make only two more revolutions before twelve, now you are going to bed for the last time." Nothing of the sort. Perhaps I am a little cracked. For I cannot deny that I am in really high spirits. I only pray to God in heaven to sustain me in this mood, for surely it is easier for the flesh to die in this state. How merciful the Lord has been to me! Even at the risk of sounding hysterical — I am so full of thanks that there is actually no room for anything else. He has guided me so firmly and clearly during these two days. The whole courtroom might have roared, like Herr Freisler* himself, and all the walls might have rocked — it would have made no difference to me. It was just as is written in Isaiah 43:2: "When thou passest through the waters, I will be with thee;

* President of the People's Court.

and through the rivers, they shall not overflow thee: when thou walkest through the fire, thou shalt not be burned; neither shall the flame kindle upon thee." That is to say, upon your soul. When I was called up for my last words, I was in such a frame of mind that I nearly said, "I have only one thing to add to my defense. Take my goods, my honor, my child and wife; the body they may kill; God's truth abideth still, his kingdom is for ever." But that would only have made it harder for the others; therefore I said only, "I do not intend to say anything, Herr President."

Therefore I can say only one thing, dear heart. May God be as merciful to you as to me — then even the death of a husband matters not at all. For he can demonstrate his omnipotence even when you are making pancakes for the boys, or when you have to take Puschti out of the room (although I hope that isn't necessary any more). I should be saying farewell to you — I can't do it. I should be mourning and regretting the drabness of your everyday life — I can't do it. I should indeed be thinking of the burdens that will now fall upon you — I can't do it. I can say only one thing to you: if you attain to a feeling of supreme security — if the Lord gives you that which, had it not been for this period in our lives and its conclusion, you would never have had, then I am leaving you a treasure that cannot be confiscated, a treasure compared to which even my life is of small account.

The decisive pronouncement in my trial was: "Count Moltke, Christianity and we National Socialists have one thing in common, and one thing only: we claim the whole man." Did he realize what he was saying? Just think how wondrously God prepared this unworthy vessel of his: at the very moment when there was danger of my being drawn

into active preparations for the coup I was taken out of it,
so that I am free and remain free of any connection with
the use of violence. In addition, God had implanted in me
that socialistic trait which freed me, although owner of a
great estate, from any suspicion of representing vested interests. Then he abased me as I have never been abased
before, so that I have had to give over all pride, so that
after thirty-eight years I finally understand my sinfulness,
so that I am learning to pray for his forgiveness, to entrust
myself to his mercy. Then he caused me to come here,
that I might see you standing fast, and that I might be
freed of all thoughts of you and the boys, that is to say, all
anxious thoughts. He is giving me time and opportunity
to put in order everything that can be put in order, so that
all earthly cares can fall away. Then he permitted me to
experience, to an unheard-of depth, the anguish of parting
and the fear of death and the terror of hell — so that this
too is over and done with.

Then he endowed me with faith, hope, and love, all this
in a plenitude truly lavish. . . . And then your husband
was selected to be attacked and condemned, as a Protestant,
above all because of his friendship with Catholics. And
thus he stood before Freisler not as a Protestant, not as a
landed proprietor, not as a nobleman, not as a Prussian,
not as a German — all that was explicitly eliminated in the
main hearing (for example, Sperr said: "I thought, what an
extraordinary Prussian") — but as a Christian and as nothing else.

Katharine Trevelyan

Niece of the celebrated historian George Macaulay Trevelyan, she was born in 1909. She published her "autobiography of a natural mystic," *Through Mine Own Eyes*, in 1963. It first appeared in England a year earlier as *Fool in Love*.

From THROUGH MINE OWN EYES

When I knew myself nothing but a prize fool in love, I took my pain and foolishness in both hands and quite simply offered them to God, whom I recognized through this last anguish to be the backcloth of my life and my eternal love.

What followed was beyond me to understand.

Whether it was predestined or whether the Heavens had been waiting with an open question to hear an uncomplaining acceptance of this last sorrow, I cannot say.

It felt as though an infinitely complex machine had in all its parts, between one moment and the next, clicked silently into gear and started to work with inexorable power.

I saw face to face at last.

Light streamed down from the sky such as I have never beheld. The sun shone with a new light, as though translucent gold were at its heart. I saw not only the physical sun but the spiritual sun also, which poured down on me as I walked in the garden at Coombe.

The wonder was beyond anything I have ever read or imagined or heard men speak about. I was Adam walking alone in the first Paradise. That it was a garden near the outskirts of London in the twentieth century made no difference, for time was not, or had come round again in a full circle. Though I was Adam, I had no need of Eve, for both combined within me. Marriage and maternity fulfilled and surpassed, I had run beyond womanhood and become a human being.

Every flower spoke to me, every spider wove a miracle of intricacy for my eyes, every bird understood that here was Heaven come to earth. Turner must have been seeing the skies as I saw them then — living cloud shapes crossing and recrossing each other as though conversing in form or singing in color.

But there was something more wonderful than the Light within the light — more wonderful than the standstill of time. It was that God walked with me in the garden as He did before the Fall. Whether I sat, whether I walked, He was there — radiant, burningly pure, holy beyond holy.

When I breathed, I breathed Him; when I asked a question He both asked and answered it.

My heart was unshuttered to Him and He came and went at will; my head had no limit or boundary of skull, but the Spirit of God played on me as though my mind were a harp which reached the zenith.

Every prayer was fulfilled, every possible desire for the whole world consummated; for His Kingdom had come and I had beheld it with my very eyes. Never again the need to meditate for He was here, to be STOOD in, SAT in, as a child might play on the edges of a great sunny river. And, indeed, I found myself only a child, playing in Him, laughing with Him at the way He was visiting His world. When I stood within Him, He gave and was everything. The years to come, which He showed me as easily as a father shows his child a curious shell beside the great river, held in them no surprise; only wonder and joy.

Loren Hurnscot

This is the pseudonym of an Englishwoman whose spiritual and emotional history between the two World Wars is told in A *Prison, A Paradise* (1959).

From A PRISON, A PARADISE

Just at dusk, I was there on the rock by the river. I had to wait in the woods for people to go. There was silence at last. I burnt a card — the nine of diamonds — that I had seen in a street in Bloomsbury and picked up, out of some queer whim, wondering why it was not the nine of spades. The subcurrents of lunacy had been swaying through me for a long time.

The sheer evil of the place was growing. The water was still and oily below the spume. "If a man fell in there by sheer accident, he'd be damned for a thousand years," I thought. I felt the presence of past suicides, evil and despairing, all round me. "Is that the company I'm going to keep?"

The last light died out on the grey-green woods. I sat on, on the rocks. It was time. Was it time? And suddenly I knew that if I did this thing, I should be making an unbreakable link between myself and all the evil in the world. It came over me, blindingly, for the first time in my life, that suicide was a wrong act, was indeed "mortal sin." In that moment, God stopped me. I did not want my

life, but I knew I was suddenly forbidden by something outside myself to let it go.

I cried hopelessly for a long while. I looked again at the
water, and thought of the Dial in my bag, that I'd meant
to swallow to deaden consciousness. A tremendous "NO"
rose — within me? outside me? I don't know. "I can't do
it — I'm held back — I know beyond all doubt that it is
absolutely *wrong.*"

Some blind instinct made me pull off my "disguise." It
began to rain. There were seven shillings in my bag, dark
was falling, and I was two hundred miles from home. I
walked back to the village in the darkness, sobbing and
talking to God. There was no earthly help for me anywhere, but I knew I was no longer alone; that God was
there. It had always been pride that had held me off from
Him. Now it was broken the obstacle was gone. One is
never simple enough, while things go well.

"I'm in Your hands," I kept whispering. "You stopped
me. You must show me what to do." I got back as far as
the hotel, and asked about a bus to Sherston. They had all
gone. "You might get a lift," someone said. I stood in the
rain, on the bridge, crying, utterly down and out, praying
in my heart all the time. Out of the rainy darkness a voice
called out, "Mrs. Mitchell might put you up — first house
on the left, over the bridge."

I forget the journey. Perhaps I slept. Once more I went
to Robin's basement, retrieved my property, posted the
cheque and sent a telegram. Then I went down to Well-
bridge, where Bee and Angus met me. It was lovely to see
her good kind face at the station, after all I'd gone through.
They were very sweet to me and I spent a happy ten days
there, mostly out in the hopfields, getting well. The old
persecution-complex melted away; a bad dream. A little
money was promised me till Christmas, so that I could

just live. Everything in me was very quiet, waiting. And when I came back to Tripoly, the peace of God seemed to enter my heart.

I feel that it all had to happen, and happen in just that way. Nothing else would have removed the suicide-obsession I've cherished secretly, ever since I was a child. Those hours by the northern river had to be, when I was beyond all human help, and knew at last that God was there.

The future looks most uncertain. But my faith is certain now. "You've been given a very great grace," said that little priest, "to have been stopped on the last edge like that." And I knew he understood.

October 2nd. The present is being a sort of holiday, a holy day. Life won't go on like it — it may be the best that I shall ever know. There is a radiance within. The screen my bitter "outcast" pride put between God and me has gone, and I know both in spirit and (in a strange inexplicable way) even in body that it is true that God is love.

October 4th. Mist and cold, after yesterday's Indian summer. It was one of the perfect days — the high tide of this present time. I went out for a walk, then picked blackberries on Periton Hill, in that far clump at the edge of the downs. For a long time I sat on the crumbling turf, sheltered from the wind, with the blue distances below, and warm sun lying over this lovely autumn land. And suddenly I was swept out of myself — knowing, knowing, knowing. Feeling the love of God burning through creation, and an ecstasy of bliss pouring through my spirit and down into every nerve. I'm ashamed to put it down in these halting words. For it was ecstasy — that indissoluble mingling of fire and light that the mystics know. There was a scalding sun in my breast — the "kingdom of God within" — that rushed out to that All-Beauty.

November 24th. There were some wonderful days in October when I was burning and consumed for hours in the love of God — the "sun flower" experience, a bliss I never dreamed of. But I never tried to invoke it, I feared to use it as a sort of indulgence so I dared not pray for it, though it seemed to me that if the self-screen could be withdrawn, it could be almost constant.

But there have been distractions: that short job I did for the little evacuee children, in that oppressive house in Sussex; then a visit to Alison that had some ugly elements. I wondered if the "sun flower" would ever come back. This evening at Tripoly, washing up in the tiny kitchen, having thought and prayed all day, I was suddenly overwhelmed once more by the deepest bliss, the burning love of God. Tears poured down my face and I did not even know they were there until afterwards.

January 5th 1948. The highlight of my visit, and one of the occasions of our lives, came on New Year's Eve. Alison and I went by a variety of buses to Ripon, and set off on a cloudy winter afternoon, in a taxi, to the gates of Fountains Abbey. I had clamoured for years to revisit it, for I had loved it as a child and had never seen it since. We dismissed the taxi at the gates, walked by frost-whitened paths between silvery evergreens, then down towards the roar of the Skell and the dim lovely ruins. Repair-work was going on and scaffolding towered above the Chapel of the Nine Altars. As dusk fell, we stood together on the south side of the cloister-garth, looking north, towards the cedar and the great grass-grown walls and the tower. And as we stood silently watching, they began to change. A soft, silvery-amber and quite unearthly light like warm moonlight lay over them. But there was no moon; it was not due to rise for hours yet. In utter silence — where was the roar of the Skell? — the whole ruin changed, rebuilt itself: the walls were intact, the church and the Chapel of the Nine Altars became roofed and perfect. The pinnacled tower stood out newly finished, a deeper amber than the rest. The entire structure was silver-gilt in colour, and this colour seemed to be struck out of it by the silvery light in which it was bathed. We both stood awestruck, wordless, not moving, for what seemed a long time. "There's no scaffolding," breathed Alison at last in a soft amazed tone. I didn't answer, for I thought, "Why should there be scaffolding? We're seeing as it was about 1520, when Huby's tower was finished, and they've only just removed the scaffolding." But then I realised that we were both seeing the same thing. She said later that she had meant the scaffolding that showed above the Chapel of the Nine Altars, where (certainly from the time and place in which we now were) there was no scaffolding.

We saw no Cistercian monks, brought back no useful information whatever, we merely stood for a timeless moment, for eternities or for ten minutes, seeing Fountains as it was a few years before the Reformation.

Last night, as usual, I sat and composed myself. It was about a quarter to eleven by my very wrong clock. And almost at once, something akin to the "sun flower" came back — that indescribable sense of the inflooding, enfolding, brimful-filling of God's burning love, and the knowledge that the material universe, the atmosphere, world, body are screens of mercy, which in our fallen state are there as a protection. That God's love meeting only foulness would destroy and disintegrate it; that the screen is our shelter and our opportunity. But it is no more than a screen; there is no least corner of the universe where God's love is not.

And for the first time I began to understand this strange

idea: the spatial location of the Heavenly Heart. It was like "the fifth month, when the child moves." For the second time in ten years, there's hope.

Anonymous

— • —

This contemporary Episcopalian author, who prefers to remain anonymous, also wrote *The Golden Fountain* and *The Romance of the Soul.*

From THE PRODIGAL RETURNS

VI

With recovered health, I married, and knew great happiness; but as a bride of four months I had to part from my husband, who went to the South African War. Always, always this terrible pain of love that must part. Always it was love that seemed to me the most beautiful thing in life, and always it was love that hurt me most. He was away for fifteen months. I made no spiritual advance whatever. Mystified by so much pain, I now began to regard God if not as the actual Author of all pain, at any rate as the Permitter of all pain. More and more I fell back in alarm at the discovery of the depths of my own capacities for suffering. A tremendous fear of God now commenced to grow up in me, which so increased that after a few years I listened with astonishment when I heard people say they were afraid of *any* person, even a burglar! I could no longer understand feeling fear for anyone or anything save God. All my actions were now governed solely by this sense of weighty, immediate fear of Him. This continued for some ten years.

VIII

One day I returned from a walk, and hardly had I entered my room when I commenced thinking with great nearness and intimacy of Jesus; and suddenly, with the most intense vividness, He presented Himself before my consciousness so that I inwardly perceived Him, and at once I was overcome by a great agony of remorse for my unworthiness: it was as though my heart and mind broke in pieces and melted in the stress of this fearful pain, which continued — increased — became unendurable, and lasted altogether an hour. Too ignorant to know that this was the pain of Repentance, I did not understand what had happened to me; but now indeed at least I knew beyond a doubt that I had a soul! My wonderful Lord had come to pay me a visit, and I was not fit to receive Him — hence my agony. I would try with all my strength to improve myself for Him.

I was at first at a standstill to know even where to commence in this improvement, for words fail to describe what I now saw in myself! Up till now I had publicly confessed myself a sinner, and privately calmly thought of myself as a sinner, but without being disturbed by it or perceiving how I was one! I kept the commandments in the usual degree and way, and was conscientious in my dealings with others. Now all at once — by this Presentment of Himself before my soul — which had lasted for no more than one moment of time — I suddenly, and with terrible clearness, saw the whole insufferable offensiveness of myself.

Two years went by, and on Easter morning, at the close of the service as I knelt in prayer in the church, He suddenly presented Himself again before my soul, and again I saw myself, and again I went down and down into those terrible abysses of spiritual pain; and I suffered more than I suffered the first time: indeed, I have never had the courage to quite fully recall the full depths of this anguish to mind.

After this my soul knew Jesus as Christ the Son of God, and my heart and mind accepted this without any further wonder or question, and entirely without knowing how this knowledge had been given, for it came as a gift.

A great repose now commenced to fill me, and the world and all its interests and ways seemed softly and gently blown out of my heart by the wings of a great new love, my love for the Risen Christ.

X

It was summer-time: a great battle was raging in France. A friend wrote me that my husband was up in the very foremost part of it. I heard no word from my husband; weeks passed, and still the same ominous silence. At last day came when the shadow of these two fearful years rose up and overwhelmed me altogether. I went up on to the wild lonely hill where I so often walked, and there I contended with God for His help. For the first time in my life there was nothing between God and myself — this had *continually* happened with Jesus Christ, but not with God the Father, Who remained totally inaccessible to me. Now, like a man standing in a very dark place and seeing nothing but knowing himself immediately near to another — so I knew myself in very great nearness to God. I had no need for eyes to see outwardly, because of the immense magnetism of this inward Awareness. At one moment my heart and mind ran like water before Him — praying Him, beseeching Him for His help; at another my soul stood straight up before Him, contending and claiming because she could bear no more: and it felt as though the Spirit of God stood over against my spirit, and my spirit wrestled with God's Spirit for more than an hour. But He gave me than I suffered the first time: indeed, I have never had the courage to quite fully recall the full depths of this anguish to mind.

After this my soul knew Jesus as Christ the Son of God, and my heart and mind accepted this without any further wonder or question, and entirely without knowing how this knowledge had been given, for it came as a gift.

A great repose now commenced to fill me, and the world and all its interests and ways seemed softly and gently blown out of my heart by the wings of a great new love, my love for the Risen Christ.

X

It was summer-time: a great battle was raging in France. A friend wrote me that my husband was up in the very foremost part of it. I heard no word from my husband; weeks passed, and still the same ominous silence. At last day came when the shadow of these two fearful years rose up and overwhelmed me altogether. I went up on to the wild lonely hill where I so often walked, and there I contended with God for His help. For the first time in my life there was nothing between God and myself — this had *continually* happened with Jesus Christ, but not with God the Father, Who remained totally inaccessible to me. Now, like a man standing in a very dark place and seeing nothing but knowing himself immediately near to another — so I knew myself in very great nearness to God. I had no need for eyes to see outwardly, because of the immense magnetism of this inward Awareness. At one moment my heart and mind ran like water before Him — praying Him, beseeching Him for His help; at another my soul stood straight up before Him, contending and claiming because he could bear no more: and it felt as though the Spirit of God stood over against my spirit, and my spirit wrestled with God's Spirit for more than an hour. But He gave me

idea: the spatial location of the Heavenly Heart. It was like "the fifth month, when the child moves." For the second time in ten years, there's hope.

Anonymous

This contemporary Episcopalian author, who prefers to remain anonymous, also wrote *The Golden Fountain* and *The Romance of the Soul.*

From THE PRODIGAL RETURNS

VI

With recovered health, I married, and knew great happiness; but as a bride of four months I had to part from my husband, who went to the South African War. Always, always this terrible pain of love that must part. Always it was love that seemed to me the most beautiful thing in life, and always it was love that hurt me most. He was away for fifteen months. I made no spiritual advance whatever. Mystified by so much pain, I now began to regard God if not as the actual Author of all pain, at any rate as the Permitter of all pain. More and more I fell back in alarm at the discovery of the depths of my own capacities for suffering. A tremendous fear of God now commenced to grow up in me, which so increased that after a few years I listened with astonishment when I heard people say they were afraid of *any* person, even a burglar! I could no longer understand feeling fear for anyone or anything save God. All my actions were now governed solely by this sense of weighty, immediate fear of Him. This continued for some ten years.

VIII

One day I returned from a walk, and hardly tered my room when I commenced thinking nearness and intimacy of Jesus; and suddenly, most intense vividness, He presented Himself consciousness so that I inwardly perceived Hi once I was overcome by a great agony of remo unworthiness: it was as though my heart and in pieces and melted in the stress of this fearful continued — increased — became unendurable, altogether an hour. Too ignorant to know th the pain of Repentance, I did not understan happened to me; but now indeed at least I kn doubt that I had a soul! My wonderful Lord pay me a visit, and I was not fit to receive H my agony. I would try with all my strength to self for Him.

I was at first at a standstill to know even mence in this improvement, for words fai what I now saw in myself! Up till now I had fessed myself a sinner, and privately calmly t self as a sinner, but without being disturbe ceiving how I was one! I kept the commar usual degree and way, and was conscientio ings with others. Now all at once — by this Himself before my soul — which had last than one moment of time — I suddenly, a clearness, saw the whole insufferable offer self.

Two years went by, and on Easter morn of the service as I knelt in prayer in the denly presented Himself again before m I saw myself, and again I went dowr those terrible abysses of spiritual pain; a no answer, no sign, no help. He gave me nothing but that awful silence which seems to hang for ever between God and Man. And I became exhausted, and turned away in despair from God, and from supplication, and from striving, and from contending, and, very quiet and profoundly sad, I stood looking out across the hills to the distant view — how gentle and lovely this peace of the evening sky, whilst on earth all the nations of the world were fighting together in blood and fury and pain!

I had stood there for perhaps ten minutes, mutely and sadly wondering at the meaning of it all, and was commencing to walk away when suddenly I was surrounded by a great whiteness which blotted out from me all my surroundings. It was like a great light or white cloud which hid all my surroundings from me, though I stood there with my eyes wide open: and the cloud pricked, so that I said to myself, "It is an electric cloud," and it pricked me from my head down to my elbows, but no further. I felt no fear whatever, but a very great wonder, and stood there all quite simple and placid, feeling very quiet. Then there began to be poured into me an indescribably great vitality, so that I said to myself, "I am being filled with some marvellous Elixir." And it filled me from the feet up, gently and slowly, so that I could notice every advance of it. As it rose higher in me, so I grew to feel freed: that is to say, I had within me the astounding sensation of having the capacity to pass where or how I would — which is to say I felt freed of the law of gravity. I was like a free spirit — I felt and knew within myself this glorious freedom! I tasted for some moments a new form of living! Words are unable to convey the splendour of it, the boundless joy, the liberty, the glory of it.

And the incomprehensible Power rose and rose in me until it reached the very crown of my head, and immediately it had quite filled me a marvellous thing happened —

the Wall, the dreadful Barrier between God and me, came down entirely, and immediately I loved Him. I was so filled with love that I had to cry aloud my love, so great was the force and the wonder and the delight and the might of it.

And now, slowly, the vivid whiteness melted away so that I saw everything around me once more just as before; but for a little while I continued to stand there very still and thoughtful, because I was filled with wonder and great peace.

One night I compose myself as usual for sleep, but I do not sleep, neither can I say that I am quite awake. It is neither sleep, nor is my wakefulness the usual wakefulness. I do not dream, I cannot move. My consciousness is alight with a new fiery energy of life; it feels to extend to an infinite distance beyond my body, and yet remains connected with my body. I live in a manner totally new and totally incomprehensible, a life in which none of my senses are used and which is yet a thousand, and more than a thousand, times as vivid. It is living at white heat — without forms, without sound, without sight, without anything which I have ever been aware of in this world, and at a terrible speed. What is the meaning of all this? I do not know: my body is quite helpless and is distressed, but I am not afraid. God is teaching me something in His own way. For six weeks every night I enter this condition, and the duration and power or intensity of it increase by degrees. It feels that my soul is projected or travels for incalculable distances beyond my body — (long afterwards I understand through experience that this is not the mode of it, but that the soul *remaining in the body* is by some de-insulation exposed to the knowledge of spirit-life as and when free of the flesh) — and I learn to comprehend and to know a new manner of living, as a swimmer learns a new mode of progression by means of his swimming, which is not his natural way.

By the end of three weeks I can remain nightly for many hours in this condition, which is always accompanied by an intense and vivid consciousness of God.

As this consciousness of God becomes more and more vivid so my body suffers more and more. By day I can only eat the smallest morsels of food, which almost choke me, but I drink a great quantity of water. I am perfectly healthy, though I have hardly any sleep and very little, indeed almost no, food — the suffering is only at night with the breathing and the heart when in this strange condition. But I have no anxiety whatever; I am glad that He shall do as He pleases with me. Nothing but love can give us this supreme confidence.

During the whole of these experiences I live in a state of very considerable abstraction. But this now suddenly increases, increases to such an extent that I hardly know whether to call it abstraction or the extremity of poverty. I now become divested of all interests outside and inside, divested of the greater part of my intelligence, divested of my will. I am of no value value whatever, less than the dust on the road.

In this awful nothingness I am still I. My consciousness continues and is not confounded with or lost in any other consciousness, but is reduced to stark nakedness and worth nothing: and this worthless nothing is hung up and, as it were, suspended nowhere in particular as far from earth as from heaven, totally unknown and unwanted by both God and Man. I am naked patience — waiting. I have a few thoughts, but very few: I think one thought where in normal times I should think ten thousand. I feel and know that I am nothing, and I feel that this has been done to me; just as before, all that I had was also done to me and was a gift. So I acknowledge that I once had and was perhaps something and that now I possess and certainly am nothing — I acknowledge it, I accept it, without hesitation, without protest. One of my few thoughts is that I shall remain for the rest of my natural life in this pitiful state where, however, I shall hope to be preserved from further sinning simply because I have not a sufficiency of will, intelligence, or thought with which to sin! I am too completely nothing to be able to sin. I have another thought, which is that as I no longer have any intelligence with which to deal with the ordinary difficulties of life, such as street life and traffic, I shall shortly be run over and killed; and so I put a card with my address on it into my little handbag, for the convenience of those who shall be obliged to deal with my body afterwards.

I have just sufficient capacity left me to automatically, mechanically, go through with the necessities of life. I have not become idiotic. I live in a tremendous and profound solitude, such a solitude as would frighten many people greatly. But my beautiful pastime had accustomed me to solitude and also to something of this nothingness — a brief nothingness was a necessary part of the beautiful pastime: so I have no fears now of any kind; but I wonder. Perhaps I am just four things — wonder, patience, resignation, and nothing.

This period of intense abstraction, this strange valley of humiliation, poverty, solitude, seemed a necessary prelude to the great, the supreme, experience of my life. As I came slowly out of this poverty and solitude, the joyousness of my spiritual experience increased: the nights were no longer at all a time of sleep or repose, but of rapturous living.

The sixth week came, and I commenced to fear the nights and this tremendous living, because the happiness and the light and the poignancy and the rapture of it were becoming more than I could bear. I began to wonder secretly if God intended to draw my soul so near to Him that I should die of the splendour of this living. My raptures were not only caused by the sense of the immediate Presence of God — this is a distinctive rapture running through and above all raptures, but there are lesser ecstasies caused by the meeting of the soul with Thoughts or Ideas, with melodies which bear the soul in almost unendurable delight upon a thousand summits of perfection; and with an all-pervading rapturous Beauty in a great light. There is this peculiarity about the manner of these thoughts and melodies and beauties — they are not spoken, heard, or seen, but *lived*. I could not pass these things to my reason and translate the Ideas into words or the melodies into sounds, or the beauty into objects, for spirit-living is not translatable to earth-living, and I found in it no words, no sounds, no objects, and I comprehended and I lived with that in me which is above Reason and of which I had, previously to these experiences, had no cognisance.

There came a night when I passed beyond Ideas, beyond melody, beyond beauty, into vast lost spaces, depths of untellable bliss, into a Light. And the Light is an ecstasy of delight, and the Light is an ocean of bliss, and the Light is Life and Love, and the Light is the too deep contact with God, and the Light is unbearable Joy; and in unendurable bliss my soul beseeches God that He will cover her from this most terrible rapture, this felicity which exceeds all measure. And she is not covered from it. And she beseeches Him again; and she is not covered; and being in the last extremity from this most terrible joy, she beseeches Him again: and immediately is covered from it.

Part III

I

Wonderful, beautiful weeks went by, filled with divine, indescribable peace. The Presence of God was with me day and night, and the world was not the world as I had once known it — a place where men and women fought and sinned and toiled and anguished and wondered horribly the meaning of this mystery of pain and joy, of life and death. The world was become Paradise, and in my heart I cried to all my fellow-souls, "Why fret and toil, why sweat and anguish for the things of earth when our own God has in His hand such peace and bliss and happiness to give to Every man? O come and receive it, Every man his share."

And the glamour of life in Unity with God became past all comprehension and all words.

III

One evening as I knelt to say my prayers, which were never long, because since the Visitation on the hill my natural habit — whether walking, sitting, working, travelling, or on my bed — had come to be a continual sending up from my heart and mind the tenderest and most adoring, the most worshipping and thanking little stream of thoughts to God (very much as a flower, if we could but see it, sends its scent to the sun).

And because this mode of prayer is so smooth and joyous, so easy, so unutterably sweet, in that during it the Presence of God laves us about as the sun laves the flower — so because of this it was only for short and set times that I worshipped Him as the creature in prayers upon its knees; but those few moments of prayer would always be intense, the heart and the mind with great power bent wholly and singly upon God.

So now, this evening as I knelt and dwelt in great singleness on God, He drew me so powerfully, He encompassed me so with His glamour, that this singleness and concentration of thought continued much longer than usual on account of the greatness of the love that I felt for Him, and the concentration became an intensity of penetration because of this magnetism, He turned on to me, and my mind became faint, and died, and I could no longer think of or on God, *for I was one with Him.* And I was still I; though I was become Ineffable Joy.

When it was over I rose from my knees, and I said to myself, for five wonderful moments I have been in contact with God in an unutterable bliss and repose: and He gave me the bliss tenderly and not as on that Night of Terror; but when I looked at my watch I saw that it had been for between two and three hours.

Then I wondered that I was not stiff, that I was not cold, for the night was chilly and I had nothing about me but a little velvet dressing-wrapper; and my neck was not stiff, though my head had been thrown back, as is a necessity in Communion with God; and I thought to myself, it is as if my body also had shared in the blessing.

And this most blessed happening happened to me every day for a short while, usually only for a few moments. In this way God Himself caused and enabled me to contemplate and *know* Him; and I saw that it was in some ways at one with my beautiful pastime, but with this tremendous difference in it — that whereas my mind had formerly concentrated itself upon the Beautiful, and remaining Mind had soared away above all forms into its nebulous essence in a strange seductive anguish, it now was drawn and magnetised beyond the Beautiful directly to the Maker of it: and the soaring was like a death or swooning of the mind, and immediately I was living with that which is above the mind: in this living there was no note of pain, but a marvellous joy.

Slowly I learnt to differentiate degrees of Contemplation, but to my own finding there are two principal forms — Passive and Active (or High) Contemplation.

In meditation is little or no activity, but a sweet quiet thinking and talking with Jesus Christ. In Passive Contemplation is the beginning of real activity; mind and soul without effort (though in a secret state of great love-activity) raise themselves, focussing themselves upon the all-unseen Godhead: now is no longer any possible picture in the mind, of anyone nor anything, not even of the gracious figure or of the ways of Christ: here, because of love, must begin the sheer straight drive of will and heart, mind and soul, to the Godhead, and here we may be said first to commence to breathe the air of heaven.

There is no prayer, no beseeching, and no asking — there are no words and no thoughts save those that intrude and flash unwanted over the mind, but a great undivided attention and waiting upon God: God near, yet never touching. This state is no ecstasy, but smooth, silent, high living in which we learn heavenly manners. This is Passive or Quiet Contemplation.

High Contemplation ends in Contact with God, in ecstasy and rapture. In it the activity of the soul (though entirely without effort on her part) is immensely increased). It is not to be sought for, and we cannot reach it for ourselves; but it is to be enjoyed when God calls, when He assists the soul, when He energises her.

And then our cry is no more, Oh, that I had wings! but, Oh, that I might fold my wings and stay!

Ancilla

———•–•———

This is the pseudonym of a contemporary Episcopalian American writer. *The Following Feet* was published in 1957.

From THE FOLLOWING FEET

From the lyric beauty of that mountain-land we descended to Nuremberg, arriving in mid-afternoon. It was a hot, rather stifling August day, with thunder in the offing.

We were affected differently. Dissension arose and was dispelled. We drew perhaps closer together as a party, but I think we were all a little glad when we moved on. And yet it was in Nuremberg, evil-smelling Nuremberg, that this thing happened to me that changed my whole way of thinking.

If I had invented the setting I should have reversed it, and sought the mountains last. From the heights of the Delectable Mountains Bunyan's pilgrims caught their first glimpse of the Holy City, yet this happened in the City of the Plain. Like everything else about it to me it is inexplicable.

It happened on Wednesday, the 22nd of August. Of this I am certain since I kept scattered notes in a diary; but of my state of mind I am less sure, and of my relations with the party, a group of former pupils and colleagues with whom I had worked in the normal give-and-take of college life. Having helped to organize the holiday I felt rather anxiously responsible for its success.

I think that I mainly wanted to be admired, to be regarded as competent, perhaps to be regarded as travelled, as a woman with some knowledge of the world, as well-read, above all as a humanist.

Some time during the afternoon I reached St. Sebalduskirche. I had read it up, but it was not until 1952 that I knew that the director of the mediaeval school held in this church was the mystic Hans Denck (born c. 1495).

I recollect an impression of masses of gilding and a wide space filled with light: light from the windows, nothing strange, only an effect of luminous space.

I was looking and thinking very idly, my eyes wide open, not screwed to attention. How do I know that my eyes were open? I just know, just as I know that I was sitting down. I had a complete feeling of my whole self. I know that my feet ached a little, but that my body was quiet and, as it were, happy.

The notebook continues: 'Saw renunciation.' I do not know why I wrote 'saw.' I think that my mind in my quiet body was recalling in a detached, tranquil fashion, the dissent that had arisen and been checked in the party. I saw it from a distance as a struggle to be first in the regard of other people. I think I knew, not with my intellect alone, but with my whole being, that as a 'self' I really did not matter, and was wholly glad of it. I am quite willing to assent to this as a proposition as I write. Indeed, I should like to do so. But at that moment I knew quite differently, and only once since have I got back to it. It was as if I had moved, in my mind, away from the central place, as if I had always sat on a throne in mid-consciousness, administering my affairs, and had stepped down. It was positive, and I cannot, by taking thought, repeat it. It had the stillness of humility shining with surprised joy, the quality of joy seen sometimes on the face of a very young child when he recognises, unexpectedly, someone he loves. I had the impression that it was momentary, the time taken to switch on a light, or to press a button.

Then, precisely as if that moving off the centre of my own consciousness had set some machinery going, it happened. How can I explain! I can only use negatives.

I saw nothing, not even a light.

I heard nothing, no voice, no music, nothing.

Nothing touched me. Nor was I conscious of any Being, visible or invisible.

But suddenly, simply, silently, I was not there. And I was there. It lasted for a moment, yet it was eternal, since there was no time.

And I knew, as certainly as I know I am trying to write it down, as certainly as I know that I live and eat and walk and sleep, that this world, this universe, is precisely as we see it, hear it, know it, and is at the same time completely different. It is as we see it because we are of it; it is also and at the same time wholly *other*.

A completely colour-blind person suddenly aware of colour? More fundamental than this.

A dog in a library sniffing his master's familiar book suddenly enabled to read it?

Robert Bridges's wolf and the first inklings of thought? But it was not an inkling, it was complete. Yet I do not know in what ways the earth appeared different. It was not different materially. It still had form, and colour, even good and evil, and animals and people, but it was conceived differently, as a whole, perhaps, as a spiritual entity. And it filled me with awe and grave joy and certainty, since I knew for always that so it was and no other, and that all was well; that it was the answer to all questions. I had no vision of God, or of any person, no vision of Christ, or of any spiritual being. Yet it was all that is, and there was no God, and equally no Not-God. It was whole and of the spirit. No words can make it clear. All I can say is that the wholeness seemed akin to that part of me that I should call spirit, as if my spirit were part of it and could not be separated from it.

How long the experience lasted I have no idea, but I think it was momentary. When it ceased I felt as though I had expended a great deal of time, and that, equally, there was no time in that moment. That timelessness was the clearest impression.

I came to, as after an anaesthetic, rather slowly. I recollect three clear and definite stages. First, the timeless moment distinctly ended, as if a curtain fell, and I returned to my bodily senses, proclaiming in a kind of fierce silence: 'So now I know, and it is all true, *and I have always known it.*' That phase was happy, wondering, elated. It settled later into an assertion in my mind that the world is spiritual; but the words did not mean what they would have meant the day before. To me their content was fuller, and deeper, and contained the notion that I belonged to that world in my essence, being fashioned for it and newlyborn into it.

The second stage I disliked intensely, feeling it to be humiliating and gross. I still dislike the idea, since it seems ribald. Yet it happened, and I think that if anything else had happened I might ultimately have persuaded myself that I had imagined the first part, but I should never have imagined this. I think now that my senses had been out of action and were returning, the oldest and most stable perchance, first. I know that I gradually saw the shrine again, that I looked round hastily to see if anyone was there who might have noticed anything strange about me. I think a bell rang, or a clock chimed. But, before any of these things happened I tasted food, yet it was not food in my mouth with bulk that can be felt, rather was it the idea of food, a taste-image only. And how it enraged me! So sordid, such a bump to the earth!

During the third stage of my coming-to I experienced a definite prohibition, not in words yet clear and precise, that I must tell no one at all, nor write it down (hence the seven cryptic words standing alone in my journal), nor even hint at what I had known. It was there, as one puts a secret into a child's hand, and closes his fingers over it. It was whole, complete, and not to be analysed, fussed over, frittered away. It was within me and would grow like the mustard-seed of the parable and fill all my mind, though I did not know that then.

I shied off it, I dared not even finger it; I held my mind still and looked within; and I was desperately afraid that it would happen again, since I felt that I could not bear it.

N. W. Clerk

This is the pseudonym of a distinguished contemporary English writer and theologian. *A Grief Observed* (1963) attempts an exact account of his reactions to the lingering death of his wife.

From A GRIEF OBSERVED

Meanwhile, where is God? This is one of the most disquieting symptoms. When you are happy, so happy that you have no sense of needing Him, so happy that you are tempted to feel His claims upon you as an interruption, if you remember yourself and turn to Him with gratitude and praise, you will be — or so it feels — welcomed with open arms. But go to Him when your need is desperate, when all other help is vain, and what do you find? A door slammed in your face, and a sound of bolting and double bolting on the inside. After that, silence. You may as well turn away. The longer you wait, the more emphatic the silence will become. There are no lights in the windows. It might be an empty house. Was it ever inhabited? It seemed so once. And that seeming was as strong as this. What can this mean? Why is He so present a commander in our time of prosperity and so very absent a help in time of trouble?

I tried to put some of these thoughts to C. this afternoon. He reminded me that the same thing seems to have happened to Christ: "Why hast thou forsaken me?" I know. Does that make it easier to understand?

Of course it's easy enough to say that God seems absent

at our greatest need because He *is* absent — non-existent. But then why does He seem so present when, to put it quite frankly, we don't ask for Him?

One thing, however, marriage has done for me. I can never again believe that religion is manufactured out of our unconscious, starved desires and is a substitute for sex. For those few years H. and I feasted on love; every mode of it — solemn and merry, romantic and realistic, sometimes as dramatic as a thunderstorm, sometimes as comfortable and unemphatic as putting on your soft slippers. No cranny of heart or body remained unsatisfied. If God were a substitute for love we ought to have lost all interest in Him. Who'd bother about substitutes when he has the thing itself? But that isn't what happens. We both knew we wanted something besides one another — quite a different kind of something, a quite different kind of want. You might as well say that when lovers have one another they will never want to read, or eat — or breathe.

Feelings, and feelings, and feelings. Let me try thinking instead. From the rational point of view, what new factor has H's death introduced into the problem of the universe? What grounds has it given me for doubting all that I believe? I knew already that these things, and worse, happened daily. I would have said that I had taken them into account. I had been warned — I had warned myself — not to reckon on worldly happiness. We were even promised sufferings. They were part of the programme. We were even told "Blessed are they that mourn" and I accepted it. I've got nothing that I hadn't bargained for. Of course it is different when the thing happens to oneself, not to others, and in reality, not in imagination. Yes; but should it, for a sane man, make quite such a difference as this? No. And it wouldn't for a man whose faith had been real faith and whose concern for other people's sorrows had been real concern. The case is too plain. If my house has collapsed at one blow, that is because it was a house of cards. The faith which "took these things into account" was not faith but imagination. The taking them into account was not real sympathy. If I had really cared, as I thought I did, about the sorrows of the world, I should not have been so overwhelmed when my own sorrow came. It has been an imaginary faith playing with innocuous counters labelled "Illness," "Pain," "Death" and "Loneliness." I thought I trusted the rope until it mattered to me whether it would bear me. Now it matters, and I find I didn't.

Something quite unexpected has happened. It came this morning early. For various reasons, not in themselves at all mysterious, my heart was lighter than it had been for many weeks. For one thing, I suppose I am recovering physically from a good deal of mere exhaustion. And I'd had a very tiring but very healthy twelve hours the day before, and a sounder night's sleep; and after ten days of low-hung grey skies and motionless warm dampness, the sun was shining and there was a light breeze. And suddenly at the very moment when, so far, I mourned H. least, I remembered her best. Indeed it was something (almost) better than memory; an instantaneous, unanswerable impression. To say it was like a meeting would be going too far. Yet there was that in it which tempts one to use those words. It was as if the lifting of the sorrow removed a barrier.

Why has no one told me these things? How easily I might have misjudged another man in the same situation? I might have said, "He's got over it. He's forgotten his wife," when the truth was, "He remembers her better *because* he has partly got over it."

Such was the fact. And I believe I can make sense out

of it. You can't see anything properly while your eyes are blurred with tears. You can't, in most things, get what you want if you want it too desperately: anyway, you can't get the best out of it. "Now! Let's have a real good talk" reduces everyone to silence, "I *must* get a good sleep to-night" ushers in hours of wakefulness. Delicious drinks are wasted on a really ravenous thirst. Is it similarly the very intensity of the longing that draws the iron curtain, that makes us feel we are staring into a vacuum when we think about our dead? "Them as asks" (at any rate "as asks too importunately") don't get. Perhaps can't.

And so, perhaps, with God. I have gradually been coming to feel that the door is no longer shut and bolted. Was it my own frantic need that slammed it in my face? The time when there is nothing at all in your soul except a cry for help may be just the time when God can't give it: you are like the drowning man who can't be helped because he clutches and grabs. Perhaps your own reiterated cries deafen you to the voice you hoped to hear.

On the other hand, "Knock and it shall be opened." But does knocking mean hammering and kicking the door like a maniac? And there's also "To him that hath shall be given." After all, you must have a capacity to receive, or even omnipotence can't give. Perhaps your own passion temporarily destroys the capacity.

Sources

Martin Luther — *Career of the Reformer IV*, edited by Lewis W. Spitz and Helmut T. Lehmann (vol. 34 of Luther's *Works*, Philadelphia: Muhlenberg, 1960), p. 336.

John Donne — Joan Bennett, *Four Metaphysical Poets* (New York: Vintage, 1960), pp. 169-170.

Jakob Boehme — *The Way to Christ*, translated by Stephen Hobhouse (London: John M. Watkins, 1911), pp. 170-171.
   The Confessions of Jakob Boehme, translated by Frederick D. Maurice, compiled and edited by W. Scott Palmer, introduction by Evelyn Underhill (London: Methuen, 1920), pp. 15-25.

John Amos Komensky — *The Labyrinth of the World and the Paradise of the Heart*, edited and translated by Count Lutzow (London: J. M. Dent, 1905). pp. 197-198, 201-205.

George Herbert — Joan Bennett, *Four Metaphysical Poets* (New York: Vintage, 1960), pp. 175-177.

Samuel Rutherford — *The Letters of Samuel Rutherford* (Edinburgh: Oliphant, Anderson and Ferrier, 1881), pp. 57, 204-206.

Jeremy Taylor — *Holy Living and Dying*, revised and edited by the Rev. Thomas Smith, D.D. (London: Henry G. Bohn, 1851), pp. 20-23.

Richard Baxter — *The Saints' Everlasting Rest* (Westwood, N. J.: Fleming H. Revell, 1962).

Henry Vaughn — Joan Bennett, *Four Metaphysical Poets* (New York: Vintage, 1960), pp. 205, 214-215.

George Fox — *A Journal or Historical Account of the Life, Travels, Sufferings, Christian Experience and Labour of Love, etc., of George Fox* (Philadelphia: Friends' Book Store, 189?), pp. 60-63, 69, 70.

John Bunyan — *The Pilgrim's Progress*, edited by the Rev. Robert Philip (London: George Virtue, 1848), pp. 202-207.
   The Riches of Bunyan, selected from his *Works* by the Rev. Jeremiah Chaplin (New York: American Tract Society, 1850), pp. 390-395.

Thomas Traherne — *Centuries of Meditations*, edited by Bertram Dobell (London: published by the editor, 1908), pp. 157-158.

Charles Marshall — *The Journal, together with Sundry Epistles and Other Writings of Charles Marshall* (London: Richard Barrett, 1844), pp. 2-8.

Pierre Poiret — *La Paix des Bonnes Ames*, (Amsterdam: Theodore Boetman, 1687) translated by Anne Fremantle, Section VI, pp. 101-102.

Johannes Kelpius — *A Method of Prayer*, edited and with an introduction by E. Gordon Alderfer (New York: Harper, in association with Pendle Hill, 1950), pp. 75-77, 86-91, 116-117.

William Law — *Selected Mystical Writings of William Law*, edited by Stephen Hobhouse (London: Rockliff, 1948), pp. 35-51, 67-68, 72, 81-83, 100-101, 186-187, 210-211.

Emanuel Swedenborg — *The Memorabilia of Swedenborg*, with an introduction by George Bush (New York: J. Allen, 1846), part 1, pp. 18-21.

Spiritual Diary, translated by J. H. Smithson (New York: Lewis C. Bush, 1850), vol. I, part 1, pp. 40-41, 43, 62-63.

Spiritual Diary, translated by George Bush, edited by Samuel Beswick (Boston: Henry H. & T. W. Carter, 1871), vol. II, part 1, pp. 9, 17, 99; vol. II, part 2, p. 51.

Gerhard Tersteegen — *Life and Character of Gerhard Tersteegen*, translated by Samuel Jackson (London: Black, Young and Young, 1834), pp. 29, 48, 50-52.

Jonathan Edwards — *The Life and Character of the Late Reverend, Learned and Pious Mr. Jonathan Edwards*, edited by S. Hopkins (Northampton, Mass.: printed by A. Wright for S. & E. Butler, 1804), pp. 24-35.

David Brainerd — Jonathan Edwards, *An Account of the Life of the Late Reverend David Brainerd* (Boston: D. Henchman, 1749), pp. 44-45, 70-71, 74-75.

John Wesley — *The Heart of John Wesley's Journal*, edited by Percy Livingston Parker (London: Fleming H. Revell, n.d.), pp. 28-30, 43-45, 253, 313.

John Woolman — *The Quaker Reader*, selected and introduced by Jessamyn West (New York: Viking, 1962), pp. 250-253, 268-270.

Johann Wolfgang von Goethe — (*Dichtung und Wahrheit*) *Goethe's Popular Works*, Cambridge Edition, translated by John Oxenford (Boston: Estes and Lauriat, 1883), vol. I, pp. 36-38.

Faust, translated and with an introduction by Philip Wayne (Baltimore: Penguin Books, 1959), part 2, p. 25.

William Blake — *The Portable Blake,* selected and arranged with an introduction by Alfred Kazin (New York: Viking, 1946), pp. 192-124, 207-210, 487.

Hölderlin, Johann Christian Friedrich — *An Anthology of German Poetry from Hölderlin to Rilke,* edited by Angel Flores (New York: Doubleday, Anchor, 1960), pp. 31-33, 34-40.

William Wordsworth — *Poets of the English Language,* edited by W. H. Auden and Norman Holmes Pearson (New York: Viking, 1950), vol. IV, *Blake to Poe,* pp. 193-196, 205-207, 214-215.

The Viking Book of Poetry of the English-Speaking World, edited by Richard Aldington (New York: Viking, 1941), pp. 662-667.

Novalis — *Hymns and Thoughts on Religion,* translated and edited by W. Hastie (Edinburgh: T. & T. Clark, 1888), pp. 97, 120.

An Anthology of German Poetry from Hölderlin to Rilke, edited by Angel Flores (New York: Doubleday, Anchor, 1960), pp. 83-86.

The Disciples of Sais, translated by Eileen Hutchins (London: Methuen, 1903), pp. 79, 92-95.

Jacob Bower — William Warren Sweet, *Religion on the American Frontier: The Baptists, 1783-1830* (New York: Holt, 1931), pp. 190-195.

John Keats — *Letters of John Keats,* edited by Sidney Colvin (London: Macmillan, 1891), pp. 73-75.

Ralph Waldo Emerson — *Emerson: A Modern Anthology,* edited by Alfred Kazin and Daniel Aaron (Boston: Houghton Mifflin, 1959), pp. 151-152, 170-171.

Alfred, Lord Tennyson — *Poetical Works, including the Plays* (London: Oxford University Press, 1953), pp. 257, 262-263.

Kierkegaard, Sören Aabye — *Kierkegaard,* selected and introduced by W. H. Auden (London: Cassell, 1955), pp. 180-183.

Henry David Thoreau — *The Journal of Henry D. Thoreau,* edited by Bradford Torrey and Francis H. Allen (Boston: Houghton Mifflin, 1906), vol. I, pp. 296, 320-322; vol. II, pp. 306-307, 314-315, 468-471.

Emily Brontë — *The Oxford Book of English Verse,* edited by Sir Arthur Quiller-Couch (Oxford: Oxford University Press, 1939), pp. 893-894.

Poets of the English Language, edited by W. H. Auden and

Norman Holmes Pearson (New York: Viking, 1950), vol. V, *Tennyson to Yeats*, pp. 203-204.

Walt Whitman — *Specimen Days* (New York: New American Library, Signet, 1961), pp. 161-162.

The City Without Walls, an anthology arranged by Margaret Cushing Osgood (London: Jonathan Cape, 1932), pp. 306-307.

Henri Frederic Amiel — *Amiel's Journal*, translated and with an introduction and notes by Mrs. Humphry Ward (New York: A. L. Burt, 1899), pp. 28-29, 55-56, 135.

George Macdonald — *The Visionary Novels of George Macdonald*, edited by Anne Fremantle, with an introduction by W. H. Auden (New York: Noonday, 1954), pp. 237-239, 250-253.

Emily Dickinson — *Selected Poems and Letters by Emily Dickinson*, edited by Robert N. Linscott (New York: Doubleday, Anchor, 1959), pp. 48, 61, 67, 72-73.

Letters of Emily Dickinson, edited by Mabel Loomis Todd, with an introduction by Mark Van Doren (New York: Grosset & Dunlap, 1962), pp. 286, 362-363.

Hannah Whitall Smith — *The Christian's Secret of a Happy Life* (Westwood, N. J.: Fleming H. Revell, 1952), pp. 202-204.

W. H. Hudson — *Far Away and Long Ago* (New York: E. P. Dutton, 1918), pp. 34-38.

William James — Victor Gollancz, *From Darkness to Light* (New York: Harper, 1956), pp. 217-218.

Richard Jefferies — *The Story of My Heart*, edited by Samuel J. Looker (London: Constable, 1947), pp. 76-79.

Vincent Van Gogh — *Van Gogh: A Self-Portrait*, letters revealing his life as a painter, selected by W. H. Auden (Greenwich, Conn.: New York Graphic Society, 1961), pp. 52-56, 185-187.

George Gissing — *The Private Papers of Henry Ryecroft* (New York: New American Library, Signet, 1961), pp. 118-121, 125-126.

Rufus Jones — *The Quaker Reader*, selected and introduced by Jessamyn West (New York: Viking, 1962), pp. 404-405, 406.

William Butler Yeats — *The Celtic Twilight*, and a selection of early poems (New York: New American Library, Signet, 1962), p. 79.

Forbes Robinson — *Forbes Robinson, Disciple of Love*, selections from his letters and addresses, edited and with an introduction by M. R. J. Manktelow (London: S.P.C.K., 1961, pp. 51-52.

Æ — *Song and Its Fountains* (London: Macmillan, 1932), pp. 1-4.

Johannes Anker-Larsen — *With the Door Open,* translated by Erwin and Pleasaunce von Gaisberg (London and New York: Macmillan, 1931), pp. 21-23, 29-33, 37-39, 42-43, 48-51, 62-63, 70-75.

John Masefield — *So Long to Learn* (New York: Macmillan, 1952), pp. 9, 139-140, 179-180.

Margaret Prescott Montague — *Twenty Minutes of Reality* (New York: E. P. Dutton, 1917), pp. 1-3, 5-11.

Stark Young — *The Pavilion* (New York: Scribner's, 1951), p. 192.

Virginia Woolf — *A Writer's Diary* (New York: Harcourt, Brace, 1954), pp. 85, 100, 110, 165.

Frank C. Laubach — *Letters by a Modern Mystic* (New York: Student Volunteer Movement, 1937), pp. 10-11.

Edwin Muir — Victor Gollancz, *From Darkness to Light: A Confession of Faith in the Form of an Anthology* (New York: Harper, 1956), pp. 131-132.

    An Autobiography (London: Hogarth Press, 1954), pp. 245-246.

    Collected Poems, 1921-1951 (London: Faber, 1952), pp. 173-175.

T. S. Eliot — *Four Quartets* (New York: Harcourt, Brace, 1943), pp. 127-128.

Thomas Raymond Kelly — *A Testament of Devotion,* with a biographical memoir by Douglas V. Steere (New York: Harper, 1941), pp. 35-47.

Edward Estlin Cummings — *I: Six Nonlectures* (Harvard University Charles Eliot Norton Lectures 1952-1953, Cambridge, Mass.: Harvard University Press, 1954), pp. 32-33, 91.

C. S. Lewis — *Surprised by Joy* (New York: Harcourt, Brace, 1956), pp. 16, 224-225.

    The Screwtape Letters (New York: Macmillan, 1943), pp. 156-160.

John Betjeman — *Summoned by Bells* (Boston: Houghton Mifflin, 1960), pp. 75-77.

Dietrich Bonhoeffer — *Christians and Unbelievers,* translated by Geoffrey Winthrop Young, in *Prisoner for God,* edited by Eberhard Bethge (London: Student Christian Movement Press, 1954), pp. 167-168.

Helmuth James, Count von Moltke — *Dying We Live,* translated by Reinhard Kuhn and edited by Helmut Gollwitzer, Kathe Kuhn and Reinhold Schneider (New York: Pantheon, 1956), pp. 124-125, 129-130.

Katherine Trevelyan — *Through Mine Own Eyes* (New York: Holt, Rinehart and Winston, 1963), pp. 219-220.

Loren Hurnscot — *A Prison, A Paradise* (New York: Viking, 1959), pp. 198, 201-203, 230-231, 251.

Anonymous — *The Prodigal Returns* (London: John M. Watkins, 1921), pp. 34-87.

Ancilla — *The Following Feet* (Greenwich, Conn.: Seabury, 1963, pp. 17-23.

N. W. Clerk — *A Grief Observed* (Greenwich, Conn.: Seabury, 1963), pp. 9-10, 31, 37-38.